Submarine and Anti-Submarine

"WHOSE CREW ABANDONED SHIP
AND THEN ALL STOOD UP AND CURSED US."

Submarine and Anti-Submarine

The Allied Under-Sea Conflict During the First World War

Henry Newbolt

LEONAUR

Submarine and Anti-Submarine
The Allied Under-Sea Conflict During the First World War
by Henry Newbolt

First published under the title
Submarine and Anti-Submarine

Leonaur is an imprint of Oakpast Ltd
Copyright in this form © 2013 Oakpast Ltd

ISBN: 978-1-78282-082-6 (hardcover)
ISBN: 978-1-78282-083-3 (softcover)

http://www.leonaur.com

Publisher's Notes

The views expressed in this book are not necessarily
those of the publisher.

Contents

To
JOHN BUCHAN

CHAPTER 1

The Spirit of Submarine War

It is probable that a good deal of the information contained in this book will be new to the public; for it has been collected under favour of exceptional circumstances. But the reader will gain little if he cannot contribute something on his side—if he cannot share with the writer certain fundamental beliefs. The first of these is that every nation has a spirit of its, own—a spirit which is the mainspring of national action. It is more than a mechanical spring; for it not only supplies a motive force, but determines the moral character of the action which results. When we read the history of nations, and especially the history of their explorations, wars, and revolutions, we soon recognise the spirit of each, and learn to expect its appearance in every moment of crisis or endurance. If it duly appears, our impression is confirmed; if it fails on any occasion, we are disappointed.

But the disappointments are few—nations may at times surprise us; but, as a rule, they are like themselves. Even when they develop and seem to change, they are apt, under the stress of action, to return to their aboriginal character, and to exhibit it in their old historic fashion. To attempt, then, to give an account of any national struggle, without paying attention to the influence of the characteristic spirit of the country or countries concerned, would be a difficult undertaking, and a mistaken one. Even in a short crisis, a great people will probably display its historic colours, and in a long one it certainly will. To ignore this, to describe national' actions without giving a sense of the animating spirit, would be not only a tame and inadequate method; it would lower the value of life itself by making mere prose of what should, by right, partake of the nature of poetry.

History cannot often be entirely poetical, or poetry entirely historical. When Homer told the tale of Troy, he did not make prose—or even history—of it. He everywhere infused into it 'an incomparable ardour'—he made an epic. But Mr. Thomas Hardy wrote history in *The Dynasts*, and made it an epic too. An epic—the common definition tells us is—'a theme of action treated in heroic proportions and style.' *The Dynasts* certainly is that—the struggle is great, the issues are great, the men are great. Even more than their heroic fighting, their speech and manners in the moment of action are such as to show unfailingly by what a distinctive and ever-present spirit national life may be sustained and magnified.

When we come to nearer times, and more familiar events, the same necessity is upon us. What writer of artistic sense, or scientific honesty, would touch, for example, the history of modern Egypt without attempting to understand the character of such men as Gordon and Cromer, and the spirit which (however personal and diverse in its manifestations) they both drew from the nation that sent them forth? Such an understanding would enable the narrator to carry us all with him. For every man of our national birth and breeding would feel, when he was told the story of such heroes, not only their superiority but their likeness to himself. 'There,' he would say, 'but for lack of fortune, or opportunity, or courage, or stature, there goes John Smith.' It is admiration which helps us to feel that, and a mean spirit which conceals it from us.

Further, it is my belief that the historian who would deal adequately with our present war must have an even wider understanding and sympathy. He must have a broad enough view to recognise all the various motives which impelled us, section by section, to enter the struggle; and a deep enough insight to perceive that, below all motives which can be expressed or debated in words, there was an instinct—a spontaneous emotion—which irresistibly stirred the majority of our people, and made us a practically unanimous nation. He must be able to see that this unanimity was no freak—no sudden outburst—but the natural fulfilment of a strong and long-trained national character; and he must trace, with grateful admiration, the national service contributed by many diverse classes, and by a large number of distinguished men—the leaders and patterns of the rest.

However scientific the historian's judgments, and however restrained his style, it must be impossible for any reader to miss the real point of the narrative—the greatness of the free nations, and the nobility of their heroes. Belgians, Serbians, French, Italians, Americans—all must hear their great men honoured, and their corporate virtues generously recognised. We Britons, for our own part, must feel, at every mention of the names of our champions, the fine sting of the invisible fire with which true glory burns the heart.

It must never be possible to read, without an uplifting of the spirit, the achievements of commanders like Smith-Dorrien, Haig, and Bird-wood—Plumer and Rawlinson, Allenby and Byng, and Home; or the fate of Cradock and Kitchener; or the sea-fights of Beatty and Sturdee, of Keyes and Tyrwhitt. It must be clear, from the beginning to the end of the vast record, that the British blood has equalled and surpassed its ancient fame—that in every rank the old virtues of courage, coolness, and endurance, of ordered energy and human kindliness, have been, not the occasional distinction, but the common characteristics of our men. Look where you will on the scene of war, you must be shown 'a theme of action treated in heroic proportions and style'—fit, at least, to indicate the greatness of the national spirit.

In this book our concern is with the war at sea, and with a part only of that gigantic effort. But of this part, every word that has been said holds good. The submarine and anti-submarine campaign is not a series of minor operations. Its history is not a mere episode among chapters of greater significance. On the contrary, the fate of Britain, and the fate of Germany, were speedily seen to be staked upon the is-sue of this particular contest, as they have been staked upon no other part of the worldwide struggle. The entrance of America into the fel-lowship of nations was involved in it. The future of civilisation de-pends upon it. Moreover, in its course the British seaman has shown himself possessed, in the highest degree, of the qualities by which his forefathers conquered and kept our naval predominance; and finally, it is in the submarine war that we see most sharply the contrast of the spirit of chivalry with the spirit of savagery; of the law of humanity with the lawlessness of brute force; of the possible redemption of so-cial life with its irretrievable degradation. It is a subject worthy, thrice over, of treatment in a national epic.

The present book is not an epic—it is not a poetical work at all. Half of it is mere technical detail; and the rest plain fact plainly told. But it is far from my intention that the sense of admiration for na-tional heroes, or the recognition of national greatness, shall be absent from it. I have used few epithets; for they seemed to me needless and inadequate. The stories of the voyages and adventures of our own submarines, and of the fighting of our men against the pirates, need no heightening. They need only to be read and understood; and it is chiefly with a view to their better understanding, that the reader is offered a certain amount of comment and description in the earlier chapters. But a suggestion or two may be made here, at the very beginning, in the hope of starting a train of thought which may accompany the narrative with a whisper of historic continuity—a reminder that as with men, so with nations—none becomes utterly base on a sudden, or utterly heroic. Their vices and their virtues are the harvesting of their past.

Let us take a single virtue, like courage, which is common to all nations but shows under a different form or colour in each, and so becomes a national characteristic, plainly visible in action. A historical study of British courage would, I believe, show two facts: first, that the peculiar quality of it has persisted for centuries; and, secondly, that if our people have changed at all in this respect, they have only changed in the direction of greater uniformity. Once they had two kinds of courage in war; now they have but one, and that by far the better one. In the old days, among the cool and determined captains of our race, there were always a certain number of hot heads—'men of courage without discipline, of enthusiasm without reason, of will without science.' The best of them, like Sir Richard Grenville, had the luck to die conspicuously, in their great moments, and so to leave us an example of the spirit that defies odds, and sets men above the fear of death. The rest led their men into mad adventures, where they perished to the injury of their cause. Most Englishmen can understand the pure joy of onset, the freedom of the moment when everything has been given for the hope of winning one objective; but it has been the more characteristic way of our people—at any rate for the last five centuries—to double courage with coolness, and fight not only their hardest but their best.

From Cressy to Waterloo, and from Mons to Arras, we have won many battles by standing steadily and shooting the attack to pieces. Charges our men have made, but under discipline and in the nick of opportunity. The Black Prince charged fiercely at Poitiers; but it was only when he had broken three attacks, and saw his chance to win. The charge of the Worcesters at Gheluvelt, the charge of the Oxfords at Nonneboschen, and a hundred more like them, were as desperate as any 'ride of death;' but they were neither reckless nor useless, they were simply the heroic move to win the game. Still more is this the rule at sea. Beatty at Jutland, like Nelson and Collingwood at Trafalgar, played an opening in which he personally risked annihilation; but nothing was ever done with greater coolness, or more admirable science. The perfect picture of all courage is, perhaps, a great British warship in action; for there you have, among a thousand men, one spirit of elation, of fearlessness, of determination, backed by trained skill and a self-forgetful desire to apply it in the critical moment.

The submarine, and the anti submarine ship, trawler or patrol-boat are, on a smaller scale, equally perfect examples; for there is no hour of their cruise when they are not within call of the critical moment. In the trenches, in the air, in the fleet, you will see the same steady skilful British courage almost universally exemplified. But in the submarine war, the discipline needed is even more absolute, the skill even more delicate, the ardour even more continuous and self-forgetful; and all these demands are even more completely fulfilled.

This is fortunate, and doubly fortunate; for the submarine war has proved to be the main battlefield of our spiritual crusade, as well as a vital military campaign. The men engaged in it have been marked out by fate, as our champions in the contest of ideals. They are the patterns and defenders of human nature in war, against those who preach and practise barbarism. Here and nowhere else so clearly as here the world has seen the death struggle between the two spirits now contending for the future of mankind. Between the old chivalry, and the new savagery, there can be no more truce; one of the two must go under, and the barbarians knew it when they cried *Weltmacht oder Niedergang*.

Of the spirit of the German nation it is not necessary to say much. Everything that could be charged against them has been already proved, by their own words and actions. They have sunk without warning women and children, doctors and nurses, neutrals and wounded men, not by tens or hundreds but by thousands. They have publicly rejoiced over these murders with medals and flags, with songs and school holidays. They have not only broken the rules of international law; they have with unparalleled cruelty, after sinking even neutral ships, shot and drowned the crews in open boats, that they might leave no trace of their crimes. The men who have done—and are still doing—these things have courage of a kind. They face danger and hardship to a certain point, though, by their own account, in the last extreme they fail to show the dignity and sanity with which our own men meet death.

But their peculiar defect is not one of nerve, but of spirit. They lack that instinct which, with all civilised races, intervenes, even in the most violent moment of conflict or desperation, and reminds the

13

combatant that there are blows which it is not lawful to strike in any circumstances whatever. This instinct—the religion of all chivalrous peoples—is connected by some with humanity, by some with courtesy, by ourselves with sport. In this matter we are all in the right. The savage in conflict thinks of nothing but his own violent will; the civilised and the chivalrous are always conscious of the fact that there are other rights in the world beside their own.

The humane man forbears his enemy; the courteous man respects him, as one with rights like his own; the man with the instinct of sport knows that he must not snatch success by destroying the very game itself. The civilised nation will not hack its way to victory through the ruins of human life. It will be restrained, if by no other consideration, yet at least by the recollection that it is but one member of a human fellowship, and that the greatness of a part can never be achieved by the corruption of the whole.

The German nature is not only devoid of this instinct, it is roused to fury by the thought of it. Any act, however cruel and barbarous, if only it tends to defeat the enemies of Germany, is a good deed, a brave act, and to be commended. The German general who lays this down is supported by the German professor who adds:

> The spontaneous and elementary hatred towards England is rooted in the deepest depths of our own being—there, where considerations of reason do not count, where the irrational, the instinct, alone dominates. We hate in the English the hostile principle of our innermost and highest nature. And it is well that we are fully aware of this, because we touch therein the vital meaning of this war

Before the end comes, the barbarian will find this hostile principle, and will hate it, in the French, the Italians, the Americans—in the whole fellowship of nations against which he is fighting with savage fury. But, to our satisfaction, he has singled us out first; for, when we hear him, we too are conscious of a spontaneous hatred in the depths of our being; and we see that in this we do 'touch the vital meaning of this war.'

CHAPTER 2

The Evolution of the Submarine

Many are the fables which the Germans have done their best to pass off for truth among the spectators of the present war; but not one is more wilfully and demonstrably false, than their account of the origin of the submarine. According to the story which they have endeavoured to spread among the unthinking public in neutral countries, the under-sea boat—the arm with which they claim to have revolutionised naval warfare—is the product of German ingenuity and skill. The French, they say, had merely played with the idea; their submarines were costly toys, dangerous only to those who tried to navigate them. The Americans had shown some promise half a century ago; but having since become a pacifist race of dollar-hunters, they had lost interest in war, and their boats would be found useless in practice. 'As for the British, the day of their naval power was past; they had spent their time and money upon the mania for big ships, and neglected the more scientific vessel, the submarine, which had made the big ships obsolete in a single year's campaign. The ship of the future, the U-boat, was the national weapon of Germany alone.

The claim was unjustified; but, so far, it was not—to an uninstructed neutral—obviously unjustified. The Americans were not yet at war; the submarines of France and Britain were hardly ever heard of. Our boats had few targets, and their operations were still further restricted by the rules of international law, which we continued to keep, though our enemies did not. Moreover, whatever our service did achieve was done secretly; and even our successes were announced so briefly and vaguely as to make no impression. The result was that the Germans were able to make out a plausible title to the 'command of the sea beneath the surface;' and they even gained a hearing for the other half of their claim, which was unsupported by any evidence whatever. The submarine is not, in its origin, of German invention; the idea of submarine war was not a German idea, nor have Germans contributed anything of value to the long process of experiment and development by which the idea has been made to issue in practical underwater navigation

From beginning to end, the Germans have played their characteristic part. They have been behind their rivals in intelligence; they have relied on imitation of the work of others; on discoveries methodically borrowed and adapted; and when they have had to trust to their own abilities, they have never passed beyond mediocrity. They have shown originality in one direction only—their ruthless disregard of law and humanity. These statements are not the outcome of partisanship, but of a frank study of the facts. They are clearly proved by the history of submarine war.

That history may be said to begin with the second half of the sixteenth century, when the two main principles or aims of submarine war were first set forth—both by English seamen. Happily the records remain. Sir William Monson, one of Queen Elizabeth's admirals, in his famous *Naval Tracts*, suggests that a powerful ship may be sunk much more easily by an under-water shot than by ordinary gunfire. His plan is 'to place a cannon in the hold of a bark, with her mouth to the side of the ship: the bark shall board, and then to give fire to the cannon that is stowed under water, and they shall both instantly sink: the man that shall execute this stratagem may escape in a small boat hauled the other side of the bark.'

This is the germinal idea from which sprang the submarine mine or torpedo; and the first design for a submarine boat was also produced by the English Navy in the same generation. The author of this was William Bourne, who had served as a gunner under Sir William Monson. His invention is described in his book of *Inventions or Devices* published in 1578, and is remarkable for its proposed method of solving the problem of submersion. This is to be achieved by means of two side-tanks, into which water can be admitted through perforations, and from which it can be blown out again by forcing the inner side of each tank outwards. These false sides are made tight with leather suckers, and moved by winding hand-screws—a crude and inefficient mechanism, but a proof that the problem had been correctly grasped. For a really practical solution of this, and the many other difficulties involved in submarine navigation, the resources of applied science were then hopelessly inadequate. It was not until after more than three hundred years of experiment that inventors were in a position to command a mechanism that would carry out their ideas effectively.

The record of these three centuries of experiment is full of interest; for it shows us a long succession of courageous men taking up, one after another, the same group of scientific problems and bringing them, in spite of all dangers and disasters, gradually nearer to a final solution. Many nations contributed to the work, but especially the British, the American, the Dutch, the French, the Spanish, the Swedish, the Russian, and the Italian. The part played by each of them has been, on the whole, characteristic. The British were the first, as practical seamen, to put forward the original idea, gained from the experience of their rivalry with Spain. They have also succeeded, at the end of the experimental period, in making the best combined use of the results of the long collaboration.

A Dutchman built the first practical submarine, and achieved the first successful dive. The Americans have made the greatest number of inventions, and of daring experiments in earlier wars. The French have shown, as a nation, the strongest interest in the idea, and their navy was effectively armed with submarines ten years before that of any other power. To them, to the Dutch, and to the Italians, the credit belongs of that indispensable invention, the optic tube or periscope. The Swedes and Russians have the great names of Nordenfelt and Drzewiecki to their credit. The Germans alone, among the eight or nine nations interested in the science of naval war, have from first to last contributed almost nothing to the evolution of the submarine. The roll of submarine inventors includes about 175 names, of which no less than 60 belong to the English-speaking peoples, but only six to Germany.

Among these six, the name of Bauer is remembered as that of a courageous experimenter, persevering through a career of repeated failures; but neither he, nor any of his fellow countrymen, advanced the common cause by the suggestion of a single idea of value. Finally, when the German Admiralty, after the failure of their own Howaldt boat, decided to borrow the Holland type from America, it was no German, but the Franco-Spanish engineer d'Equevilley, who designed for them the first five U-boats, of which all the later ones are modifications. The English Admiralty were in no such straits. They were only one year before the Germans in adopting the Holland type; but the native genius at their disposal has enabled them to keep ahead of their rivals from that day to this, in the design, efficiency, size, and number of their submarine vessels. And this result is exactly what might have been expected from the history of submarine invention.

The construction of a workable submarine depends upon the discovery and solution of a number of problems, the first five of which may be said to be the problems of

1. Submersion.
2. Stability.
3. Habitability.
4. Propulsion and Speed.
5. Offensive Action.

If we take these in order, and trace the steps by which the final solution was approached, we shall be able to confirm what has been said about the work contributed by successive inventors.

1. *Submersion.*—We have seen that for submersion and return to the surface, Bourne had at the very beginning devised the side-tank to which water could be admitted, and from which it could be 'blown out' at will. Bushnell, a remarkable inventor of British-American birth, substituted a hand-pump in his boat of 1771, for the mechanism proposed by Bourne. In 1795, Armand-Maizière, a Frenchman, designed a steam submarine vessel to be worked by 'a number of oars vibrating on the principle of a bird's wing.' Of these 'wings,' one lot were intended to make the boat submerge. Nothing came of this proposal, and for more than a century tanks and pumps remained the sole means of submersion. In 1893 Haydon, an American, invented a submarine for the peaceful purpose of exploring the ocean bed. Its most important feature was the method of submersion.

This was accomplished by means of an interior cylindrical tank, with direct access to the sea, and fitted with two powerfully geared pistons. By simply drawing the pistons in, or pushing them out, the amount of water ballast could be nicely regulated, and the necessity for compressed air or other expellants was avoided. This device would have given great satisfaction to William Bourne, the Elizabethan gunner, whose original idea, after more than two centuries, it carried out successfully. Finally, in 1900, the American Inventor, Simon Lake, in his *Argonaut II.*, introduced a new method of diving. For the reduction of the vessel's floatability he employed the usual tanks; but for 'travelling' between the surface and the bottom, he made use of 'four big hydroplanes, two on each side, that steer the boat either down or up.' Similar hydroplanes, or horizontal rudders, appeared in the later Holland boats, and are now in common use in all submarine types.

Lake was of British descent, his family having emigrated from Wales to New Jersey; but he owed his first interest in submarine construction, and many of his inventive ideas, to the brilliant French writer, Jules Verne, whose book *Twenty Thousand Leagues under the Sea* came by chance into his hands when he was a boy ten years old, and made a lasting impression upon him.

2. *Stability.*—Next to the power of submersion, the most necessary quality in a submarine is that of stability under water. The most obvious method of securing this is by water ballast, which was probably the first means actually employed. Bushnell, in 1771, substituted a heavy weight of lead, as being more economical of space and better suited to the shape of his boat, which resembled a turtle in an upright position. The leaden ballast, being detachable at will, also acted as a safety weight, to be dropped at a moment of extreme urgency. In the *Nautilus*, built in 1800 by the famous engineer, Robert Fulton, an American of English birth and education, the leaden weight reappeared as a keel, and was entirely effective.

The inventor, in a trial at Brest in 1801, dived to a depth of 25 feet, and performed successful evolutions in different directions for over an hour. Bauer, fifty years later, returned to the ballast principle, and used both a water-tank and a safety weight in the same boat. The results were disastrous. His first submarine sank at her first trial in Kiel harbour, and was never refloated. His second was built in England; but this, too, sank, with great loss of life. His third, *Le Diable Marin*, after several favourable trials at Cronstadt, fouled her propeller in a bed of seaweed, and the releasing of the safety weights only resulted in bringing her bows to the surface. The crew escaped with difficulty, and the vessel then sank.

Three years later, in 1861, Olivier Riou designed two boats, in both of which stability was to be preserved automatically by the device of a double hull. The two cylinders which composed it, one within the other, were not fixed immovably to one another, but were on rollers, so that if the outer hull rolled to the right the inner rolled to the left. By this counterbalancing effect, it was estimated that the stability of the vessel would be absolutely secured; but nothing is recorded of the trials of these boats. The celebrated French inventors, Bourgois and Brun, reintroduced the principle of water-tanks combined with a heavy iron ballast keel.

But in 1881, the Rev. W. Garrett, the English designer of the Nordenfelt boats, invented a new automatic mechanism for ensuring stability. This consisted of two vertical rudders with a heavy pendulum weight so attached to them that, if the boat dipped out of the horizontal, the pendulum swung down and gave the rudders an opposite slant which raised the vessel again to a horizontal position. This arrangement, though perfect in theory, in practice developed fatal defects, and subsequent types have all returned to the use of water-tanks, made to compensate, by elaborate but trustworthy mechanism, for every loss or addition of weight.

3. *Habitability.*—For the habitability of a submarine the prime necessity is a supply of air capable of supporting life during the period of submersion. The first actual constructor of a submarine, Cornelius van Drebbel, of Alkmaar, in Holland, was fully aware of this problem, and claimed to have solved it, not by mechanical but by chemical means. His improved boat, built in England about 1622, carried twelve rowers, besides passengers, among whom King James I. is said to have been included on one occasion, and was successfully navigated for several hours at a depth of ten to fifteen feet. Robert Boyle says in 1662:

> Drebbel conceived that 'tis not the whole body of the air, but a certain quintessence (as chymists speake) or spirituous part of it that makes it fit for respiration, which being spent, the grosser body or carcase (if I may so call it) of the air, is unable to cherish the vital flame residing in the heart: so that (for aught I could gather) besides the mechanical contrivance of his vessel he had a chymical liquor, which he accounted the chief secret of his submarine navigation. For when from time to time, he perceived that the finer and purer part of the air was consumed or over-clogged by the respiration and steames of those that went in his ship, he would, by unstopping a vessel full of the liquor, speedily restore to the troubled air such a proportion of vital parts as would make it again for a good while fit for respiration.'

Drebbel, who was a really scientific man, may possibly have discovered this chemical secret. If so, he anticipated by more than 200 years a very important device now in use in all submarines, and in any case he was the originator of the idea. But his son-in-law, a German named Kuffler, who attempted after Drebbel's death to exploit his submarine inventions, was a man of inferior ability, and either ignorant of the secret or incapable of utilising it. For another century and a half, submarine designers contented themselves with the small supply of air which was carried down at the time of submersion. Even the *Turtle*—Bushnell's boat of 1776, which has been described as 'the first submarine craft which really navigated under serious conditions' was only built to hold one man with a sufficient supply of air for half an hour's submersion. This was a bare minimum of habitability, and Fulton, twenty-five years later, found it necessary to equip his *Nautilus* with a compressed air apparatus. Even with this, the crew of two could only be supplied for one hour.

In 1827, the very able French designer, Castera, took out a patent for a submarine life-boat, to which air was to be supplied by a tube from the surface, protected by a float, from which the whole vessel was suspended. The danger here was from the possible entry of water through the funnel, and the boat, though planned with great ingenuity, was never actually tried. Bauer, in 1855, fitted his *Diable Marin* with large water-tubes, running for thirty feet along the top of the boat and pierced with small holes from which, when desired, a continual rain could be made to fall. This shower-bath had a purifying effect on the vitiated air, but it had obvious disadvantages; and there is no record of its having been put into actual use before the unfortunate vessel sank, as before related.

In the same year, a better principle was introduced by Babbage, an English inventor, who designed a naval diving-bell, fitted with three cylinders of compressed air. His method was followed by Bourgois and Brun, whose boats of 1863-5 carried steel reservoirs with compressed air, at a pressure of at least 15 atmospheres. The principle was now established, and was adopted in Holland and Lake boats, and in all subsequent types, with the addition of chemical treatment of the vitiated air.

4. *Propulsion.*—The various solutions of this problem have naturally followed the successive steps in the development of machinery. Drebbel made use of oars. Bushnell, though he speaks of 'an oar,' goes on to describe it as 'formed upon the principle of the screw—its axis entered the vessel, and being turned one way rowed the vessel forward, but being turned the other way rowed it backward: it was made to be turned by the hand or foot.' Moreover, he had a similar 'oar' placed at the top of the vessel, which helped it to ascend or descend in the water. The conclusion seems unavoidable that to this designer belongs the honour of having invented the screw propeller, and also

of having put it into successful operation. Fulton adopted the same method of propeller and hand-winch in his *Nautilus*; but his huge vessel, the *Mule*, built in 1814 to carry 100 men, was driven by a silent steam-engine. He died during the trials of this boat, and further experiment with it seems to have been abandoned, possibly owing to the great interest excited by his first war steamer, which was building at the same time

A regrettable set-back was thus caused. For forty years no one experimented with any kind of propulsory engine. Bauer, in 1855, could devise no better method of working his propeller than a system of 7-foot wheels, turned by a pair of men running on a treadmill. At the same moment, however, a more fruitful genius was at work. A French professor, Marié-Davy, designed a submarine in which the propeller was driven by an electro-magnetic engine placed in the stern of the ship, with batteries forward. The idea was a valuable one, with a great future before it, though for the moment it achieved no visible success. A year later, in 1855. the famous British engineer, James Nasmyth, designed a 'submerged mortar,' which was in reality a ram of great weight and thickness, capable of being submerged level with the surface, and driven at a speed of over 10 knots by a steam-engine with a single high-pressure boiler.

But in spite of the simplicity and power of this boat, it was finally rejected as being neither invisible nor invulnerable to an armed enemy; and in their desire to obtain complete submersion, the French inventors of the next few years—Hubault, Conseil, and Masson—all returned to the hand-winch method of propulsion. Riou, however, in 1861, adopted steam for one of his boats, and electric power for the other; and in 1883 the American engineer, Alstitt, built the first submarine fitted with both steam and electricity. Steam was also used in the *Plongeur* of Bourgois and Brun, which was completed in the same year.

The American Civil War then gave a great opportunity for practical experiments in torpedo attack; but the difficulty of wholly submerged navigation not having been yet solved, the boats used were not true submarines, but submersibles. Their propulsion was by steam, and their dimensions small. A more ambitious invention was put forward in 1869 by a German, Otto Vogel, whose design was accepted by the Prussian Government. His submersible steamship was to be heavily armed, and was 'considered the equal of a first-class iron-clad in defensive and offensive powers.' These powers, however, never came into operation.

Inventors now returned to the designing of true submarines; and after the Frenchman, Constantin, the American, Halstead, and the Russian, Drzewiecki, had all made the best use they could of the hand-winch or the pedal for propulsion, three very interesting attempts were made in 1877-8 to secure a more satisfactory engine. Olivier's boat, patented in May 1877-8, was to be propelled by the gases generated from the ignition of high explosives, the massed vapours escaping through a tube at the stern. This ingenious method was, however, too dangerous for practical use. Surman's design of 1878 included a propeller, rotated by com-pressed air. But the English boat of the same date, Garrett's *Resurgam*, was much the most noteworthy of the three, and introduced a method which may in the future be brought to perfection with great results. In this boat, the motive force was steam, and propulsion under water, as well as on the surface, was aimed at and actually attained.

In her trials, the vessel showed herself capable of navigating under water for a distance of 12 miles, by getting up a full head of steam in a very powerful boiler, with the aid of a blower, before diving; then by shutting the fire-door and chimney, and utilising the latent heat as long as it would last. When the heat was exhausted, it was, of course, necessary to return to the surface, slow up the fire again and recharge the boiler with water. The vessel was remarkably successful, and had the great merit of showing no track whatever when moving under water. She was lost by an accident, but not until she had impressed Nordenfelt, the Swedish inventor, so strongly that he secured the services of her designer, Garrett, for the building of his own submarine boats. The first of these appeared in 1881.

In the same year were patented Woodhouse's submarine, driven by compressed air, and Génoud's, with a gas-engine worked by hydrogen, which is said to have attained a speed of between four and five knots. Blakesley, in 1884, proposed to use steam raised in a fireless boiler heated by a chemical composition. In 1884, too, Drzewiecki produced the fourth of his ingenious little boats, driven this time not by pedals but by an electric motor. His example was followed by Tuck of San Francisco shortly afterwards, and by Campbell and Ash in their *Nautilus*, which in 1886 underwent very successful trials in the West Indian Docks at Tilbury, near London.

In 1886 D'Allest, the celebrated French engineer, designed a submarine fitted with a petrol combustion engine. But the question of propulsion may be said to have been finally settled, within a few months after this, in favour of the electro-motor. For Gustave Zédé's famous *Gymnote*, which was actually put on the stocks in April 1887, attained in practice a surface speed of 10 knots, and a maximum of 7 to 8 under water. This success saved future designers the trouble of further experiments with ingenious futilities.

6. *Offensive Action.*—We have so far been considering the development of the submarine as a vessel navigable under water, without reference to the purpose of offence in war. But this purpose was from the first in view; and with almost all the inventors recorded, it formed the main incentive of their efforts. The evolution of the submarine weapon has been much simpler, and more regular, than that of the vessel which was to use it; but it has been equally wonderful, and the history of it is equally instructive. Briefly, the French, in this department as in the other, have shown the most imaginative enthusiasm, the Americans the greatest determination to achieve results—even with crude or dangerous means—while the English have to their credit both the earliest attempts in actual war, and the final achievement of the automobile torpedo. Of the Germans, as before, we must record that they have contributed nothing of any scientific value.

Sir William Monson's device of a bark, with an underwater cannon and an accompanying boat was soon developed by the English navy into the more practicable mine, self-contained and floating, to be towed by boat or submarine. In January, 1626, the king gave a warrant to the Master of the Ordnance, 'for the making of divers water-mines, water-petards, and boates to goe under water.' In June of the same year, the Duke of Buckingham, then commanding the naval expedition for the relief of La Rochelle, issued a warrant for the delivery of '50 water-mynes, 290 water-petards, and 2 boates to conduct them under water.' Pepys in his *Diary* for March 14, 1662, mentions a proposal by Kuffler of an 'engine to blow up ships.' He adds, 'We doubted not the matter of fact, it being tried in Cromwell's time, but the safety of carrying them in ships;' and probably this distrust of Drebbel's German subordinate proved to be justified, for nothing more is heard of the design.

The attempt referred to as made 'in Cromwell's time' may have been Prince Rupert's attack on Blake's flagship, the *Leopard*, in 1650. The engine then used was not a submarine one but an infernal machine, concealed in an oil-barrel, brought alongside in a shore boat by men disguised as Portuguese, and intended to be hoisted on board the ship and then fired by a trigger and string. A more ingenious 'ship-destroying engine' was devised by the Marquess of Worcester in 1655. This was evidently a clock-machine, for it might be affixed to a ship either inside, by stealth, or outside by a diver, 'and at an appointed minute, though a week after, either day or night, it shall infallibly sink that ship.'

The clock machine was actually first tried in action in 1776 by Bushnell, or rather by Sergeant Lee, whom he employed to work his *Turtle* for him. The attack by this submarine upon the *Eagle*, a British 64-gun ship lying in the Hudson River, was very nearly successful. The *Turtle* reached the enemy's stern unobserved, carrying a mine or magazine of 150 lbs. of powder, and provided with a detachable wood-screw which was to be turned until it bit firmly on the ship's side. The mine was then to be attached to it, and the clockwork set going. The wood-screw, however, bit upon some iron fittings instead of wood, and failed to hold; the tide also was too strong for Lee, who had to work the wood-screw and the propeller at the same time. He came to the surface, was chased by a guard-boat, and dived again, abandoning his torpedo, which drifted and blew up harmlessly when the clockwork ran down. Lee escaped, but the *Turtle* was soon after-wards caught and sunk by the British. Bushnell himself, in the follow-ing year, attacked the *Cerberus* with a 'machine' consisting of a trigger-mine towed by a whale-boat. He was detected, and his mine captured by a British schooner, the crew of which, after hauling the machine on deck, accidentally exploded it themselves, three out of the four of them being killed.

In 1802 Fulton's *Nautilus*, in her trials at Brest, succeeded in blow-ing up a large boat in the harbour. In 1814 his submersible, the *Mute*, was armed with 'columbiads,' or immensely strong underwater guns, which had previously been tried with success on an old hulk. Simi-lar guns were tried nearly fifty years later by the Spanish submarine designer Monturiol. But the offensive weapon of the period was the mine, and the ingenuity of inventors was chiefly directed to methods of affixing it to the side or bottom of the ship to be destroyed. One of these was the use of long gloves of leather or rubber, protruding from the interior of the submarine, invented by Castera in 1827, and adopted by Bauer, Drzewiecki, and Garrett in succession. But the de-vice was both unhandy and dangerous; there would often be great difficulty in manoeuvring the boat into a position in which the gloves would be available, and they could not be made thick enough to withstand the pressure of any depth of water.

Practical military instinct demanded a method of launching the mine or torpedo against the target, and the first attempts were made by placing a trigger-mine at the end of a spar carried by the nose of the attacking boat. In October, 1863, during the American Civil War, the forts of Charleston were in danger from the accurate fire of the Federal battleship *Ironsides*, and Lieut. Glassell was ordered to attack her in the submarine *David*. He had no difficulty in getting near his enemy and exploding his torpedo, but he had misjudged his distance, and only succeeded in deluging the *Ironsides* with a column of water. The submarine was herself severely injured by the explosion and had to be abandoned.

A second *David*, commanded by Lieut. Dixon, in February, 1864, attacked the *Housatonic*, off the same harbour, and in spite of the greatest vigilance on the part of Admiral Dahlgren's officers, succeeded in reaching the side of the battleship, where she lay for the space of a minute making sure of her contact. The mine was then fired: the *Housatonic* rose on a great wave, listed heavily, and sank at once. The *David*, too, disappeared, and it was found three years afterwards that she had been irresistibly sucked into the hole made in her enemy's side. After this, experiments were made with drifting and towing mines, and with buoyant mines to be released at a depth below the enemy's keel; but by 1868 the invention of the automobile torpedo by the English engineer, Whitehead, of Fiume, solved the problem of the submarine offensive in the most sudden and conclusive manner.

The Torpedo.—Whitehead's success arose out of the failure of an enterprising Austrian officer, Captain Lupuis, who had been trying to steer a small fireship along the surface of the water by means of ropes from a fixed base either on shore or in a parent ship. The plan was a crude one and was rejected by the Austrian naval authorities; it was then entrusted to Whitehead, who found it incapable of any practical realisation. He was, however, impressed with Lupuis' belief in the value of a weapon which could be operated from a distance, and though he failed in designing a controllable vessel, he conceived the idea of an automobile torpedo, and, after two years' work, constructed it in a practical form. It has been spoken of as 'the only invention that was perfect when devised,' and it certainly came very near perfection at the first attempt, but it was erratic and could not be made to keep its depth.

In 1868, however, Whitehead invented the 'balance-chamber,' which remedied these defects, and brought two finished torpedoes to England for trial. They were fired by compressed air from a submerged tube, and at once proved capable of averaging 7½ to 8½ knots up to 600 yards and of striking a ship under way up to 200 yards. The target, an old *corvette* in the Medway, was sunk on to the mud by the first shot, at 136 yards, and immediately after the trials the British Government bought the secret, and other rights. Imitations were, of course, soon attempted in other countries, and a type, called the Schwartzkopf, was for some years manufactured in Berlin and used in the German and Spanish navies; it was also tried by the Italians and Japanese, but it failed in the end to hold its own against the Whitehead.

The automobile torpedo was at first used only for the armament of ordinary warships; it was not until 1879 that an American engineer named Mortensen designed a submarine with a torpedo-tube in the bows. His example was followed by Berkeley and Hotchkiss in 1880, by Garrett in his first Nordenfelt boat of 1881, and by Woodhouse and by Lagane in the same year. Even after this Drzewiecki, Tuck, and D'Allest designed their submarines without torpedo-tubes, but they were, in fact, indispensable, and the use of the Whitehead torpedo has been for the last twenty years assumed as the main function of all submarines designed for war.

The Submarine in War.—The difficulties of construction, propulsion, and armament having now been solved, the submarine at last took its place among the types of warships in the annual lists. From the first England and France held a marked lead, and in Brassey's *Naval Annual* for 1914 the submarine forces of the chief naval powers were given as follows: Great Britain, 76 vessels built and 20 ordered; France, 70 and 23; the U.S.A., 29 and 31; Germany, 27 and 12. The technical progress of the four services was probably more equal than their merely numerical strength; but it was not altogether equal, as may be seen by a brief comparison of the development of the British and German submarine types between 1904 and 1914.

The eight British A-boats of 1904 had a displacement of 180 tons on surface/207 tons submerged; the German Ul of 1904-6 was slightly larger (197/236) but in every other respect inferior—its horsepower was only 250 on surface/100 submerged, against 550/150, its surface speed only 10 knots against 11.5, and it was fitted with only a single torpedo-tube instead of the A-boat's two. This last deficiency was remedied in 1906-8, but the German displacement did not rise above 210/250 nor the horse-power above 400/150, while the British advanced to 550/600 and 1200/550. By 1913 the Germans were building boats of 650/750 displacement and 1400/500 horse-power, but the British were still ahead with 725/810 and 1750/600, and had also a superiority in speed of 16/10 knots to 14/8.

The last German boats of which any details have been published are those of 1913-14, with a displacement of about 800 tons on the surface and a maximum speed of 18/7 knots. The British F-boats of the same date are in every way superior to these, with a displacement of 940/1200 a speed of 20/12 knots, and an armament of six torpedo-tubes against the German four. The comparison cannot be carried, in figures, beyond the date of the outbreak of war, but it is well known among the allies of Great Britain that the superiority has been amply maintained, and, in certain important respects, materially increased.

The four years of conflict have, however, afforded an opportunity for a further, and even more important, comparison. The problems of submarine war are not all material problems: moral qualities are needed to secure the efficient working of machinery, the handling of the ship under conditions of danger and difficulty hitherto unknown in war, and the conduct of a campaign with new legal and moral aspects of its own. In two of these departments, those of efficiency and seaman-ship, the Germans have achieved a considerable show of success, though it could be, and in time will be, easily shown that the British naval service has been more successful still.

But in the domain of policy and of international morality, the comparison becomes no longer a comparison but a contrast; the new problems have been dealt with by the British in accordance with the old principles of law and humanity; by the Germans they have not been solved at all, the knot has simply been cut by the cruel steel of the pirate and the murderer. The methods of the U-boat campaign have not only brought successive defeats upon Germany, they will in the end cripple her commerce for many years; and, in addition to her material losses, she will suffer the bitter consequences of moral outlawry.

Of the general efficiency of the German submarines it is too soon to speak, but it may be readily admitted that they have done well. We know, of course, many cases of failure—cases in which boats have been lost by defects in their engines, by running aground through mishandling in shoal waters, or by inability to free themselves from British nets. On the other hand, the German patrol has been kept up with a degree of continuity which, when we remember the dislocation caused by their severe losses, is, at least, a proof of determination. But the British submarine service has to its credit a record of work which, so far as can be judged from the evidence available, is not only better but has been performed under more difficult and dangerous circumstances. In the North Sea patrolling has been carried out regularly, in spite of minefields and of possible danger from the British squadrons, which must, of course, be avoided as carefully as if they were enemies.

The German High Seas Fleet has been, for the most part, in hiding, but on the rare and brief occasions when their ships have ventured on one of their furtive raids British submarines have done their part, and the only two German Dreadnoughts which have risked themselves outside Kiel since their Jutland flight were both torpedoed on the same day. Better opportunities, as we shall see later, were found in the Baltic, where British submarines, in spite of German and Swedish nets, ice-fields, and the great distance of bases, succeeded in establishing a complete panic, by torpedoing a number of German war vessels and the cargo ships which they were intended to safeguard.

But it was in the Gallipoli campaign that the conditions were most trying and most novel. The British submarines detailed for the attack in Turkish waters had to begin by navigating the Dardanelles against a very rapid current, setting strongly into a succession of bays. They had to pass searchlights, mines, torpedo-tubes, nets and guard-boats; and in the Sea of Marmora they were awaited by a swarm of cruisers, destroyers, and patrol-boats of all kinds. Yet, from the very first, they were successful in defeating all these. Boat after boat went up without a failure, and maintained herself for weeks at a time without a base, returning with an astonishing record of losses inflicted on the enemy. These records will be given more fully in a later chapter; but that of E. 14, Lieut.-Commander Courtney Boyle, may be quoted here as an example, because it is no exceptional instance but merely the earliest of a number, and set a standard which was well maintained by those who followed.

The passage of the narrows was made through the Turkish mine-field, and its difficulty may be judged by the fact that E. 14, during the first 64 hours of the voyage, was diving for 44 hours and 50 minutes. After she began her patrol work, there was more than one day on which she was under fire the whole day, except when she dived from time to time. The difficulty of using her torpedoes was extreme; but she succeeded in hitting and sinking two transports, one of which was 1,500 yards distant and escorted by three destroyers. Finally when, after twenty-two days' patrolling, she began her return voyage, she was shepherded by a Turkish gunboat, a torpedo-boat, and a tug, one each side of her and one astern, and all hoping to catch her in the net; but by deep and skilful diving she escaped them, and cleared the net and the mine-field at a speed of 7 knots.

Her second patrol extended over twenty-three days. This time the tide was stronger, and the weather less favourable. The total number of steamers, grain dhows and provision ships, sunk on this patrol, amounted to no less than ten, and the return voyage was success-fully accomplished, the boat tearing clean through an obstruction off Bokali Kalessi.

The third patrol was again twenty-two days. An hour after starting, E. 14 had her foremost hydroplane fouled by an obstruction which jammed it for the moment, and threw the ship eight points off her course. After a quick scrape she got clear, but found afterwards that her guard wire was nearly cut through. On this trip the wireless apparatus was for a time out of order, but was successfully repaired; eight good ships were burnt or sunk, one of them being a supply ship of 5,000 tons. The return voyage was the most eventful of all. E. 14 came full against the net at Nagara, which had apparent been extendedly since she went up. The boat was brought up from 80 feet to 45 feet in three seconds, but broke away uninjured, with her bow and periscope standards scraped and scored.

The efficiency of the boat and her crew were beyond praise. Since leaving England E. 14 had run over 12,000 miles and had spent nearly seventy days at close quarters with the enemy in the Sea of Marmora; she had never been in a dockyard or out of running order; she had had no engine defects except such as were immediately put right by her own engine-room staff. Yet she made no claim to be better than her consorts. Nor did she make any boast of her humane treatment of captured enemies; she merely followed the tradition of the British Navy in this matter, and the principles of law as accepted by all civilised nations. The commander of a submarine, whether British or German, has to contend with certain difficulties which did not trouble the cruiser captain of former wars.

He cannot spare, from his small ship's company, a prize crew to take a captured vessel into port; he cannot, except in very rare cases, hope to take her in himself; and, again, if he is to sink her, he cannot find room in his narrow boat for more than one or two prisoners. What he can do is to see that non-combatants and neutrals, at least, shall be exposed as little as possible to danger or suffering; he can give them boats and supplies and every opportunity of reaching land in safety. No one needs to be told how the Germans, either of their own native cruelty or by the orders of a brutal and immoral Higher Command, have in such circumstances chosen to deal with their helpless fellow-men, and even with women and children, and with the wounded and those attending them. But it may be well to put in evidence some of the brief notes in which a typical British submarine commander has recorded as a matter of course his own method on similar occasions.

May 8. Allowed two steamers full of refugees to proceed.'

June 20. Boarded and sank 3 sailing *dhows*; towed crew inshore and gave them some biscuit, beef, and rum and water, as they were rather wet.'

June 22. Let go passenger ship.

June 23. Burnt two-master and started to tow crew in their boat, but had to dive. Stopped 2 *dhows*: crews looked so miserable that I only sank one and let the other go.

June 24. Blew up 2 large *dhows*; saw 2 heads in the water near another ship; turned and took them up exhausted, gave them food and drink and put them on board their own ship.'

July 30. Burnt sailing vessel with no boat and spent remainder of afternoon trying to find a craft to get rid of her crew into. Found small sailing boat and got rid of them.'

August 3. Burnt large *dhow*. Unfortunately, 9 on board, including 2 very old men, and their boat was small, so I had to take them on board and proceed with them close to the shore—got rid of them at 9.30 p.m.'

As for the hospital ships, there were numbers of them coming and going; but, empty or full, it is inconceivable that the British Navy should make war upon hospital ships. Victory it will desire, but not by villainy; defeat it will avoid strenuously, but not by the destruction of the first law of human life. The result is none the less certain: in the history of submarine war, as in that of all naval war, it will inevitably be seen that piracy and murder are not the methods of the strong.

CHAPTER 3

The Submarine of Today

The feelings of the average landsman, when he sets foot for the first time in a submarine, are a strong mixture of curiosity and apprehension. The curiosity is uppermost—the experience before you is much more novel than, for example, that of a first trip in an aeroplane. From a mountain or tower, a great wheel or a balloon, you have seen the bird's-eye view of the earth and felt the sensation of hanging over the aerial abyss. But even the fascinating pages of Jules Verne have not told you all that you will feel in a submarine, and nothing but physical experience can do so. You are eager to see the working of new mechanical devices in a wholly strange element, and to learn the use of a new weapon in a wholly strange kind of war.

But with this eagerness, there is an underlying sense of uneasiness, a feeling that you are putting yourself into a position where you are as helpless as a mouse in a patent trap. The cause of this is not fear of war risks, for it is equally strong in harbour, or in time of peace. It is probably connected with the common dread of suffocation, which may be an instinct inherited from ages of primitive life in the open. They will tell you, in the submarine service, that it is a mere habit of mind and very soon forgotten. There is even a story of an officer who, on coming ashore from a year's work in an E-boat, refused to travel in the Tube railway, because it looked so dangerous. He preferred the risks he was used to, and so do most of us.

You stand, then, at the foot of the narrow iron ladder down which you have come from the upper air, you gag your inherited instinct, and let your curiosity loose. Before the boat dives, there is time for a good deal to be taken in. The interior seems large beyond expectation. This is partly an illusion, produced by the *vista* of the compartments, fore and aft of the central control where you are standing. The bulk-head doors being all open at this moment, you can see into the engine and motor rooms towards the stern, and forward through the battery compartment to the bow torpedo-tubes.

The number of men seems large too, and they are all busy; but you note that every part of them is more active than their feet—there is very little coming and going. In the control, close to you, are the captain, a lieutenant, a steersman, and seven or eight other men for working the ballast tanks, air valves, electrical apparatus, and hydroplanes. The last two of them have just come down from deck—the hatches are closed—the engines have already been running for some minutes, though the order escaped your observation.

You are invited 'to see her dive.' You go up to the forward conning-tower scuttle and flatten your face against the thick glass. An order is given. You hear the hissing of air, as the ballast tanks are filled. You expect to see the forward part of the boat dip down into the water in which she is heaving. Instead of that, it is apparently the sea which lifts itself up, moves along the deck, and seems to be coming in a huge slow wave over your scuttle. The light of day gives place to a green twilight, full of small bubbles. Mentally you feel a slight chill; but physically, a warm and sticky sensation. As there is nothing more to be seen out of window, you return to your instructor. He explains to you that the ship is now running on her motors, and that her speed is therefore low—not nearly enough to overhaul a vessel or convoy of any power. On the surface, with her other engines, she could far more than double the pace; and even with the motors, she could do a spurt for a short time—but spurts are very expensive; for they use up the battery power with ruinous rapidity, and then a return to the surface will be necessary, whether safe or not.

At this point it may strike you suddenly that you are now under water—you begin to wonder how deep you are, and why you have not perceived any change in the boat's position. The answer is that the depth marked on the gauges is only twenty feet, and the angle of descent was therefore very slight—much too slight to be perceptible in the short length of a single compartment. The depth of twenty feet is now being maintained with surprising steadiness; the explanation is that two entirely separate forces are at work. First, there are the horizontal rudders or hydroplanes, fitted outside the vessel both fore and aft, by which she can be forced down, provided she has sufficient way on, in much the same fashion as an ordinary vertical rudder forces a ship to one side or the other.

But this is only the diving apparatus; to keep her down, there is her water ballast—the water which was taken into her main ballast tanks, when the order to submerge was given. These tanks contain a sufficient weight of water to counteract the normal buoyancy of the boat, by which she would naturally float upon the surface. When they are emptied, she will neither sink nor rise of her own motion—she will lie or run at whatever depth she is placed, by her hydroplanes or otherwise.

These, you will have noticed, were called the 'main' ballast tanks—there would seem then to be others. There are, and several kinds of them. First, there is an auxiliary ballast tank, which has a peculiar use of its own. A submarine must be able to float or submerge in fresh water as well as at sea; for her base or harbour will often be in the mouth of a river, or she may have to navigate a river, a canal, or a lake. It is a point that would not probably have occurred to you, but the difference between the density of fresh and salt water is sufficiently great to make a real difficulty here. Everyone knows that it is less easy to float in fresh water, and less easy to sink in salt. For practical purposes, a submerged boat is less buoyant in fresh water by 26 tons in 1000, and *vice versa*; so that when a submarine of 1000 tons leaves a river for the sea, she must take an extra 26 tons of ballast to keep her down, and when she comes home again she must get rid of 26 tons, or she will sink so much deeper in the fresh water. For this purpose she has a special tank of the right size, proportioned to her tonnage; and it is placed in the middle of the ship, in order that it may not interfere with her trim when it is filled or emptied.

That last remark will put you in mind that, in any kind of navigation, the trim of the boat is a delicate and important matter. Even in very large and heavy ships you may be able, by shifting guns or cargo, to slip off a shoal, or right a leaking vessel after a collision. In a tickle boat like a submarine, it is necessary to have some means of trimming, the vessel, fore or aft, at any moment, and especially when about to dive, or when caught by some under-water obstruction. Tanks are therefore fitted for this purpose at each end of the boat. They are comparatively small, because the effect required is in ordinary circumstances very limited, and in a desperate emergency they may need to be supplemented by rushing the crew fore or aft, as living ballast. An example of this will be found in a later chapter.

You may now feel that you have heard enough of tanks; but your instructor will insist on showing you a whole additional series. He will

35

make a point of your recognising that a submarine, when submerged, is in reality hanging in the water as a balloon hangs in the air, and for every loss of weight she must be instantaneously compensated, or she will begin to rise. What loss of weight can she suffer while actually under water? It is not perhaps very hard to guess. There is, first of all, the consumption of oil by the engines; secondly, the consumption of food and fresh water by the crew; and thirdly, the departure from time to time of torpedoes. Also, when on the surface, there may be gun ammunition fired away, or other things heaved overboard, and allowance must be made for this when the boat goes down again. The modern submarine is prepared to keep her balance under all such circumstances. She has compensating tanks, and they are placed as near as possible to the oil-tank, fresh-water tank, or torpedo-tube, for whose diminished weight they are to compensate.

You are probably more interested in the torpedo-tubes than in the oil-tanks. It is time then to go forward. You pass through the battery compartment, where the officers' quarters are, and are shown (under the floor) the accumulators, ranged like the honey sections in the frames of a beehive, and very carefully covered over with flexible waterproof covering as well as with close-jointed planking. What would happen if water did find its way down to the batteries? An instant discharge of chlorine gas, blinding and suffocating. What would you do then? Come to the surface at all costs—and lucky it you are in time! The Germans know all about that—and not long ago one of our own boats was only saved by the good goal-keeping of a lieutenant, who caught up a lid of some sort, and stood by the leak, neatly fending off the water spurt from the door of the battery compartment.

Now you are in the forward torpedo compartment, and there are the tubes. I need not say anything about their size or number—you will realise at a glance that when a couple are loosed off at once, a good deal of weight goes out of the ship. The ordinary 18-inch fish is 17 feet long, and takes some handling. The explosive alone in her war-head weighs as much as a big man, say 12 ½ stone, and a 21-inch fish carries twice as much as that, packed in some four feet of her length. Behind that comes the air chamber—another ten feet—with the compressed air to drive the engine, which is in her stern. The air is stored at a pressure of over 2000 lbs. to the square inch; so the steel walls of the chamber must be thick, and this makes another heavy item. Lastly, there is the engine-box with its four-cylinder engine, two propellers, gyroscope and steering gear. Altogether, an 18-inch fish will weigh nearly three-quarters of a ton, and a 21-inch over 2000 ls., so that the amount of compensation needed when you fire, is considerable.

To see how it is done, we will imagine ourselves firing this starboard tube. The torpedo is got ready, and special care is taken to make sure that the firing-pin in her nose is not forgotten. Cases have been known in which a ship has been hit full by a torpedo which did not explode—just as a good many Zeppelin bombs were found in London, after the early raids, with the detonating pin not drawn. The fish is now ready to come alive, and is slid into the tube. The door is shut behind it, and the water-tight outer door, at the other end of the tube, is now ready to be opened by powerful levers. But the immediate result of this opening would be an inrush of sea-water which would weigh the boat's head down; for though the fish's belly fits the tube pretty closely, there is a good deal of empty space where it tapers towards the nose and tail. Here comes in-the tank system. When the tube is loaded, this empty space is filled by water from within the ship, so that no change of weight occurs when you open the outer door.

But when the firing-button has been pushed, and the torpedo has been shot out by an air-charge behind it there is no possibility of preventing the whole tube from filling with water, and this water must be got rid of before the tube can be reloaded. To do this, you first close the outer door again; then you have to deal with the tubeful of water. A good part of it is what the ship herself supplied to fill the space round the torpedo; and this must be pumped back into the special tank it came from. The remainder is the sea-water which rushed in, to take the place left empty by the departing torpedo: and this must be pumped into another special tank to prevent the ship feeling the loss of the torpedo's weight. When you get a fresh supply of torpedoes, these special compensating tanks (which are really a kind of dummy torpedoes) will be emptied out, one for each new torpedo. Meantime, you have now got the tube empty, and can open the inner door and reload.

But what of the torpedo which has been fired? It is travelling towards its mark at a speed of between thirty-five and forty knots, if we suppose the range to be an ordinary one, under 1000 yards, and the torpedo to have been 'run hot,' i.e. driven by hot air instead of cold. The compressed air is heated mechanically inside the torpedo, in the act of passing from the air chamber to the machinery, and this increases both the speed and range. But it is not always convenient or possible to start the heating apparatus, and even when 'run cold' the fish will do thirty knots. This speed is amazing, but it is one of the least wonderful of the torpedo's qualities. The steering of the machine is a double miracle. One device makes it take, after the first plunge, exactly the depth you desire, and another—a gyroscope fitted inside the rudder—gear keeps it straight on its course; or makes it, if you wish, turn in a circle and strike its prey, boomerang fashion.

The head of the fish can also be fitted with cutters which will cut through any torpedo-netting that a ship can afford to carry. The only thing that no ingenuity can accomplish is to make a torpedo invisible during its run. The com-pressed air, when it has passed through the engine, must escape, and it comes to the surface in a continuous boiling line of bubbles. This is visible at a considerable distance; and though, when the track is sighted by the look-out, the torpedo itself is of course always well ahead of the nearest spot where the bubbles are seen rising, it is surprising how often ships do succeed in avoiding a direct shot.

A prompt cry from the look-out, a steersman ready to put his helm over instantly, and the torpedo goes bubbling past, a few feet ahead or astern, or comes in on a tangent and runs harmlessly along the ship's side without exploding. Then away it goes across the open sea, until the compressed air is exhausted, the engine stops, and the mechanical sinker sends it to the ocean bed, which must be fairly strewn with dead torpedoes by this time; for as we know, to our advantage, the proportion of misses to hits is very large in the U-boat's record.

Now that you have seen the weapon—and can at any rate imagine the handling of it you are naturally keen to sight the game, and realise the conditions of a good shot. You go back to the central compartment, where the commander is ready to show you a ship through the periscope. Not, of course, an enemy ship—in this war, if you want a shot at an enemy ship, you must go into his own waters—into the Bight or the Baltic—to find him; and even there he is probably tucked up very tight in his berth, with chained barges and heavy nets all round him, and mines all up the approach. But there are plenty of our own ships out every day—sweeping, cruising, trading; and transporting men, food, mails, and munitions. And what you see will help you to understand why the Germans have spent so many torpedoes, and sunk so comparatively small a proportion of our enormous tonnage.

The boat is now less deep in the water; the gauges mark 15 feet, and you are told that the top of the periscope is therefore some two feet above the surface. The shaft of it is round, like a large vertical piston; but at the bottom it ends in a flattened box, with a hand-grip projecting on each side. You take hold of the grips and look into the box. Nothing is visible but an expanse of water, with a coastline of low hills beyond it—all in miniature. The commander presses the back of your left hand on the grip, and you move round slowly as the periscope revolves. The coastline goes out of the picture, the sea lies open to the horizon, and upon it appears a line of odd-looking spots. They are moving; for the nearest one, which was narrow a moment ago, is now three or four times as broad, and is in a different place in the line.

The line, you are told, is not a line at all, but a convoy, in fairly regular formation. The nearest spot is a destroyer, zigzagging on the flank; the others are ships which have been so effectively 'dazzled' that their shapes are unrecognisable. You carry on, in hope of something nearer, and suddenly a much larger object comes into the field of vision. A ship, of course, though it does not look like any ship you have ever seen; and you are asked to guess its distance and direction. You are bewildered at first; for as you were moving the lens rapidly to starboard, the vessel came in rapidly to port, and as her dazzle-paint makes her stern indistinguishable from her bows, you continue to think she is steaming in that direction.

After a more careful observation, this mistake is corrected. She is crossing us from port to starboard. But at what angle? This is vitally important, for the possibility of getting in a successful shot would depend entirely upon the answer. We are ourselves heading about due north: she is crossing to the east: if her course is south of east, she is coming nearer to us, and our torpedo would strike her before the beam—the most favourable chance. If, on the contrary, her course is north of east she is going away, and the torpedo would have a poor chance of hitting her abaft the beam. In fact, it would not be worthwhile to risk losing so costly a shot. A torpedo at present prices is worth not far short of £2000, and we only carry two for each tube.

You look long and hard at this dazzle-ship. She doesn't give you any sensation of being dazzled; but she is, in some queer way, all wrong—her proportions are wrong, she is somehow not herself, not what she ought to be. If you fix your attention on one end of her, she seems to point one way—if you look away at her other end, she is doing something different. You can't see the height of her funnels clearly, or their relative position. But, with care, you decide that she is coming about south-east and will be therefore your bird in two minutes' time. The

'DOES NOT LOOK LIKE ANY SHIP YOU HAVE EVER SEEN.'

commander is interested. He takes a look himself, laughs, and puts you back at the eye-piece. You hold on in hope that he may, after all, be wrong; but the bird ends by getting well away to the north-east. Your error covered just ninety degrees, and the camouflage had beaten you completely. You begin to think that the ingenuity at command of the nation has been underestimated. But this ship is nothing of a dazzle, the commander tells you—he can show you one whose cut-water seems always to be moving at a right angle to her stern!

He adds that he knew all about that cruiser, and she knew all about him. Otherwise he would not have shown even his periscope; and if he had, she would have had a shell into him by now, and a depth-charge to follow. A depth-charge is perhaps the most formidable weapon against which the submarine has to be on guard. It is a bomb, with a detonator which can be set to explode when it reaches any given depth. A small one would need to hit the mark full, or be very close to it, in order to get a satisfactory result; but the newer and larger ones will seriously damage a submarine within an area of forty yards. The charge is either dropped over the stern of the pursuing vessel, when she is thought to be just over or just ahead of the enemy; or it is fired out of a small and handy short-range howitzer—a kind of lob-shot, a number of which can be made by several patrol boats acting together, so as to cover a larger area with much less risk of embarrassing each other. Even if the submarine is not destroyed outright, the chances are in such a case that she will be so damaged as to be forced to the surface or to the bottom, and then the end is certain. A bad leak would bring her up—an injury to her tanks or rudders might drive her down.

You are uncomfortably reminded once more of that inherited dislike of death by suffocation. If a submarine cannot rise to the surface, you ask, is there no possible means of escape? The answer is that it may be possible, with great difficulty, to get out of the boat; but there is very little chance that you would survive. The lungs are not fitted to bear so great and sudden a change of pressure as that felt in passing from the boat to the water, and from the deep water to the surface. You are perhaps surprised; but the pressure of sea-water at 160 feet is equal to five atmospheres, or about 75 lbs. to the square inch. To pass safely through this to the ordinary surface atmosphere would need a long and gradual process, and not a sudden rise of a few seconds.

A very brave attempt was made on one occasion, when a British submarine had gone to the bottom during her trials, and could not be got up by any effort of her crew. The agony of the situation was intensified by the fact that help was close at hand, if only the alarm could be given, and the whereabouts of the submarine communicated to the rescuers. The officers of the sunken boat were, of course, perfectly aware of the danger from sudden change of pressure; but one of them volunteered to go to the surface, alive or dead, and carry a message on the chance of attracting some ship's attention. To lessen the risk as far as possible, it was arranged that he should go up into the conning-tower, and that the hatch should then be closed beneath him and the water gradually admitted. As it flowed slowly in, and mounted round him, the air in the top of the conning-tower would diminish in extent but increase in pressure. When it reached his neck, the internal pressure would be nearly equal to the external. He would be able to open the top, possibly to make his escape, and conceivably to reach the surface without his lungs being fatally injured. If he failed, he would at any rate have given his life for the chance of saving his comrades.

The commander accompanied him into the conning-tower, meaning, it is said, to return into the ship himself when he had seen to all the arrangements. But when the water was admitted, the two of them were shot out together, and as it happened it was the volunteer who was killed, by striking against the superstructure, while the commander came up alive. In no long time—though it must have seemed unendurably long to those below, waiting in complete uncertainty—the rescuers were informed, found the submarine, and got a hawser under her stern. They raised her high enough out of the water, vertically, to open a hatch and save the crew. Then the hawser gave, and the boat went down again.

That story is not unlikely to haunt you all the way home, and for a long time afterwards. It may even make a difference to your whole feeling about the war under water, as waged by our own service. The submarine is not merely an incredibly clever box of mechanical toys, nor is it only the fit weapon of a cruel and ruthless enemy; it is also a true part of the navy without fear and without reproach, whose men play the great game for each other and for their country, and play it more greatly than we know. The tune of their service is a kind of undertone; but it is in the heroic key, and cannot fall below it.

CHAPTER 4

A British Submarine Base

Our submarine now returns to the surface. She is proceeding on patrol, and her commander, as he bids us goodbye, recommends us to put into the port from which he has just come, and see what a submarine base is like. We take his advice, and return to our trawler. Her head is turned westward and signals are made and answered. The skipper informs us that we are about to pass through a mine-field where the mines are as thick as herring-roe. It is some consolation to hear that 'The Sweep' has already done its daily morning work, and that the channel is presumably clear.

The East Coast of England, from Tynemouth to Thames mouth, is pierced with some ten or a dozen estuaries, all more or less suitable for flotilla bases. It is unnecessary to say how many of these are used by our submarines, or which of them it is that we are about to enter. But a short description can do no harm, because one of these bases is very like another, and all are absolutely impervious to enemy craft. Even if they could navigate the mine-field, so thickly strewn with both our mines and their own, and so constantly and thoughtfully rearranged, they would not find it possible to slip, as we are doing, past the elaborate boom at the harbour mouth, or to escape being sunk by the guns which dominate it, and the seaplanes which are constantly passing over it.

And now that we are inside, it looks an even more dangerous place for an intruder—a perfect hornets' nest. Close to us on the left lies a small pier, with buildings on a hill behind—it the commodore's house and offices, seamen's training-school, and gymnasium. At the pier-head are two or three picket-boats; and a little further on, a light cruiser with her observation balloon mounted. The vast sheds beyond are the hangars of the Air Service. They are painted in a kind of Futurist style, which gives them a queer look from below, but makes them, when seen from a thousand feet up, either invisible or like a landscape of high roads, cornfields, haystacks and groups of trees—objects quite uninviting to any stray air-raider. But their best protection is the efficiency of the machines and men inside them.

Over on the opposite side of the river stretches a long quay. The background of it is a naval railway station; the ships lying in front of it are partly supply ships, partly merchant vessels brought in under convoy, and two of them are depot ships, moored permanently there, and used as headquarters for the submarine, destroyer, and other services. Out in the centre of the harbour lies a still larger depot ship, the floating head-quarters of the admiral who is commodore of the port; and behind her, in two long lines, stretching away upstream into the far distance, lies an apparently inexhaustible force of light cruisers, destroyers, and destroyer-leaders, with here and there a submarine—one is slung aloft in a dry-dock for overhauling. A side creek to the left is crowded with trawlers and drifters, whose men are now ashore 'between sweeps.' At this hour of the day the place is at its fullest, for the daily 'Beef Trip,' or food convoy, has just come in, and the dozen destroyers which escorted it are all lying at their moorings, on both sides of the main stream line. There they will be till to-night, when at 7 o'clock to the second they will all slip away again into the twilight like thin grey ghostly dogs, shepherding another flock of very substantial sheep.

The trawler puts us aboard the depot ship; but the admiral is not there. A picket-boat takes us over to his pier, and we find him in his chart-room, surrounded by maps marked with spots and figures in different colours, quite unintelligible except to those who have the key, and even to them no subject for conversation at large. But the admiral is a good talker, his mind is an encyclopaedia of submarine war and the working of a naval base, and he is amazingly quick in separating the facts which interest you, and yet are fit for repetition outside, from those which you must forget as soon as you have heard them. He begins by explaining the daily routine of the port—the mine-sweeping, which is done regularly twice a day, but at what times the enemy can only guess, and the mine-laying, which is a game of brain against brain, each side trying to see through the other's devices and catch him with their own.

An elementary example would be the obvious dodge of moving the enemy's mine a short distance, instead of removing it altogether—

so that when next he comes that way, he shall run into it unexpectedly, and perish by his own trap. But this, as I have described it, is too simple a device to be successful, and the ingenuity of our mine-layers has improved upon it by a dozen skilful variations. Much can be done by studying carefully the habits of the German mind. One officer, who is specially skilled in this matter, has the credit of being able to make a U.C.-boat lay her eggs just where he pleases, and of knowing exactly when it will be time to go and collect them.

Our own mine-laying and coastal patrol would be more exciting if the possible successes were not limited to an occasional submarine. It is a little dull to be always laying traps for a flotilla that never comes. The work of our coastal submarines is therefore monotonous; but it is none the less invaluable. Besides making sure, it trains a continual succession of crews for oversea work, and gives experience to young commanders. The number of boats increases every year, and the flow of volunteer entries keeps pace with it. The standard demanded is very high, and it is fully maintained. The prize of efficiency is immediate entry into the hardships and dangers of the oversea patrol.

There is no doubt that the hardships are more trying to our men than the dangers. The oversea-patrol is kept up through the winter. The weather off the enemy's coast is often very severe, and boats have to be shut down for long periods. In summer, the work of diving patrols is almost equally arduous, owing to the longer hours of daylight. Boats must frequently be submerged for nineteen or twenty hours at a time; and after the first twelve of these, the air, in spite of purifiers, becomes oppressive to breathe—not even the head of a match will burn. Then there are two special conditions tending towards depression.

First, the positive results are few, and form no measure of the work or the risks. Results are obtained, but never in proportion to the devotion and sanguine hopes of the service. It is a baffling and trying experience to live for days with your eye glued to a periscope—the field of vision is contracted, and too close to the water. The psychological effect of the strain would be bad in the case of any but highly trained and selected officers—as one of them has said, the sighting of a surface enemy is a relief seldom obtained. The Germans are fortunate in the daily, almost hourly, sighting of targets. But their officers, in consequence of continual heavy losses, are commonly sent to sea undertrained, and their results are naturally poor in proportion to the torpedoes expended.

The second of the two causes which would discourage any but

the finest spirit, is the fact that an almost complete silence broods over the Submarine Service. Not only is the work done mostly in the deep-sea twilight; but, however arduous and creditable it may be, it is seldom recognised publicly. Rewards are given, but not openly. A commander may reappear for a day or two among his friends, wearing the ribbon of the D.S.O. or the V.C., or both, but little or nothing will be published of the actions by which he won them. It is not only that information must be kept from reaching the enemy—and naturally the German Admiralty is always anxious to know how their boats are lost—but there is also a settled custom in our navy, a custom older than the Submarine Service, by which 'mention in despatches' is confined to incidents during which one or both sides have been under fire, from gun or torpedo.

Custom in the navy is generally a sound rule; but in this particular instance, the custom did not grow up to fit the case, and does not fit it. The admiral does not say anything on this point; but he tells us that the real danger a submarine commander has to face is not the gun or the torpedo. He may come off his patrol without having been shot at by either, and yet may be entitled to the credit of having been in action for days and nights on end. In fact, every minute that he is in enemy waters he is in danger from mines, and from a host of formidable pursuers—aeroplanes and Zeppelins with bombs, and fast anti-submarine craft with depth-charges and explosive sweeps. No doubt all ships are to some extent in danger from mines, but no other class of vessel is asked to run the. gauntlet on the enemy's coast to anything like the same extent.

If surface ships are sent, they are sent for a single operation, the ground is prepared for them as far as possible, the period of exposure is short, and when the work is done the force is withdrawn. But our submarines are, for days and weeks at a time, close to known minefields and in areas most likely to bold new or drifted mines. They are harassed by hunters to whom they can make no reply, and particularly by aircraft, which can detect them even at sixty feet below the surface. The areas in which they work are comparatively narrow, and so closely patrolled by small craft that it is seldom possible to come to the surface in daylight; navigation, too, is very difficult, and the rapidly changing densities of the water off the enemy's coast make the trimming of the boat and the depth control a matter of constant anxiety.

Yet not only are officers and men found in plenty to enter this service of twilight and silence, but the keenness they show for it is unfailing. The work itself is their one ambition, and their records are astounding. Ask the Captain (S.) of this port. In two years he has organised 370 cruises, lasting in all 1680 days, and extending over a surface mileage of more than 200,000 miles. There was only a single breakdown, and that ended in a triumph; for the commander got himself towed back by an enemy trawler, neatly captured for the purpose. Another—Commander Talbot—made twenty-one cruises; Lieutenant C. Turner, nineteen; Commanders Good hart and Leir, seventeen each; Commander Benning and Lieut. C. Moncreiffe, sixteen. More wonderful still is the fact that the first two of these officers spent fifty-six and sixty-five days respectively in enemy waters, and the other four from thirty-six to forty-nine days each.

The most interesting part of their adventures cannot yet be told; but much may be guessed from an outline or two. Commander Leir, or instance, was repeatedly in action with Zeppelins, seaplanes, and anti-submarine craft, one of which he sank. He was present at the action in the Heligoland Bight in August 1914, and brought home some German prisoners. Commander Benning was also repeatedly in action. Once, after torpedoing an armed auxiliary cruiser, he was forced by enemy sweepers to dive into a German mine-field. There he had to stay, with batteries exhausted, till night gave him a chance of recharging. Another time he went down into a mine-field of his own will, to lie in wait for an armed auxiliary. He was there for three hours, but ambushed her success-fully in the end, close to the German coast.

Lieut.-Commander Turner covered 20,000 miles to his own score, and passed much of his time actually in the swept channels, with enemy patrols in sight the whole day. Sometimes he came up and fought them, sometimes they hunted him with depth-charges. For those who sleep in beds and travel in buses, it is an almost unimaginable life. 'Yes,' says the admiral, 'in this service, officers need a two-o'clock-in-the-morning courage every hour they are at sea: and they have it.'

The charts are put away. We move out, first to the gymnasium, where physical drill is going on, then towards the great air-sheds. As we approach the first of these, an officer meets us and hands a block to the admiral with the morning report upon it.

The admiral's face lights up as he reads. 'A lucky chance—something to interest you.' The Beef Trip, it appears, which has just returned, was escorted as usual by two seaplanes, flying ahead of the convoy. The starboard one of these had sighted a submarine at 8.30 a.m. and swooped towards her instantly. She was nearly submerged

'TOWED BACK BY AN ENEMY TRAWLER.

when the seaplane passed over her, but the two big depth-charges which were dropped in a flash, fell right into her wash and close to the conning-tower, which disappeared in the explosion.

An excellent bit of work! But the face of the officer standing by shows a distinct cloud. 'What is it?' Well, the fact is that the pilot of the other seaplane, a mile and a half away to port, had an impression that the submarine was British.

The pilot of the bomb-dropper is sent for and comes out at once—a fair-haired and very young lieutenant, with an air of perfectly undisturbed serenity. He is sure nothing is wrong—it is 'only a muddle.' His companion pilot had certainly sighted and spoken a British submarine some quarter of an hour earlier; but this was not the one. Also another boat, E. 134, was out on patrol in that precise direction, but she was not due in that spot till 11 o'clock, B.S.T., and it was highly improbable she would be there so much before her time. Besides, he knew the colour of a Hun conning-tower. Undoubtedly it was 'only a muddle.' The explanation sounds a good one, but it is a speculation, not a certainty; and on further inquiry, it appears that nothing has since been heard of E. 134. The admiral sends off the young pilot with a word of good cheer; but when he has gone, he hands back the report with a serious look. The incident has become too interesting. It is no longer something to tell a visitor. We go into the sheds and spend the remainder of our time in viewing the huge Americas and Handley-Pages.

The rest of the story comes after lunch, when we go to visit the Captain (S.) in his depot ship. He has heard all about our pilot, and our submarine too. E. 134 lay all night in her billet, resting on the bottom at 140 feet and listening with all her hydrophones. In the morning her watch was rewarded; she heard, first, the monotonous low ticking of a German submarine's motors passing near her on the outward patrol—then at 8.30 the heavy dull boom of two explosions close together—then not a sound more! Finally, at her appointed time, noting that the U-boat had never stirred again, she rose to the surface and came home in rear of the sweep. The muddle is cleared up, and in the best manner.

We discuss the dead submarine and ask whether she would be, or would have been, more formidable when used against a convoy than against a single ship. The Captain (S.) who has already been torpedoed once himself, thinks there can be no doubt on this subject.

'SHE WAS NEARLY SUBMERGED WHEN THE SEAPLANE
PASSED OVER HER.'

A single ship is much more easily approached than a convoy—she has only one set of eyes on the look-out, from one position, and the enemy can stalk her without fear of being trodden on from other quarters. Convoys ought to escape nearly every time, and they do. Look at the record of this port—not one loss in two years.

This opinion is based on experience, but the matter looks different from the point of view of the convoy escort, whose responsibility weighs upon him every day afresh. This we discover when we pass on to visit a destroyer-leader, at a later hour in the evening. She is being got ready for the night's work and it is now just six, but her captain assures us that what remains of his time is entirely ours. He takes us down to his own room, an elegant and almost spacious apartment, very unlike anything to be seen in a destroyer of the ordinary type; and he, too, answers our question positively.

Which is easiest—to hit a single ship or a convoy? The question answers itself—a submarine ought to get at least one bird out of a covey every time! She does not do it, perhaps; but look at the trouble we take to prevent her. Think of all the work put in by the auxiliary patrol to keep the sea fairly clear to start—with armed yachts, trawlers, whalers, drifters, motor-launches, mine-sweepers, net-drifters and motor-boats, out day and night all round the whole coast of the U.K. That is their routine work; and besides that they supply escorts to individual ships of special value and to ocean convoys, when they have arrived at their port of initial entry, and are to be taken on elsewhere. Then there are the various kinds of protective devices for the ships themselves—the dazzle-painting, the smoke-boxes on broads, and the smoke-boxes for floating behind you. And since we *are* talking of these things, there is the work of the destroyers and trawlers on regular convoy.

This is, of course, the captain's own job, and we naturally bint a desire that he should pursue the subject.

There is no difficulty about it—the Germans already know all that they can ever know of our convoy system—how it is or-ganised in the form of group-sailings on definite routes, and worked, as far as possible, at night, with extra protection given by daylight and during moonlight hours—above all, how successful it is, and how, little by little, they have given up the chase of mercantile convoys for the attack of transports and single ships of great size and value. In one month, for instance, of the present year, 690 vessels were convoyed from England to France, of which only three were attacked, and only two sunk, including one small sailing ship. More astonishing still, out of 693 convoyed from France to England in the same month not one was touched, or even attacked. Then there are the Dutch and Scandinavian lines.'

We should like to know exactly how it is done, and especially what part the destroyers play in the game. Briefly, but very sharply, the picture is drawn for us. You see a fine August day, off the coast of Scotland, with white summer clouds over a rippling sea; a compact convoy of eight ships sailing in two columns, with a ninth lagging on the left, three times her proper distance to the rear. Their speed is slow; they are flanked on both sides, fore and aft, by armed trawlers, with one just ahead of the two columns, and they are covered by two fast destroyers. The first of these is ahead of the convoy, zigzagging continuously from side to side across the whole front. The second is zigzagging in another direction. Suddenly, from this second destroyer, a signal is seen to fly. Her look-out has spotted the wake of a periscope 1000 yards away on her starboard bow, moving to cut off the convoy, from the right column of which it is already not more than 1500 yards distant.

A torpedo fired at this moment should cross the convoy formation exactly in the middle, and would have an excellent chance of sinking either of the centre ships in either column—it could hardly miss all four. But the destroyer has in a moment altered course 8 points to starboard, and is prolonging this zigzag directly towards the enemy at thirty-odd knots, with her forward guns blazing. The U-boat captain, no doubt, longs to take his shot into the brown; but he has less than one minute in which to perform the more urgent duty of saving his own ship. Down he goes, with a depth-charge after him, and is not seen or heard of again in this story. The convoy calls up its lame duck and goes safely to its destination.

'Yes,' says the captain, 'we get them through, and it all looks very simple; but it's mostly a matter of ten seconds, and you can't grow fat on a daily margin of ten seconds.'

'But the admiral has something to say on your report? '

'The admiral writes outside, "Good look-out and prompt action of *Swallow* probably averted a casualty to the convoy." He has to write that most days—he must be tired of writing it.'

It is now two minutes to seven. As we drop into our picket-boat, the destroyer slips silently from her moorings and fades away down-stream with eleven other thin grey phantoms.

CHAPTER 5

Submarines and War Policy

The *Encyclopaedia Britannica* says:

Strategy has been curtly described as the art of concentrating an effective fighting force at a given place at a given time, and tactics as the art of using it when there.

In less scientific language, you fight a battle by means of tactics, and a campaign by means of strategy. But when nations live, as we have all been living for many years past, in constant preparation for war, there must be forethought as to the means and methods to be employed. Each nation has broad general plans, ready for the moment when fighting is decided upon, and ships, guns, and armies are provided accordingly. This is what is meant by war policy; and examples will come to mind at once. We live in a group of islands, with dominions and other possessions overseas, and we have no desire to attack our continental neighbours.

British war policy has therefore always been chiefly directed to the provision of an invincible navy for defending our shores and our commerce. The German Empire, on the other hand, is practically self-contained; it lies on the continent, with land powers for neighbours whom it has long hoped and intended to dominate. German war policy, therefore, concerned itself until quite recently with plans for aggression by land, and only provided a powerful fleet when it became desirable to have a weapon in hand against England—not necessarily to fight us on equal terms, but, as they said themselves, to make us hesitate to take sides against them.

In this way it came about that both countries had a great naval war policy, and watched each other carefully, building dreadnoughts against dreadnoughts, and cruisers against cruisers. We made great and successful efforts to keep the lead; for sea power is a matter of life and death to us; and the Germans were spending every mark they could spare, to get more and more nearly upon even terms. It is certain that the war policy of both powers took account of the possible uses of submarine boats; but the lines of thought which they followed were in some ways widely different, and they led, when war came, to unexpected developments. Let us consider for a few moments what the British admirals on the one hand, and the German on the other, intended to do with their submarine forces, and what they actually did when the time for action came.

British war policy was essentially non-aggressive. The navy had but one possible antagonist of the first rank at sea, and that one we should never have fought with, except in a war of defence. Our submarines, therefore, had two obvious duties marked out for them. They would help in coast defence by making it dangerous for ships of war or transports to approach, and they might be used, if an opportunity arose, to attack a fleet in harbour, or a cruiser at sea. There was every probability that any fleet of a power at war with us would sooner or later have to spend a good deal of time in port, and it would certainly be well to have the means to attack it there. But, important as this function was, the idea of defence against invasion probably came first, and there is no doubt that an efficient submarine force is a very formidable addition to our flotilla for coast defence.

Perhaps we thought, in those years of perpetual preparation, too much about the 'Invasion of England' and too little about the duty of supporting our Allies on land; and we had this much justification, that the power from which we had every reason to expect an attack, was one directed by men of great energy and determination, certain to be relentless in pressing a war home upon us, even at the risk of a heavy loss. On the other hand, those who spoke and wrote most about invasion, nearly always failed to realise the immense difficulty of the undertaking; and they failed especially to see that, in modern times, the conditions had changed very considerably in favour of the defence. The initial problem of an invader by sea must always be the provision of transport sufficient for a large body of troops, with arms, equipment, and supplies of food and munitions.

Even if we allow only two tons of shipping per man—the Japanese allowed six tons—the transport of 100,000 men would take twenty vessels of 10,000 tons each, and to collect these and load them would be a big operation, difficult to conceal. In fact to conceal it, for a sufficiently long time, from a defence force well supplied with wireless telegraphy, fast scouts, and aerial observation, would now be a practical impossibility. But even if we suppose such an expedition to be able (under cover of fog, or by a complete surprise) to cross the North Sea unobserved, there remains the further difficulty of the landing. A place must be found where the invaders could obtain immediate control of supplies and communications; there are but half a dozen such places at most upon our eastern coast-line, and these are all prepared for a strenuous defence by land. If we add to the land defence a mine-field and the presence of an unknown number of submarines, the attempt be-comes one involving the certainty of immense losses, and the extreme probability of failure. Even the German war-lords have not yet made up their minds to the risk of seeing eight or ten divisions drowned in an hour.

Besides coast defence and harbour attack, there might possibly be a chance for our submarines in a fleet action. Of that, all that can be said now is that our Submarine Service is believed to have shown greater promptness and ingenuity in its preparations than the German Admiralty, and awaits the next naval engagement with eager anticipation. But already it has been found practicable to use our submarines for two very important kinds of work, to an extent which was certainly quite unforeseen. One of these is the chase and destruction of enemy submarines—a kind of service which has been pronounced impossible, even in books written during the later stages of the war, but actual examples of which will be given in one of the chapters which describe our hunting methods. The other kind of work is the blockade of the enemy's shipping trade and supply service, to be described when we come to the account of our submarine campaigns in the Baltic and Dardanelles.

If we turn now to German naval policy, we shall come at once upon an interesting point, which has not been generally understood. We have been told that the German Admiralty, before the war, was completely deceived as to the value of the submarine. And Mr. Marley Hay has been often quoted as saying that, in several conversations in 1911, Admiral von Tirpitz 'expressed emphatically his opinion that he considered submarines to be in an experimental stage, of doubtful utility, and that the German Government was not at all convinced that they would form an essential or a conspicuous part of their future naval programme.' Mr. Hay shows clearly that this was not said with the object of misleading; for he was urging Tirpitz to build, and the admiral continued to refuse.

When war broke out, the German Navy had only twenty-seven submarines built against seventy-six British and seventy French boats, and she was only building twelve more, against the twenty and twenty-three on our side. This may have been partly due to a miscalculation of their efficiency; but the main reason was probably that the directors of German war policy were (at that time) preparing for a war in which our navy was to take no part. The account with England was to be settled at a later date. The immediate intention was to deal with France and Russia, and the assistance of the Austrian and Italian submarines in the Mediterranean was of course reckoned upon.

When war came these calculations were falsified. The German High Seas Fleet found itself unable to stand up to ours, and German war policy was forced to take a different direction. The U-boats' first allotted task was the legitimate one of reducing our margin of superiority in battle-ships and cruisers. While our fleet was certain to keep the sea, and protect our long coast-line and huge merchant tonnage, the German High Seas Fleet must lie in the Kiel Canal, risking only furtive and futile rushes into the open. But if the U-boats could hit a sufficient number of our more active warships, they might bring the forces nearer to an equality, and perhaps establish a prestige for their own service. How they failed in this attempt we shall see presently.

When their failure in the game of attrition became evident, the U-boats were utilised in a different way. A submarine blockade of the British Isles was plainly threatened by Admiral von Tirpitz towards the end of 1914; and the official announcement of it was made on February 4, 1915. By this document it was declared that on and after February 18, every British or French merchant vessel found in the waters of the 'war region round these islands will be destroyed, without its always being possible to warn the crews or passengers of the dangers threatening.' Neutral ships, it was added, would not be attacked unless by mistake; but they are warned not to take the risk.

Those who know even a little of the history of our old wars will see at a glance that this is a new move in naval war policy, and one made by the Germans to get over certain difficulties which arise from the very nature of submarine boats, and which are especially embarrassing when the submarines belong to a navy decidedly inferior to its enemies at sea. The old and well-established rules of naval war laid down that you could only interfere with merchant shipping if it were engaged in carrying contraband of war. To ascertain whether the ship you had sighted was carrying contraband or not, you had to board and search her. If innocent, you must let her proceed on her voyage. If apparently guilty, you took over her men or otherwise placed them in safety, put a prize crew on board and sent her home to a port of your own, to be tried legally by a properly constituted tribunal called a Prize Court. If this court decided that she was, in fact, carrying contraband, she was your prize. If you were forced by stress of circumstances to destroy the prize, instead of sending her into port, you took every care to remove everyone on board before doing so; and when you had not room for so many people, you released the prize rather than endanger or sacrifice the lives of non-combatants.

All these humane rules could well be observed by any ordinary cruiser; and they were, in fact, kept by the *Emden* and other German cruisers when harrying British commerce in the East. But it is obvious at the first glance that a submarine would be continually in difficulties over them. It would always be risky for so fragile and unhandy a vessel to board and search a big ship, which might prove to be armed with guns or bombs. No submarine could find room for merchant crews or passengers in her own small compartments, and no submarine could afford to spare a prize crew for even one prize, or the time and horse-power to tow her into port. In short, it was plain, from the first, that the legitimate cruiser game could not be played at all by submarine boats. The Government of the United States put the truth unanswerably in these words:

'The employment of submarines for the destruction of enemy trade is of necessity completely irreconcilable with the principles of humanity, with the long existing undisputed rights of neutrals, and with the sacred privileges of non-combatants.'

The British Navy had an advantage here—the inestimable advantage of a force that could keep the sea against all its enemies. It was, therefore, possible for our submarines to stop an occasional ship with impunity, or to call up a destroyer and send a prize into port; and in the narrow waters of the Baltic and the Sea of Marmora, supply ships and merchantmen were captured and destroyed by them with every regard for the laws of humanity. But the German submarines had no fleet at sea to back their attempted blockade, and German war policy therefore took the downward course, hacking a way through the rules, and sacrificing, for the hope of victory, the very foundations of civilised human life. The U-boats began by turning passengers and crews adrift in open boats, no matter in what weather or how far from land.

'TURNING PASSENGERS AND CREWS ADRIFT IN OPEN BOATS.'

They went on to sink even great liners without search, and without warning; and they came finally down to the destruction of helpless men and women in boats, in order that the ships they had torpedoed might disappear without a trace—*spürlos versenkt.*

CHAPTER 6

Submarine v. Warship

The use of the submarine for attacking warships is, of course, perfectly legitimate, and the powers and possibilities of this weapon were
much discussed before the war. Some writers of note believed that
the day of the big battleship was practically over—that such vessels
could be 'pulled down' with certainty by any enterprising submarine commander, without any corresponding risk to his own boat.
Others, with cooler or more scientific heads, maintained that there is
an answer to every weapon, and that the introduction of submarines
would not change the principles of war. The result has shown that the
latter school of opinion was right. The submarine has achieved some
striking successes here and there against the larger ships of war, but
has not rendered them obsolete or kept them from going about their
true business, the control of the sea; and as time goes on, it is rather
the submarine than the battle-ship which is found too vulnerable to
challenge a fight, when neither has the advantage of surprise.

This legitimate use of the submarine formed part, as we have seen,
of both British and German war policy—though, in our own case, it
was originally considered rather as a means of defence against invasion;
than of offence on the high seas. It was, therefore, not unnatural that
the U-boat should score first. Besides, we were offering a hundred
targets to one. Our cruisers were all over the North Sea, while no German ships could be met there except an occasional mine-layer like the
Königin Luise. This state of things has only become more invariable as
the War has developed; and the most remarkable result, so far, of the
contest between the two submarine services is the practical equality
of the score on the two sides. With infinitely fewer and more difficult chances, the British submarine has actually surpassed the U-boat's
record, in successes obtained against enemy ships of war, and immense-

ly surpassed it in the proportion of successes to opportunities.

The first warship to fall to the torpedo of a submarine was the *Pathfinder*, a light cruiser of about 5,000 tons, with a complement of 268 officers and men, of whom some half were saved. The boat which sank her was the U. 21, commanded by Lieutenant Hersing, who raised high hopes in Germany which he was not destined to fulfil.

A greater captain is said to have been Captain Otto Weddigen, who achieved the sensational feat of pulling down three of our cruisers in one hour, and was supposed by some of his fellow-countrymen to have solved the problem of reducing the British Fleet to an equality with the German. But he owed more to luck and our inexperience than to any peculiar skill of his own; In the early morning of September 22, 1914, he stalked the armoured cruisers *Aboukir*, *Rogue*, and *Cressy*, old ships of 12,000 tons and 18 knots' speed, which were out on patrol duty in the North Sea, and were about to take up their stations for the day's work.

The danger of the submarine was hardly yet fully recognised; and when the *Aboukir*, was struck by a violent explosion, the general belief in the squadron was that she had run foul of a mine. She listed heavily and sank slowly, her funnels almost level with the water, and the smoke coming out as from the water's edge. The other two ships closed her at once, and had got within two cables of her when the *Hogue* was struck in turn by two torpedoes almost simultaneously. The effect was extraordinary. 'She seemed,' says an eyewitness, 'to give one jump out of the water and then to go straight down.' So quickly did she go, that she was out of sight long before *Aboukir*, who took twenty minutes to sink, so that her men (as one of them said) 'got time to do the best.'

The moment the *Hogue* was struck, it was realised that submarines were at work, and *Cressy* opened fire from one of her 9-2-in. guns. She was hit herself by two torpedoes immediately afterwards, and listed heavily, so that everything began to roll down the deck. But she sank slowly and her gunners kept up their fire most gallantly, giving up their chance of being saved for the hope of killing their enemy before they went down. They fired a dozen shots in all, and are said by Lieutenant Harrison to have sunk one of the attacking U-boats. A survivor from the *Aboukir* said:

> I reckon her gunners were about the bravest men that ever
> lived. They kept up the firing until she had 40 degrees of list.

They died gamely, did those fellows. (Their shipmates were worthy of them.) There was absolutely no panic on the cruiser; the men were as calm as at drill.

At last some trawlers came up; and, after two hours, some destroyers. Only 777 of the three ships' crews were saved, out of a total of about 2,100; and 60 officers were lost out of 120.

Some of our men must have been in the water for three or four hours. The *Aboukir* men were taken to the Rogue; when the Hogue was sunk, they were taken to the *Cressy*; when the *Cressy* was taken, they were thrown in the sea again. Yet here they are, and there is only one thing they want—to go to sea again and have another whack at the men who torpedoed them.'

Possibly they had their wish; for some of them may have been on board the British ship which, a few months later, destroyed U. 29 (Weddigen's boat) by a brilliant and almost reckless feat of seamanship, which, in later days, will form a favourite yarn of the service.

The only other warship lost by submarine action in 1914 was the *Hawke*, an armoured cruiser twenty-five years old, which was torpedoed while on patrol in the North Sea, and sank in ten minutes, only seventy of those on board being saved. The year 1915 began badly for us, and ended by being decidedly our worst year on one side the account, though it was our best on the other. At 2 o'clock in the morning of January 1, a squadron of battle-ships, of the older types of 1901 and 1902, was steaming down Channel in line ahead. There was a gale blowing, and the sea was running high. The last two ships of the line were the *London* and the *Formidable*, the latter of which was suddenly shaken by a violent explosion, and not long afterwards by a second one.

Even then, the ship did not sink till forty-five minutes after; and if it had not been for the rough weather and icy water, boats and rafts might have been got away with most of the crew. As it was, no steam-pinnaces could be got out, and the oars of the 42-foot cutter and other boats were nearly all smashed against the ship's sides. The whole company, from the officers, giving quiet orders on the bridge, to the men smoking on the slant deck, behaved as if at manoeuvres, and Captain Loxley, who went down with his ship, distinguished himself by signalling to the *London* not to stand by him, as there was a submarine about. One boat came ashore at Lyme Regis, with forty-six live men and nine dead in her; seventy more men were brought in after three hours' hard and dangerous work by the 50-ton smack, *Provident*, of Brixham—William Pillar, skipper. His crew consisted of three men and a cook-boy. Out of a total complement of more than 700, only 201 were saved in all. Among the lost were thirty-four officers, including eight mid-shipmen and a sub-lieutenant.

On March 11, the *Bayano*, an armed merchant-cruiser, was torpedoed off the Firth of Clyde, and went down with 170 of her 200 men. On April 11, the *Wayfarer* transport was torpedoed, and ran ashore off Queenstown. On May 1, the *Recruit*, a small torpedo-boat of 385 tons, was sunk in the North Sea, with thirty-nine out of her sixty-four officers and men.

Then came two grave losses on two consecutive days. The British Fleet off Gallipoli had already lost the *Irresistible* and *Ocean* by floating mines; and now the U-boats succeeded in inflicting another double loss on us, at a moment when the army needed the strongest support to ensure success. On May 26, a single torpedo sank the *Triumph*, while she was co-operating with the Australian and New Zealand troops before Ari Burnu. She was accompanied by an escort of two destroyers, and was about to open fire when the submarine got a shot into her. She listed till her deck touched the water, and in five minutes capsized completely, but remained floating for twenty minutes, keel upwards. Some 460 of the officers and men were saved.

The *Triumph* was not designed for our navy, but taken over from the builder's yard, and the curious arch formed by her derricks made her outline a conspicuously foreign feature in our fleet. The *Majestic*, on the other hand, which quickly followed her to destruction, was a typically British vessel, and gave her name to the whole class, built in 1895 and the following years, and then greatly admired. She also, on May 27, was supporting the army in action on the Gallipoli peninsula, when a German torpedo ended her twenty years' career. She carried about 760 officers and men, but nearly all of them were saved. In June, two torpedo-boats, the *Greenfly* and *Mayfly*, of 215 tons, were sunk; the *Roxburgh*, a 10,000-ton cruiser, was slightly damaged; and the *Lightning* torpedo-boat, of 275 tons, was disabled, but brought into harbour. On August 8, a U-boat sank one of our large auxiliary cruisers, the *India*, off the coast of Norway and in Norwegian territorial waters. By this breach of the rules, she succeeded in killing 10 officers and 150 men, cut of a complement of over 300.

The losses so far enumerated were all strictly naval losses, Up to this time, although we had been trans-porting troops by the hundred

'WERE BROUGHT IN BY THE 50-TON SMACK, *PROVIDENT*, OF BRIXHAM.'

thousand from Canada and Australia to England, and from England to France, India, Mesopotamia, Egypt, and Gallipoli, our numbers had hardly suffered the smallest diminution by submarine action. Again, during the last three years (1916-18) we have had minor losses now and then; but the one and only real disaster of this kind came upon us in 1915. On August 14, the British transport, the *Royal Edward*, was in the Ægean, carrying reinforcements for the 29th Division in Gallipoli, and details of the Royal Army Medical Corps, when she was torpedoed by a German submarine and sank rapidly. She had on board 32 military officers and 1,350 troops, in addition to her own crew of 220 officers and men.

Of all these, only 600 were saved; and for the first time in modern war we suffered the cruel loss of soldiers to the strength of a whole battalion killed—not in battle, but helpless and unresisting, without the chance of firing a shot or delivering a last charge with the bayonet. The ship herself was a less harrowing loss; but she was a fine vessel that we could ill spare—a steel triple-screw steamer of 11,117 tons and 545 feet in length. She, like her sister ship, the *Royal George*, was originally built for the Egyptian Mail Steamship Company, and ran between Marseilles and Alexandria. Her later service was carrying the mails for the Canadian Northern Steamship Company between Avonmouth and Montreal—and now she had returned to Eastern waters, only to give an isolated and inconclusive triumph to a desperate enemy.

The remainder of the year saw many attempts by the U-boat commanders to repeat this success; but they mostly ended in failure. On September 2, the transport *Southland* was hit by a torpedo, but got into Madras under her own steam, with a loss of 30 men killed in the explosion. On September 19, the *Ramazan*, with 385 Indian troops on board, was shelled and sunk by a submarine, off Antikythera. In October, the trans-port *Marquette* was sunk in the Ægean. On November 3, the transport *Mercian* was heavily shelled, and had nearly 100 killed and wounded. On November 5 the *Tara*, armed boarding-steamer, was sunk in the Bay of Sollum, on the eastern border of Egypt; and immediately afterwards two small Customs cruisers—the *Prince Abbas* of 300 tons and the *Abdul Moneim* of 450—were sunk at the same place, and no doubt by the same pair of U-boats.

The year 1916 showed clearly that, as a weapon against armed ships, the U-boat was not likely to succeed, after the first period of surprise was past. During this year we lost three mine-sweepers—*Primula*, *Clacton*, and *Genista*; two empty transports—the *Russian* and

Franconia; the *Zaida* and *Duke of Albany*, armed steamers of the auxiliary patrol; and one destroyer, the *Lassoo*, which was sunk with a loss of six men, either by mine or torpedo, off the coast of Holland. To this insignificant list must be added one disaster of a more serious kind. As we have already noted, our control of the North Sea was a continuous and effective control, and every effort was made, especially after the flight of the Germans from Jutland, to bring out the enemy fleet from its hiding-place. These efforts, of course, involved the exposure of our advanced forces to certain risks.

On August 19, there was a report that the High Canal Fleet was at sea again. Hope outstripped belief, and light cruisers were sent out in every direction to find the enemy. Two of these, the *Nottingham* and the *Falmouth*—good ships of 5,400 and 5.250 tons—were torpedoed and sunk while scouting. Here again it was the loss of the men which we felt most. The ships were new and useful ones; but they could be replaced, and they belonged to a class in which the enemy's force, since the Battle of Jutland, had been deficient, almost to a disabling degree. There was no ground for the German hope that our naval superiority could be permanently whittled away by rare and fractional losses like these. Our battle fleet continued to hold up theirs, and our blockade of their coasts was in no degree weakened.

The record of 1917, and the first half of 1918, is even more significant. The German submarine effort was more and more completely diverted from legitimate to illegitimate war—from the attack on the enemy's armed forces, to the destruction of non-combatants and neutrals in mercantile shipping of any kind. British destroyers, going everywhere, facing every kind of risk, and protecting everyone before themselves, now and again furnished an item to the German submarine bag; but the 'regardless' campaign against the world's trade and the world's tonnage was now the U-boats' chief occupation. One legitimate objective they did still set before themselves—the destruction or hindrance of transport for the United States Army between the shores of America and Europe.

Again and again during 1917, and even in the earlier days of 1918, assurances were given to the German people by Admiral von Tirpitz, by Admiral von Capelle, by the Prussian Minister of Finance in the *Diet*, and by the chief military writers in the Press, that the promise of an American army was a boast and a deception, that the American troops could not and would not cross the Atlantic, because of the triumphant activity of the U-boats. Of the complete failure to make good these assurances no better account need be given than that supplied by the German Admiralty, in answer to the complaints of their own people. Towards the end of July 1918, when there was no longer any possibility of concealing the presence of a large and victorious American force in France, Admiral von Holtzendorff, the Admiralty Chief of Staff, gave the following explanation to the *Kölnische Zeitung*. He admitted the success of the Allies in improving oversea transport, especially the transport of troops from America. But in reply to the statement that there was in Germany much disappointment that the submarines had sunk so few of the American transports, he asked, with truly Prussian effrontery, how *could* submarines be specially employed against American transports. He said:

'The Americans have at their disposition, for disembarkation, the coasts from the North of Scotland to the French Mediterranean ports, with dozens of landing-places. Ought we to let our submarines lie in wait before these ports, to see whether they can possibly get a shot at a strongly protected American transport, escorted by fast convoying vessels? The convoys do not arrive with the regularity and frequency of railway trains at a great station, but irregularly, at great intervals of time, and often at night or in a fog. Taking all this into consideration, it is evident how little prospect of success is offered for the special employment of submarines against American transports.'

This is all sound enough, and in fact the U-boats have only succeeded in killing 126 men out of the first million landed from America. But the argument of Admiral von Holtzendorff does not explain the official assurances by which the German public was deceived for more than a year, and it only partially explains the ill success of the U-boats. That could only be fully done by considering the offensive (or offensive-defensive) action of warship against submarine—which will be touched upon presently.

The record of the 'bag' made during the war by our own submarines has never yet been published in a complete form. Yet it is a most striking one, and ought effectually to remove any impression that the German Submarine Service is in any way superior—or even equal—to ours. In three years of war our boats sank over 300 enemy vessels. We lost, of course, many more; but when it is remembered that we were offering to our enemies every week more than four times as many targets as they offered us during the whole three years, it will be admitted that the comparison is not one to give them much ground for satisfaction. At present, however, this general comparison is not the one which we wish to make—we are concerned now with attacks on warships, or armed forces, and not on mercantile shipping. The greater part of our record is made up of such attacks, and it is now possible to give a short summary of them.

There have been, during this war, practically only three hunting-grounds where British submarines could hope to meet with enemy warships, transports, or supply ships. These are the North Sea, the Baltic, and the Dardanelles or Sea of Marmora. Of the work done by our submarines in the Baltic and Dardanelles we shall have separate accounts to give in later chapters. For the present, it is enough to tabulate the results. In the Baltic the bag included, besides a large number of steamers (some carrying iron ore for military use), the following warships: three destroyers, three transports, one old battleship or cruiser, one light cruiser, and one armed auxiliary. In the Dardanelles or Sea of Marmora were sunk or destroyed the following, besides a very large number of ships with stores or provisions for the troops in Gallipoli: two battle-ships, four gun-boats, one armed German auxiliary, seven transports, three ammunition ships and one ammunition train, destroyed by gun-fire.

We may add, as a note to these two parts of our record, that the work was done, not by a large number of submarines issuing in relays from a home base close at hand, and equipped with every kind of facility for repairing defects or relieving tired crews, but by an almost incredibly small number of boats, working far from their base, in closed waters, and under difficulties such as no German boat has ever successfully attempted to face.

There remains the North Sea patrol. The first success in this record stands against a famous name—that of Commander Max Horton, who (in his boat E. 9) afterwards established what has been called 'The Command of the Baltic.' In September 13, 1914, he was in the North Sea, near to enemy forces. He was submerged, and not in the happiest of circumstances, for one of his officers was ill, and to afford him some relief from the exhausted atmosphere below, it became imperatively necessary to rise to the surface. No sooner was the periscope above water, than the commander sighted a German light cruiser, the *Héla*, in a position where she might be expected to see the periscope and attack at any moment.

Fortunately a torpedo-tube was loaded and bearing. Commander Horton took a snap-shot and dived. The shot went home, and the *Héla* troubled the patrol of E. 9 no more. On October 6, a German destroyer (S. 116) fell to another shot from the same hand.

After this, game was much scarcer. The German Admiralty tried to establish a paper command of the North Sea, kept up (for the benefit of the German public) by runaway raids on our East Coast towns; but any-thing like a regular patrol was impossible to discover. In the following eighteen months, however, our submarines did succeed in two attacks on stray German destroyers, and four on armed auxiliary vessels. Lieut.-Commander Benning (E. 5) hit an auxiliary in April 1915, but did not sink her. In June, Lieut.-Commander Moncrieffe hit another, the *America*, so badly that she was run ashore. In September, Commander Benning sank a third outright; and in December, Lieut.-Commander Duff-Dunbar (E. 16) secured a larger one of 3,000 tons. Of the destroyers, the first (V. 188) was got by Commander C. P. Talbot, in E. 16, on July 26 J and the second on February 4, 1916, by Lieut.-Commander H. W. Shove, in E. 29. This was a boat of the 'S. 138' class, but she could not be further identified, nor did any British eye actually witness her final disappearance.

The rest of the bag is, for the most part, a forbidden subject. The items are many, the loss to the enemy was great; but as he is racking his brains to get or guess the details, it is no part of our business to help him. There are, however, two items of which we may speak with open satisfaction. One is the capture of a German trawler—of this we have already heard from the Admiral Commanding our Submarine Base, in Chapter 4. The simple story is that Lieut.-Commander G. Kellett, finding his boat (S. 1) so far disabled that she could not get home on her own engines, took over a German trawler by force, without attracting undue attention, and came safely into port, towed from enemy waters by an enemy boat. The remaining item hardly falls within our range; but though not submarine work, it is work actually done by a submarine, and may be classed, perhaps, with the destruction of the ammunition train by Lieut.-Commander Cochrane at Yarandji. On May 4, 1916, a Zeppelin (L. 7) fell to Lieut.-Commander F. E. B. Feilman, in E. 31, and he brought home seven of her crew as prisoners.

Even this is not all. In 1916, our submarines inflicted on the German Fleet itself four blows, which, though they were none of them actually fatal, must yet have been extremely damaging to the nerve of the Service, and certainly cost heavily for repairs both in time and labour. On August 19, the *Westfalen*—a battle-ship of 18,000 tons, built in 1908—was torpedoed by Lieut.-Commander Turner, in E. 23. On October 19, Lieut.-Commander Jessop severely damaged the light cruiser *München*, of 3,200 tons; and on November 5, Commander Lawrence (in J. 1) achieved the brilliant feat of torpedoing two German Dreadnoughts—the *Grosser Kurfürst*, which was laid down in 1913 and finished since the war began, and the *Kronprinz*, which was both laid down and commissioned since August 1914.

A success of this kind, though not final, may well be set against the sinking of much older and more vulnerable ships, like the *Formidable*, *Triumph*, and *Majestic*; and it must be remembered that the disappearance of these three from our Navy List, however regrettable, had absolutely no effect on the relative strength of the British and German Battle Fleets; whereas the loss, for some months at any rate, of two great Dreadnoughts like the *Grosser Kurfürst* and *Kronprinz*—coming as it did shortly after the Jutland losses—carried the inferiority of Admiral von Scheer's force to the point of impotence. In the match of submarine against warship, our boats had succeeded where the U-boats had signally failed.

CHAPTER 7

Warship v. Submarine

The story of the contest between our warships and their new enemy, the submarine, is the story of a most remarkable and successful adaptation. Of the six principal methods of defence used by our navy at the end of the fourth year of war, three are old and three new; and it is a striking proof of the scientific ability of the service, that the three old methods have been carefully reconsidered, and that, instead of abandoning them because, in their original use, they were apparently obsolete, our officers have turned them to even better account than the new inventions.

The oldest device for the protection of warships against torpedoes—whether fired by torpedo-boats or submarines—is the net. Our older battle-ships, as everyone will remember, were fitted with a complete set of steel nets on both sides, and with long booms for hanging then out. These booms, when not in use, were lashed diagonally along the ship's sides, like great stitches, and gave the typical vessels of the British Fleet a peculiar and decidedly smart appearance. Very smart, too, was the quickness and precision with which the order 'Out torpedo nets!' was executed; but—long before 1914—everyone was perfectly aware that the nets were practically as much out of date as masts and sails .They were so heavy, and hung so low in the water, that no ship could manoeuvre in them, and even for a fleet at anchor they had ceased to be a trustworthy defence; for the Whitehead torpedo was now fitted with cutters which could shear a way through the steel meshes.

Nets of the old type, therefore, have played no part in the present war—unless we are to believe the Turkish account of the sinking of the *Ocean* in the Dardanelles, according to which the nets were out, and were not only useless as a protection, but dragged down some of our men when they might otherwise have escaped by swimming. But, because one type of net is obsolete, the British Navy has seen no reason to reject all nets as impracticable. It is not beyond imagination to conceive a net so light and large of mesh, that it will diminish by no more than one knot the speed of the ship which carries it, and will yet catch and deflect a torpedo in the act of passing through it. For it must be remembered that the real problem is not how to stop a torpedo in its full 30-knot career, but how to prevent it from striking the ship with its head at an angle not too fine for the detonator to be fired. A turn of the helm, or the mere wave from the cut-water of a fast ship, has often sent a torpedo running harmlessly away along the quarter. The net of the future may be found equally successful in catching the fish by its whiskers and turning it forward along the bow, where the same wave will drive it outwards from the ship's course.

The second familiar means of defence was the gun. Here again there was a temptation to despair. The secondary armament of any battle-ship or cruiser was fairly certain to make short work of a tor-pedo-boat, or of a submarine visible upon the surface. But no living gunner had ever fired at the periscope of a submarine—a mark only two feet, at most, out of the water, and only four inches in diameter. To see such an object at, say, 1,000 yards, was difficult; to hit it might well seem impossible. Yet 1,000 yards was but one-tenth of the possible range at which a modern submarine might fire its torpedo.

Nevertheless the use of the gun was not discarded; and two impor-tant discoveries were made in consequence. The first of these was that gunfire may be distant, wild, or even unaimed, and yet have an excel-lent effect. The existence of a submarine is so precarious—its chance of surviving a single direct hit is so slight—that the mere sound of a gun will almost always be enough to make it submerge completely—unless it can engage the enemy, with superior gun-power, at a range of its own choosing. When Captain Weddigen had already hit the *Abou-kir*, the *Hogue*, and the *Cressy*, and all three were sinking, the sound of the *Cressy's* guns was enough to cause his disappearance, though it is very improbable that the shooting was really dangerous; for the listing of the ship was rapid, and according to eye-witnesses, the gallant gun-ners were soon firing in the air. Since then, the same thing has been repeatedly observed; and some brilliant successes by our patrol-boats and trawlers have shown that the U-boat has every right to be nerv-ous when it hears even a 6-pounder talking English.

The other discovery is a much more recent one. As soon as it was once recognised that a torpedo is just as innocuous when deflected, as when stopped or evaded, the idea was sure to strike the handiest gunners in the world that they might use their weapons to disturb the straightforwardness of the fish's onset. Even thirty knots is nothing to the velocity of a modern shell, and without hoping for a direct hit on an object from six to twenty-two feet under water, it was thought possible to give a twist to the torpedo's nose sufficient to make a potential hit into a miss or a glancing shot. This feat was actually performed by the gunners of the *Justitia*, who, with splendid coolness, shot at torpedoes as sportsmen used to shoot at oncoming tigers, and succeeded in killing or diverting several, only to fall at last before the rush of numbers.

A third weapon of the warship was the ram; and the use of this, being an offensive-defensive method, was the best of all, as we shall see presently. It was, from the beginning, present to the mind of every naval man, for A. 1 (our very first submarine) was lost, with all hands, in May, 1904, by being accidentally rammed in the act of submerging. It happened, too, that the first attack made by a submarine against British warships in the present war was beaten by this method. On August 9, 1914, a squadron of our light cruisers sighted the periscope of a German U-boat, which had succeeded in approaching to within short range of them. In the account of the affair published at the time, we were informed that H.M.S. *Birmingham* had sunk the submarine by a direct hit on the periscope, and that this was the only shot fired.

Some time afterwards, the truth became known—the *Birmingham* had to her credit, not an impossible feat of gunnery, but a brilliant piece of seamanship She had gone full speed for the enemy, and rammed him. Her captain was not led to do this by inspiration or desperation, but by a scientific knowledge of the elements in the problem. Without stopping to think afresh, he knew that a submarine takes a certain time to dive to a safe depth, and that his own ship, at 27 knots, would cover a good 900 yards of sea in one minute. When his eye measured the distance of that periscope, he saw that—given straight steering— the result was a mathematical certainty.

The new methods introduced during the war are also three in number. Of one—the use of dazzle-painting—we have already heard. It is, of course, a purely defensive measure, intended to deceive the eye at the periscope by misrepresenting the ship's size, distance, and course. Another deceptive device is the phantom ship or dummy. A vessel of comparatively small size and value is covered more or less completely

'SHE HAD GONE FULL SPEED FOR THE ENEMY, AND RAMMED HIM.'

with a superstructure of light wood-work, with sham funnels, turrets and big guns, so that she has all the appearance of a battle-cruiser or Dreadnought. The U-boat may run after her, or run from her, according to his feeling at the moment; but, in either case, he will be wasting his time and laying up disappointment for himself. In May, 1915, during the Gallipoli campaign, the Germans spent a certain amount of time and trouble in torpedoing a ship which they supposed to be H.M.S. *Agamemnon*, and in their illustrated propaganda sheets they give a picture of that ship as one of the victims of the irresistible U-boats.

For a short time the story was believed inside Constantinople, and Mr. Lewis Einstein, of the American Embassy there, relates in his diary that this success, coming (as it appeared to do) immediately after the sinking of the *Triumph* and *Majestic*, was almost more than he could bear. Fortunately for his peace of mind, he soon discovered the truth. The supposed *Agamemnon* was a dummy, and lay for some time near the entrance of the Dardanelles, with her false turrets and sham guns, exposed to the view of friends and foes on the two shores. Very possibly this dummy received a shot which might otherwise have been successfully directed against a genuine battle-ship, and the deception was thus really useful. The German cunning is expended in a very different direction. Its object is often to deceive their own people as to what has actually been lost, not to avert a possible loss at our hands.

Thus when the super-submarine *Bremen* was sunk on her outward voyage for America, one dummy *Bremen* after another was ostentatiously brought home to a German port, as if returning from a successful Atlantic passage. A more flagrant instance still was the statement that, among the German losses in the Battle of Jutland, was the sinking of the *Pommern*, a small and obsolete battle-ship of 13,000 tons, built in 1905. The British Admiralty, who knew that that older *Pommern* had been sunk in the Baltic by Commander Max Horton, nearly a year before, had no difficulty in identifying the *Pommern* lost at Jutland with a new Dreadnought of the largest type, commissioned since her predecessor's destruction and christened by her name—either then or at the moment when it became necessary to put a good face on their disasters in the battle.

It is to be hoped that this state of things may continue on both sides. The Germans are welcome to our phantom ships, if we thereby save our real ones; while, if we can sink their real ones, we may well be content to hear them given imaginary names. The two services have different ideas of what is a useful dummy.

The newest method of preserving ships from the torpedo is a purely constructional device, and very little can be said of it here. But we have been allowed to know this much—the *Marlborough* was torpedoed at Jutland, but returned to the line of battle within nine minutes, fought for three hours, and eventually came home under her own steam, defeating a submarine attack on the way. We are not told how this very satisfactory result is attained in the construction of a Dreadnought of 25,000 tons, capable of full battle-ship speed. It cannot be by the mere addition of the bulging compartments known as 'blisters,' for in the older cruisers in which these were tried they were found to cause too great a sacrifice of speed. The result, however, is there; and there can be no doubt that as the number of unsinkable ships increases, the activity of the U-boat will be very greatly discouraged.

But it would be contrary to thie principles of war and the genius of our navy, to rely upon purely defensive measures to defeat the submarine enemy. It is some-times said that the U-boat campaign took us by surprise. So far as this applies to the legitimate use of the submarine against warships, the statement is quite untrue. The campaign against merchant shipping and non-combatant passengers, waged in defiance of all inter-national law and common humanity, did certainly take us by surprise; and it is only to our credit, and the discredit of our enemies, that their barbarity was beyond our imagination. But the efforts of the U-boats against our fleet were, as we have shown in a previous chapter, actually less successful than our own attacks upon theirs, and our tacticians were never for a moment at a loss to deal with them. The principles had been thought out long ago. As early as 1907, the distinguished admiral who writes over the name 'Barfleur' clearly stated his belief that 'the untried submarine' was not likely to prove more effective than the torpedo-boat and destroyer in depriving our Battle Fleet of the control of the sea. He added:

Nothing is more to be deprecated than the attempt which has been made to enhance unduly its importance, by playing on the credulity of the public. The new instrument of war has no doubt a value, but that it is anything more than an auxiliary, with limited and special uses, is difficult to believe.

And he turned back to old and tried principles:

The traditional role of the British Navy is not to act on the defensive, but to prepare to attack the force which threatens.'

In September, 1914, when Weddigen's coup showed that the moment had come, *Barfleur* was among the first to attack the new problem tactically—he saw at once that the warship's best defence lies in the offensive power given by her immense superiority in speed and weight. And if the single ship is formidable to the submarine, a squadron is still more so. By its formation, its manoeuvres, its pace and its ramming power, it reverses the whole situation the hunter becomes the hunted, and must fly like a wolf from a pack of wolf-hounds, every one more powerful than itself.

There remains, of course, the question of the best formation for the squadron to adopt. Upon this point there are more opinions than one, and a conversation may be reported in which the merits of line abreast and line ahead were set against one another by two naval officers, and both put out of court by a third. The first two were captains commanding ships in two different squadrons. They argued the question between them with great seriousness; but in so cool and abstract a manner, that the spectator might be pardoned for suspecting—rightly or wrongly—that they were supporting doctrines which were not personal to themselves but derived from higher authority—perhaps from their respective admirals, both men of great ability and experience. It was noticeable, too, that the admiral at whose table the disputants were sitting, and who himself commanded yet another squadron, maintained an attitude of neutrality; though it is certain that he and his own officers, several of whom were present, had often discussed the problem, and were probably agreed upon the answer to it.

Captain A said 'Speed seems to be the key to the solution. It is only in line ahead that speed helps you—in fact gives you something like practical safety. If a torpedo, fired at a column in line ahead, misses the ship it is aimed at, it is very unlikely to be so wide a shot as to hit either the next ahead or next astern—it is a miss directly it crosses the line.'

Captain B remained perfectly grave, but he looked very well content with this argument. 'Yes, theoretically; but, in fact, the contrary has happened. In a column of eight ships, in line ahead, the *London* and the *Formidable* were the last two. You remember that the torpedo which sank the *Formidable* was believed to have been meant for the *London*. And anyhow, speed and stormy weather failed to save the rear ship.'

'The speed was insufficient,' replied Captain A, 'not worth calling speed. When your fleet is in line abreast, columns disposed astern, the theoretical chances of hitting are much greater. Speed is no advantage in such a formation—in fact it may be a positive disadvantage. It may actually increase the virtual target. A shot which misses the near ship of a line abreast may still hit one of the others.'

'Laurence,' said Captain B, 'when he fired at the *Moltke*, considered her, as wing ship of the squadron, to be his only chance.'

'There was no second line disposed astern,' replied Captain A; 'but even so, if his torpedo had just missed, ahead of the *Moltke*, the next or next but one in the line might have come forward just in time to receive the shot.'

'That,' said Captain B, 'is a mere question of time and distance; and, in anything like ordinary circumstances, you would not get your result. Say the ships are three cables apart, and doing only fifteen knots. The torpedo is going double the speed; but by the time it has run the three cables along the line, the next ship will have gone one and a half cables ahead and be past the danger point.'

'Your ship may be zigzagging,' replied Captain A, 'and run right into it. Line ahead has the advantage there—in fact, speaking generally, I have the power, which you have not, of immediate deployment in any direction. I can avoid mines, or turn away from the submarine altogether.'

'Certainly,' said Captain B, looking again quite well content, 'but you would not turn away in any case—you would best defend yourself by attacking the submarine.'

Captain A hesitated a moment. 'Yes,' he replied at last, 'but in line abreast your attack might be positively dangerous to yourself. Suppose your columns in line abreast to be zigzagging, as they probably would be, and imagine one of your ships to put her helm the wrong way—there would inevitably be a collision.'

'I cannot imagine such a thing,' said Captain B.

'I appeal to the admiral,' said Captain A.

It seemed an embarrassing thing, for a host and superior officer, to be called upon to give judgment between his guests on so serious an argument. But the admiral was not in the least embarrassed. He did not even express his own opinion, which was thought to favour

Captain B. 'Let me remind you,' he said, 'that you have not examined the most important witness in the case—the commander of the submarine. What order is the most dangerous for the submarine to meet? I asked Commander C, one of our best E-boat officers, this question lately, and he replied "Quarter-line, undoubtedly."'

He turned to the only landsman present, and reminded him that in a quarter-line, or bow-and-quarter line, the ships are echeloned each upon the quarter of the next ahead instead of directly astern. He added, 'A will say that this is in his favour, because ships in a quarter-line are really in line ahead, only that each one in turn is a little out of the straight. And B will claim that he wins, because a quarter-line is merely a line abreast in which each ship lags a little more behind the true front. And C will tell us that the only thing which matters is that the quarter-line gives the unhappy submarine less chance of hitting, and more chance of being sunk than either of the other two formations. And thereupon the court is adjourned.'

CHAPTER 8

British Submarines in the Baltic

The story of our submarine campaign in the Baltic is the first of two romances of the sea one Northern and one Southern—the like of which is not to be found in the annals of the last 300 years. War must often make us familiar with obscure or long-forgotten places, the scenes of old voyages, and battles long ago; but to adventure with our submarines into the Baltic, or the Sea of Marmora, is to slip through unimagined dangers into a legendary world beyond all history—sailing the seas of the past, with the captains of the future. The exploration under water of those intricate and perilous channels was alone a discovery of supreme skill and daring; and the brilliant acts of war achieved by the adventurers form only a minor part of the glory of being there at all.

The first of our submarine voyagers in the Baltic was Lieut.-Commander Max Horton, in E. 9. Before the war was a year old his fame had spread far and wide; but the details of his success are not even yet generally known, and cannot be given here. By October 6, 1914, he had sunk a German light cruiser and a destroyer, both in the 'North Sea,' and it may perhaps be guessed that he had, at any rate, thought of penetrating into the Baltic. By January, 1915, he was a full commander, and had received the D.S.O. On the 29th of that month, he was not only in the Baltic, but was sinking a destroyer there; on May 11, he bagged a transport; and on June 5, he put to the credit of E. 9 another transport and another destroyer. Finally, on July 2, he torpedoed the *Pommern*, a 13,000-ton battle-ship of an older type, but armed with 11-inch guns.

On July 29, he slipped again, in company with E. 1 (Commander N. F. Laurence), and after some independent hunting, the two boats both arrived at Reval. E. 9 had attacked a cruiser and a submarine; and, on August 18, had had a covetous look at a squadron of battle-cruisers, detailed for the German attack on the Gulf of Riga. But as they were moving constantly in regular formation, and at high speed over a large area, it was not possible to deal satisfactorily with them. E. 1, however, had had better luck. On August 19, Commander Laurence came to observation depth at 8.0 a.m., and under cover of a fog succeeded in stalking the same squadron. They were manoeuvring in line abreast, and within ten minutes came across E. 1's bows, with destroyers on both flanks. Commander Laurence had, of course, only a single ship to aim at—the battle-cruiser on the wing nearest to him, which was ascertained to have been the *Moltke*, a 22,600-ton ship. At 8.20, he fired his starboard torpedo, and at the same moment dived to avoid a destroyer which was coming straight for him. His luck was good, both ways. The torpedo got home on the battle-cruiser, and the destroyer missed E. 1 by a few feet. The next day he reported to the Russian admiral at Reval.

These two boats were followed, on August 15, by E. 8 and E. 13. The fate of E. 13 will not be forgotten while there is any rightful indignation left in Europe. On August 19. she got ashore on a neutral coas— the Danish island of Saltholm—and there, with her crew upon her, was deliberately shot to pieces by a German warship, in defiance of all humanity and international law. Her officers and men behaved with perfect courage, but many of them were killed before they could get away from the wreck of their boat.

Lieut.-Commander Goodhart's account of the voyage of E. 8 is a plain and business-like document, but to read it, with a map beside it, is to look far away into a world of historic names and ever-present dangers. It is easy enough to imagine the passage up the Skager-Rak, always remembering that we must keep well out of the central line of traffic, and that in the afternoon we have to dive and pass under a whole fleet of steam trawlers. At 7 p.m. it is possible to come to the surface again. The commander orders full speed, rounds the Skaw, and enters the Kattegat. In the fading twilight, several merchant-steamers are seen going north. The shore and island lights twinkle out one by one—Hamnskar, Vinga, Skaw, Trindelen, and Anholt. The night is short. By 3.0 a.m. we must dive again, and lie quietly on shoal ground, while the traffic goes over us. At 5.25 a..m. we venture to the surface, but are put down quickly by a steamer. At 7.0 we venture again, and do a scurry of 1½ hours in a friendly mist. Then down again, and crawl at 3 knots, till at 1.0 p.m. we are off the entrance to the Sound.

Here Commander Goodhart has to make the choice between going forward submerged, or waiting for darkness and then attempting the channel on the surface. He is confident of being able to get to his position under water, and decides accordingly to continue diving into the Sound and wait for night inside. He proceeds at fifty feet, and, by 3.6 p.m., has verified his position, coming up to twenty-one feet to do so. He goes down again to fifty feet, and alters course to pass through the northern narrows. At 4.10 p.m. he is east of Helsingör Light—'*By thy wild and stormy steep, Elsinore!*' At 5.20, after another observation, he goes to bottom in eleven fathoms, feeling comfortably certain that he has not been detected—so far—on his passage.

At 8.15 p.m. he rises to the surface. The Danish shore is bright with many lights, the Swedish shore is dark—all is exactly as it may have been a century and more ago, when Nelson was there on his way to his great battle. E. 8 goes south-westward on the surface, altering course to avoid being seen by two destroyers, who are going north, along the Danish shore, at a great pace. One of them suddenly turns south, but then stops, as if in doubt. E. 8 runs on into still more dangerous waters; the lights of Copenhagen are blazing brightly, and in Middle Ground Fort a searchlight is working. Now and again it strikes the submarine. Then come several fishing-boats, then two red lights in a small craft going south, close over to the Danish shore. She is on our starboard beam for some time, but luckily not near enough to see us, and we head boldly for Flint Channel.

Off Malmo. the shore lights are dazzling, and it is extremely hard to fix a position. There are many fishing-boats about, each carrying two bright lights. The commander orders the boat to be trimmed down, with upper deck awash, and proceeds with one engine only, at seven knots. He steadies his course through Flint Channel, passing at least twenty vessels towards the western end of it, some carrying two and some three white lights, and one making searchlight signals in the air. The majority of the fishing-boats are no sooner avoided by a change of course, than we run past a small tramp showing a green light, and then three white ones. She seems to have anchored; but two other vessels have to be dodged, and then the ship which has been signalling with searchlight. Immediately afterwards, when just N.E. of the Lightship, with her three vertical red lights, a small torpedo-boat or trawler sights us as we creep by within 200 yards of her. Probably it is the searchlight in Copenhagen which has shown us up. Anyhow it is tally-ho at last!

She lights red and green flares, and alters course in our direction. We dive, and strike bottom—'very strong bottom'—at nineteen feet on gauge, which immediately decreases to fourteen feet. At fourteen feet, then, we try to proceed on our course; but the ground is fearfully uneven, and a succession of bumps brings us to a dead stop. It is 11.40 p.m. After an anxious quarter of an hour, the commander rises to the surface. The Drogden Lightship is on our starboard quarter. A large destroyer or small cruiser is ahead of us, showing lights—she is the one who had made searchlight signals. She is only two hundred yards away, but the commander trims E. 8 deep, and steals past on motors. Four minutes this takes, and we then find a destroyer right ahead, and only one hundred yards from us. There is nothing for it but to dive. Down we go to twenty-three feet on gauge; but at sixteen feet the boat strikes bottom heavily on the starboard side, carrying away all blades of the starboard propeller. We lie on the bottom and listen to our pursuers overhead.

Life is now a matter of minutes and feet. At 12.15, the boat goes down to eighteen feet, but is still bumping badly. At 12.19, Commander Goodhart stops her and comes silently to the surface. The destroyer is there, close on our starboard beam. At 12.20, we dive again, as slowly as we dare, and at seventeen feet we glide away on our course, the depth of water mercifully increasing as we go. For a long time we seem to be escaping. Then, at 2.10 a.m., we strike bottom again at eighteen feet. An hour more, and we rise to the surface, only to see the destroyer on our port beam. Happily she is now a mile off, and does not see us. When we come up again, at 7.15, there is nothing in sight. At 8.53 we dive for a steamer, and at 10.40 for a destroyer. E. 8 is nearly out of breath now—her battery is running very low.

Commander Goodhart decides to find a good depth, go to the bottom, and lie there till darkness gives him a chance of recharging. From 10.40 a.m. till 6.40 p.m. we lie like a stone in twenty-three fathoms.

At 6.40 a Swedish steamer is still patrolling ahead. At 8.25 p.m. a patrol of three vessels is close astern, and very slowly moving east. The moon is too bright for us and we dive again. At 9.30 we try once more, but are put down by a shadowy destroyer to the south-ward. At last, ten minutes before midnight, we find a bit of sea where we and the boat can breathe in peace.

But only for two hours; daylight comes early in northern waters. It is now August 20. At 2.0 a.m. we dive again, and lie in seventeen fathoms, spending time and imagination upon the chart. We are well out of the Sound now, and clear of the Swedish coast. On our starboard beam lies the island of Rügen, where we shall never make holiday again; further back, on our quarter, is the channel that leads to Lübeck and to Kiel, which we hope to visit yet. Right ahead is the island of Bornholm, which we must pass unperceived, and beyond it the whole expanse of the Baltic lies open.

Commander Goodhart rises to the surface at 9.0 a.m., but dives again at noon. We are now not fair west of Rönne; and as he wishes to make sure of passing Bornholm unobserved, he decides to remain on the bottom till dark, then slip by and recharge his batteries, for a long run north by daylight. By 7.0 p.m. we are on our way, and eight hours later we are passing the east coast of the great island of Gotland. At 9.2 p.m. we dive for a light cruiser, which passes overhead forward; at 10.0 we return to the surface and proceed north-east, running past the entrance to the Gulf of Riga and the island of Oesel. By 1.0 a.m. on August 22, we have to dive for daylight; but by 3.0 we are up again, and going on our course full speed. At 8.30 a.m. we sight Dagerört ahead and join E. 9 (Commander Max Horton). In company with her and with a Russian destroyer, we pass into the entrance of the Gulf of Finland; and by 9.0 p.m., E. 8 is secured in Reval harbour. Within twenty-four hours, Commander Goodhart has docked and overhauled her, replaced her broken propeller, and reported her ready for sea.

The career of E. 8 in the Baltic was long and successful. It began, so far as sinkings are concerned, with the destruction of the steamer *Margarette* of Königsberg by gunfire, on October 5, 1915, and the most exciting day in the record was October 23, when the *Prinz Adalb*ert, a cruiser of nearly 9,000 tons, fell to her first shot. E. 8 was cruising off Libau when, at 8.50 a.m., Commander Goodhart observed smoke on the horizon, and altered course to intercept the ship which was soon seen to be an enemy. She had three funnels and two very high masts, and was going west with two destroyers, zigzagging—one on each bow.

Commander Goodhart ran on, at seven and a half knots, till he got within 3,000 yards, when he eased to five knots in order to lessen his wake. The wind was slight, from S.S.E., and there was bright sunlight. The conditions were ideal for an attack from the southward. All tubes were made ready; the enemy came on at an estimated speed of fifteen knots. At 9.28 the port destroyer passed ahead; four minutes later, Commander Goodhart fired his bow tube at the warship's fore-bridge and began to look out for results.

They came. After one minute he observed a very vivid flash on the water-line at the point of aim. This was immediately followed by a very heavy concussion, and the entire ship was hidden instantly in a huge column of thick grey smoke. Evidently the torpedo had exploded the fore magazine. The sky was filled with debris, and the smaller bits began falling in the water near the submarine. There was no use in spending time on the surface, and in one minute more, E. 8 was sliding down to fifty feet, where she stayed for eight minutes, to give the rest of the ship ample time to come down. At 9.42 Commander Goodhart rose to twenty feet, and took a survey through his periscope.

There was no sign of the *Prinz Adalbert*. The two destroyers had closed on to the scene of the explosion, but it was not likely that they had been able to find any survivors, for the destruction of the ship had been instantaneous and complete. Commander Goodhart decided not to attack them, because, for all he knew, they were ignorant of his presence; if so, they might very probably imagine the damage to have been done by a mine, and give him future opportunities. The shot had been a long one, about 1,300 yards, and this was in the circumstances particularly fortunate; for at a shorter distance, such as 500 or 600 yards, the submarine herself would have felt a tremendous shock from the double explosion.

An hour later he saw four destroyers hovering about the place of the wreck. He turned away, and they made no attempt to follow. At dawn next day he reported by wireless, and then proceeded to his base.

In the meantime E. 19, Lieut.-Commander F. N. Cromie, had arrived. She set to work in earnest upon the German shipping engaged in the service of the naval and military departments of the enemy, towards the western end of the Baltic. Monday, October 11, was her best day, and the beginning of a downright panic in the Hamburg trade. '8.0 A.M.,' says Lieut.-Commander Cromie, 'started to chase merchant shipping.' He had good hunting. At 9.40 a.m. he stopped the *Walter Leonhardt*, from Lulea to Hamburg, with iron ore. The crew abandoned ship, and were picked up by a Swedish steamer, considerately stopped for the purpose. A gun-cotton charge then sent the empty vessel to the bottom. By noon, E. 19 was chasing the *Germania* of Hamburg, signalling her to stop immediately.

In spite of the signals and a warning gun-shot, she continued to bolt, and soon ran ashore. Lieut.-Commander Cromie went alongside cautiously to save her crew, but found that they had already abandoned ship. He tried to tow her off, but failed to move her—small wonder, for her cargo consisted of nearly three million kgs. of the finest concentrated iron ore, from Stockholm to Stettin. He left her filling with water, and at 2.0 gave chase to the *Gutrune*. By 3.0 he had towed her crew to the Swedish steamer, and started her for the bottom with her 4,500,000 kgs. of iron ore, from Lulea to Hamburg.

The game went forward merrily. At 4.25 he began to chase two more large steamers going south. In twenty minutes he had stopped one—the Swedish boat *Nyland*, with ore for Rotterdam and papers all correct—told her to proceed, and ten minutes later caught the *Direktor Rippenhagen*, with magnetic ore from Stockholm to Nadenheim. While she was sinking he stopped another Swede bound for Newcastle, and gave her the *Direktor's* crew to take care of. An hour later, he proceeded to chase a large steamer, the *Nicomedia*, who tried to make off towards the Swedish coast. A shot across her bows brought her to a more resigned frame of mind. She proved to be a large and extremely well-fitted vessel, carrying six to seven million kgs. of magnetic ore from Lulea to Hamburg. The crew were sent ashore in boats, and E. 19 proceeded up the west of Gotland. Her cruise was marked by one more incident—a significant one.

During the morning of October 12, Lieut.-Commander Cromie stopped the *Nike*, and went alongside to examine her. He found her to be in iron ore from Stockholm to Stettin, under command of Captain Anderson, whose passport, from the Liverpool Police, proved him to be a Swede. To a Hun, this would have made no difference; but Lieut.-Commander Cromie had British ideas on international law. He sent Lieutenant Mee on board with a prize crew of two men, in the good old style of our ancestors, and ordered them to take the prize into Reval for further investigation.

After what we have already said about submarines and war policy, the point needs no pressing. War against trading vessels and non-combatants is possible within the rules, but only in certain circumstances. Even where those circumstances exist, there is no excuse for breaking the rules; and where they do not exist, only a barbarian would back his way through the net of international law and common humanity. Our navy has in all circumstances kept both these laws: the German submarines have deliberately and cruelly broken both.

Lieut.-Commander Cromie continued to have the good fortune he deserved. He ended the 1915 campaign with another warship in his bag. Cruising in the-Western Baltic on the morning of November 7, he sighted a light cruiser and two destroyers, but was disappointed in his attempt to attack. Three hours later, at 1.20, in a favourable mist, he had a second chance. A light cruiser—perhaps the same—with one destroyer in attendance, came on at fifteen knots, steaming south and east. He dived at once, and at 1.45 fired his starboard torpedo. The range was about 1,100 yards, and the shot went home on the cruiser's starboard side forward. She immediately swung round in a large circle and then stopped dead. She appeared to be on fire and sinking. But Lieut.-Commander Cromie was unwilling to leave her in uncertainty. He avoided the destroyer, passed under her stern, and manoeuvred for a second shot. This was fired at 1,200 yards, and was aimed at the cruiser's main-mast, just abaft of which it actually struck.

A double explosion followed. Evidently the after magazine had blown up, and several large smoking masses were shot out some 200 yards in the direction of the submarine. The destroyer then opened a heavy fire on the periscope with H.E. shell. Down went E. 19 for her life; but three minutes later, she was up again to see what was happening. The cruiser—she was the *Undine* of 2,650 tons—was gone. The destroyer was picking up a few survivors, and after a restless half-hour made off to the southward, leaving on the scene only a ferry-boat flying the German mercantile flag. Lieut.-Commander Cromie left also, and arrived next day at Reval, where he reported the attack and added that, under existing weather conditions, it was only rendered possible by the sound judgment and prompt action of Lieutenant G. Sharp, who was officer of the watch at the time.

E. 19 was not alone in her successful campaign against the German iron-ore trade. A week after her fine break recorded above, E. 9 arrived on the scene; and Commander Max Horton, in two successive days, sank the *Soderham*, *Pernambuco*, *Johannes-Russ*, and *Dall-Asfen*—four serious losses to the German gun factories, and even more serious blows to the courage of their carrying trade. The captain of the *Nike* told Lieutenant Mee on his voyage to Reval, that after E. 19's first raid no less than fifteen ships were held up at Lulea, awaiting convoys; and after E. 9's success, the command of the Baltic seemed to have passed for the time out of German hands.

Such a state of things could not, of course, be continuously maintained—the Baltic weather alone made that impossible. E. 1, E. 8, and E. 18 followed their leaders, and all did good service during the autumn; but their reports show how severe were the conditions when the winter really set in. E. 9 had already noted very bad weather in November, and on the 25th 'boat became covered with a large quantity of ice.' On January 10, 1916, E. 18, commanded by Lieut.-Commander R. C. Halahan, reports 'temperature very low: sea very rough; great difficulty in keeping conning-tower hatch clear of ice, as sea came over constantly and froze at once.' Two days later she proceeded to Reval in company with a Russian ice-breaker. 'The ice was very thick in places, but no difficulty was experienced in getting through.' These hindrances continued for months. As late as April 28, we find E. 18 accompanied through Moon Sound by an ice-breaker 'as there were occasional thick ice-fields.'

The next day some of these ice-fields came drifting down upon the anchorage, and E. 18 had to slip and anchor off until night. Even so, she could not be sure of escaping all danger; for the ice brought down large masses of stone, and deposited them in the channels.

In spite of all difficulties and hardships, our submarines continued their campaign indomitably, and would no doubt at this hour still hold the mastery of the Baltic trade, if the collapse of our Russian friends had not deprived them of their bases and rendered their operations useless. Early in April, 1917, it became evident that Finland must fall into German hands, and steps were taken to withdraw our naval force from the Baltic. But, for the boats themselves, there could be no return from the scene of their voyages and victories. They lay ice-bound in the harbour of Helsingfors, and there they must end their unparalleled story, for surrender to an enemy so unworthy was not to be thought of.

As soon, then, as official news came of the landing of German troops at Hango, these famous adventurers were led to their last rendezvous. The Russian ice-breakers freed them from the harbour ice. All the Russian officers who had been attached to the British flotilla, and who were then in Helsingfors, offered their assistance for the funeral rites, and soon after midday Lieut. Basil Downie, the officer in command of the submarine depot, put to sea in E. 1, followed by E. 9, E. 8, and E. 19. Each boat carried her death potion in the form of torpedo warheads with a 20-lb. dry cotton charge as primers. Three of these charges were allotted to each—one forward, one aft, and one amidships; and when the alarm-bell of the clock in each should ring, contact would be made and the end would come. The point decided on was reached at last.

The bells rang, and E. 19, E. 1, and E. 9 sank to their own thunder.

'THE RUSSIAN ICE-BREAKERS FREED THEM FROM THE HARBOUR ICE.'

E. 8, by some failure of her clock, remained unhurt, and since the ice-breaker could not stay out at sea longer, she was left to die another day, with other comrades. At 7.0 next morning, Lieut. Downie put to sea again with C. 26 and C. 35 and the torpedo-barge, with the few remaining stores. When the clocks rang this time, E. 8 sank, and C. 26 with her. The barge and C. 35 were left to wait for C. 27, the last of that victorious company. On the following morning the barge was blown up, and the two submarines were simply sunk in fifteen fathoms. They went down uninjured, but within three minutes two great explosions followed, and twelve-foot columns of water shot up. 'This, presumably,' says the report, 'was the exploding of their batteries.' Our Viking ancestors would have said, perhaps, that it was the bursting of their dragon hearts.

CHAPTER 9

British Submarines
in the Dardanelles

Our submarine campaign in the Sea of Marmora must also have a
separate chapter to itself, not only because it is now a closed episode
in the history of the war, but because it was conducted under quite
unique conditions. The scene of operations was not merely distant
from the submarine base, it was divided from it by an approach of
unusual danger and difficulty. The channel of the Dardanelles is narrow and winding, with a strong tide perpetually racing down it, and
setting strongly into the several bays. It was moreover protected, as
will appear in the course of the narrative, by forts with powerful guns
and searchlights and torpedo tubes, and by barrages of thick wire and
netting it was also patrolled constantly by armed ships.

Yet from the very first all these defences were evaded or broken
through with marvellous courage and ingenuity; for nearly a year a
succession of brilliant commanders took their boats regularly up and
down the passage, and made the transport of Turkish troops and munitions across the Marmora first hazardous, and finally impracticable.
Their losses were small; but they passed the weeks of their incredibly
long patrols in continual danger, and snatched their successes from the
midst of a swarm of vigilant enemies. Two battle-ships, a destroyer,
and five gunboats fell to them, besides over thirty steamers, many of
which were armed, nine transports, seven ammunition and store ships,
and no less than 188 sailing ships and dhows with supplies. The pages
which follow contain notes on the cruise of every British boat which
attempted the passage of the Straits; but they are far from giving an
account of all their amazing feats and adventures.

Lieutenant Norman Holbrook had the honour of being the first officer to take a British submarine up the Dardanelles. He carefully prepared his boat—B. 11—for the business of jumping over and under obstacles, by devices which have since been perfected but were then experimental. The preliminary trials turned out very satisfactorily, and on Sunday, December 13, 1914, as soon as the mainland searchlights were extinguished at dawn, he trimmed and dived for Seddul Bahr.

His main idea was to put certain Rickmers steamers out of action, and perhaps the actual object of his pursuit was the *Lily Rickmers*. He did not get her, but he got something quite as attractive. It was 9.40 a.m., or rather more than four hours from the start, when at last he put his periscope above water, and saw immediately on his starboard beam a large two-funnelled vessel, painted grey and flying the Turkish ensign. At 600 yards he fired his starboard torpedo, put his helm hard a-starboard, and dipped to avoid remonstrances. The explosion was duly audible a few seconds later, and as B. 11 came quietly up of her own motion her commander took a glimpse through the periscope. The grey ship (she was the battle-ship *Messudiyeh*) was still on his starboard beam, and firing a number of guns. B. 11 seemed bent on dipping again, but Lieutenant Holbrook was still more bent on seeing what he had done.. He got her up once more and sighted his enemy, on the port bow this time. She was settling down by the stern and her guns were no longer firing.

At this moment the man at the helm of B. 11 reported that the lenses of the compass had become fogged, and the instrument was for the time unreadable. Lieutenant Holbrook took a careful survey of his surroundings, calculated that he was in Sari Siglar Bay, and dived for the channel. The boat touched bottom and for ten minutes went hop, skip and jump along it, at full speed, until she shot off into deeper water. Her commander then brought her up again, took a sight of the European shore, steadied her by it, and ran for home. By 2 p.m. he had cleared the entrance. His feat was not only brilliant in itself; it was an act of leadership, an invaluable reconnaissance. In ten hours he had proved all the possibilities of the situation—he had forced a strongly guarded channel, surprised and sunk a battle-ship in broad daylight, and returned safely, though he had gone up without information and come down without a compass. The V.C. was his manifest destiny.

In the following spring, after the guns of the Allied fleets had failed to reduce the Turkish forts, the submarine campaign was developed. It began with a defeat—one of those defeats which turn to honour, and maintain the invincibility of our service. On April 17, while attempting a difficult reconnaissance of the Kephez minefield, E. 15 ran ashore in the Dardanelles within a few hundred yards of Fort No. 8.

Her crew were captured while trying to get her off, and there was a danger of her falling into the enemy's hands in a serviceable condition. The only remedy was to blow her up. She was no sort of a mark for the battle-ships at long range; so during the night of the 18th an attack was made by two picket boats, manned by volunteer crews. The boat of H.M.S. *Triumph* was commanded by Lieut.-Commander Eric Robinson, who led the expedition, with Lieut. Arthur Brooke Webb, R.N.R., and Midshipman John Woolley, and that of H.M.S. *Majestic* by Lieut. Claud Godwin. The fort gave them over two hundred rounds at short range, mortally wounded one man and sank the Majesties boat; but Lieut.-Commander Robinson succeeded in torpedoing E. 15 and rendering her useless. He brought both crews off, and left even the Germans in Constantinople admiring the pluck of his little enterprise. One officer is reported by Mr. Lewis Einstein, of the American Embassy there, [1] to have said, 'I take off my hat to the British Navy.' He was right—this midnight attack by a handful of boys in boats has all the heroic romance of the old cutting-out expeditions, and on Admiral de Robeck's report the leader of it was promoted to commander.

On April 25, A.E. 2 went successfully up and entered the Sea of Marmora; on the 29th, Lieut.-Commander Edward Courtney Boyle followed in E. 14. He started at 1.40 a.m., and the searchlight at Suan Dere was still working when he arrived there at 4 o'clock. The fort fired, and he dived, passing clean under the minefield. He then passed Chanak on the surface with all the forts firing at him. Further on there were a lot of small ships patrolling, and a torpedo gunboat at which he promptly took a shot. The torpedo got her on the quarter and threw up a column of water as high as her mast. But Lieut.-Commander Boyle could not stop to see more—he became aware that the men in a small steamboat were leaning over and trying to catch hold of the top of his periscope. He dipped and left them; then rounded Nagara Point and dived deep.

Again and again he came up and was driven down; destroyers and gunboats were chasing and firing in all directions. It was all he could do to charge his batteries at night. After running continuously for over fifty hours, the motors were so hot that he was obliged to stop.

---

1. *Inside Constantinople.*. This interesting book throws much light on our submarine campaign, and gives valuable confirmation of our records.

'THE FORT GAVE THEM 200 ROUNDS AT SHORT RANGE.'

The steadiness of all on board may be judged from the record of the diving necessary to avoid destruction. Out of the first sixty-four hours of the voyage, the boat was kept under for forty-four hours and fifty minutes.

On the afternoon of the 29th, he sighted three destroyers convoying two troopships; fired and dipped—for the destroyers were blazing at his periscope, and he had only that one left—the other had stopped a shot the day before. But even down below a thud was audible, and the depth gauges flicked ten feet; half an hour afterwards he saw through the periscope his own particular transport making for the shore with dense columns of yellow smoke pouring from her. And that was her last appearance. A few hours later he sighted A.E. 2 and spoke her. She had sunk one gunboat, but had had bad luck with her other torpedoes and had only one left. Lieut.-Commander Boyle arranged to meet her again next day; but next day the gallant A.E. 2 fell to a Turkish gunboat.

During these days the Sea of Marmora was glassy calm, and the patrol ships were so troublesome that Lieut.-Commander Boyle decided to sink one as a deterrent. He picked off a small mine-laying boat, and fired at a larger one twice without success, as the wake of the torpedoes was too easily seen in the clear water.

The first four days of May he spent mainly in being hunted. On the 5th, he got a shot at a destroyer convoying a transport, and made a fine right-angle hit at 600 yards, but the torpedo failed to explode. This only whetted his appetite, and for three days he chased ship after ship. One he followed inshore, but troops on board opened fire on him and hit the boat several times. At last, on the evening of May 10, after being driven down by one destroyer, he sighted another with two transports, and attacked at once. His first torpedo missed the leading transport; his second shot hit the second transport and a terrific explosion followed. Debris and men were seen falling into the water; then night came on rapidly, and he could not mark the exact moment at which she sank.

Inside Constantinople they were already telling each other yarns about E. 14, and for her incredible activity they even promoted her to the plural number. Mr. Einstein wrote on May 11:

One of the English submarines in the Marmora, is said to have called at Rodosto, flying the Turkish flag. The Kaimakam, believing the officers to be German, gave them all the petrol and provisions they required, and it was only after leaving that they hoisted their true colours.

The story will not bear examination from our side; but no doubt it very usefully covered a deficiency in the Kaimakam's store account, whether caused by Germans or by the Faithful themselves.

On May 13, Lieut.-Commander Boyle records a rifle duel with a small steamer which he had chased ashore near Panidos. On the 14th he remarks the enemy's growing shyness:

> I think the Turkish torpedo-boats must have been frightened of ramming us, as several times, when I tried to remain on the surface at night, they were so close when sighted that it must have been possible to get us if they had so desired.

The air was so clear that in the daytime he was almost always in sight from the shore, and signal fires and smoke columns passed the alarm continually. He had no torpedoes left and was not mounted with a gun, so that he was now at the end of his tether. On the 17th he was recalled by wireless, and after diving all night ran for Gallipoli at full speed, pursued by a two-funnelled gunboat, a torpedo-boat and a tug, who shepherded him one on each side and one astern, 'evidently expecting,' he thought, 'to get me caught in the nets.' But he adds, 'did not notice any nets,' and after passing another two-funnelled gunboat, a large yacht, a battle-ship and a number of tramps, the fire of the Chanak forts and the minefield as before, he reached the entrance and rose to the surface abeam of a French battle-ship of the St. Louis class, who gave her fellow crusader a rousing cheer. Commander Boyle reported that the success of this fine and sustained effort was mainly due to his officers, Lieutenant Edward Stanley and Acting-Lieutenant Lawrence, R.N.R., both of whom received the D.S.C. His own promotion to commander was underlined by the award of the V.C.

Within twelve hours of E. 14's return, her successor, E. 11, was proceeding towards the Straits. The commanding officer of this boat was Lieut.-Commander M. E. Nasmith, who had already been mentioned in despatches for rescuing five airmen while being attacked by a Zeppelin in the Heligoland Bight during the action on Christmas Day, 1914. He had been waiting his turn at the Dardanelles with some impatience, and as E. 11's port engine had been put completely out of action by an accident on the voyage from Malta, he had begged to be allowed to attempt the passage into the Marmora under one engine. This was refused, but his repairs were finished in time for him to take the place of E. 14.

He made the passage of the Straits successfully, reconnoitred the Marmora and made a neat arrangement, probably suggested by the adventures of E. 14, for saving the enemy the trouble of so much hunting. He stopped a small coastal sailing vessel, sent Lieut. D'Oyly Hughes to search her for contraband, and then trimmed well down and made her fast alongside his conning-tower. Being now quite invisible from the eastward, he was able to proceed in that direction all day without interruption. At night he released his stalking-horse and returned westward.

Early on the 23rd, he observed a Turkish torpedo-boat at anchor off Constantinople and sank her with a torpedo; but as she sank she fired a 6-pounder gun, the first shot of which damaged his foremost periscope. He came up for repairs, and all hands took the chance of a bathe. Five hours later he stopped a small steamer, whose crew did a 'panic abandon ship,' capsizing all boats but one.

> An American gentleman then appeared on the upper deck, who informed us that his name was Silas Q. Swing of the *Chicago Sun* and that he was pleased to make our acquaintance. . . . He wasn't sure if there were any stores, on board.

Lieut. D'Oyly Hughes looked into the matter and discovered a 6-inch gun lashed across the top of the fore hatch, and other gun-mountings in the hold, which was also crammed with 6-inch and other ammunition marked Krupp. A demolition charge sent ship and cargo to the bottom.

Lieut.-Commander Nasmith then chased and torpedoed a heavily laden store-ship, and drove another ashore, exchanging rifle fire with a party of horsemen on the cliff above. Altogether the day was a lively one, and the news, brought by Mr. Silas Q. Swing and his friends, shook Constantinople up severely. Mr. Einstein records that:

> The submarine came up at 20 minutes to 2 o'clock, about three hundred yards from where the American guardship *Scorpion* lay moored, and was immediately fired at by the shore batteries. It shot off two torpedoes; the first missed a transport by about fifty yards, the second struck the *Stamboul* fair, passing under a barge moored alongside, which blew up. The *Stamboul* had a gap of twenty feet on her water-line but did not sink. She was promptly towed toward Beshiktash to lie on the bottom in shallow water. The submarine meanwhile, under a perfect

'MADE HER FAST ALONGSIDE HIS CONNING-TOWER.'

hail of fire, which passed uncomfortably close to the *Scorpion*, dived and got away, steering up the Bosphorus. At Galata there was a panic, everyone closing their shops; the troops, who were already on two transports, were promptly disembarked, but later re-embarked, and still later landed once more. The total damage was inconsiderable, but the moral effect was very real.'

On the following day he adds:

S. (Swing, no doubt—Silas Q. Swing of the *Chicago Sun*) came in with an exciting tale. On his way to the Dardanelles the steamer, which carried munitions and a 6-inch gun, had been torpedoed by an English submarine, the E. 11. They allowed the crew to leave, and then sank the ship. The English officer told him there were eleven submarines in the Marmora, and these are holding up all the ships going to the Dardanelles. They had sunk three transports full of troops, out of four which had been sunk, and various other vessels, but do not touch those carrying wounded.

So, between Lieut. D'Oyly Hughes and Mr. Silas Q. Swing, the E. 11 became eleven submarines, and may go down the ages like the eleven thousand virgins of Cologne. Her commander evidently hoped to create a panic, and Mr. Einstein leaves us no doubt that the plan succeeded to the full. On May 27 he writes again:

The Marmora is practically closed by English submarines. Everyone asks where their depot is, and how they are refurnished.

May 28:

The submarines in the Marmora have frightened the Turks, and all the remaining transports, save one, lie tranquilly in the Golden Horn. Otherwise I have never seen the port so empty. One wonders where the submarines have their base, and when and how it was prepared.

He adds, with some shrewdness:

Probably, if at all, in some island of the Marmora, though the newer boats can stay out a long time.

E. 11 was far from new, as we have seen, but she was in hands that could make her stand for quality as well as quantity.

Lieut.-Commander Nasmith brought his boat safely back to

Mudros on June 7. The last hour of his trip was perhaps the most breathless, for while rushing down by Kilid Bahr he found his trim quite abnormal, and 'observed a large mine preceding the periscope at a distance of about twenty feet; which was apparently hung up by its moorings to the port hydroplane.' He could not come to the surface, as the shore batteries were waiting for him; but when outside Kum Kale, he emptied his after-tanks, got his nose down, and went full speed astern, dropping the mine neatly to the bottom.

This was good work, but not better than the skill shown in navigating shoal water, or 'the resource displayed in the delicate operation of recovering two torpedoes' without the usual derrick to hoist them—in an operation which may as well remain for the present undescribed. Admiral de Robeck, in recommending Lieut.-Commander Nasmith for the V.C., speaks of his cruise as one 'which will surely find a place in the annals of the British Navy.' It will—there can be no forgetting it. The very log of E. 11 deserves to be a classic. 'Having dived unobserved into Constantinople . . .,' says her commander soberly, and so, without a thought of it, adds one to the historic despatches of the Service.

It was now E. 14's turn again. Commander Courtney Boyle took her up on June 10, against a very strong tide. At 9 o'clock next morning he stopped a brigantine, whose crew abandoned ship:

And then all stood up and cursed us. It was too rough to go alongside her, so Acting-Lieut. R. W. Lawrence, R.N.R., swam off to her, climbed aboard, and . . . set fire to her with the aid of her own matches and paraffin oil.

On the 12th one of the Rickmers steamers was torpedoed. Shortly afterwards there was a big explosion close to the submarine. Her commander says

And I think, I must have caught the moorings of a mine with my tail as I was turning, and exploded it. . . . The whole boat was very badly shaken.'

But *Lily Rickmers* and her sister were now both removed from the Turkish service, for E. 11 had evidently accounted for one of them already. Mr. Einstein writes on June 13:

The German Embassy approached us to cable Washington to protest about the torpedoing without warning of the two Rickmers steamers in the Marmora. One of these was said to be filled with wounded, but their note neglected to say that these had been discharged from hospital and were on their way back to the Dardanelles.'

Only a German diplomatist could speak of a ship carrying troops to the front as 'filled with wounded;' and Mr. Einstein adds:

One cannot but be struck by the German inability to understand our position over the *Lusitania*.

The point is plain, and goes deep. To the modern German mind all such considerations are only a matter of words, useful for argumentative purposes that there should be any truth of reality or feeling behind them is not imaginable.

The rest of this log is a record of destruction, but destruction on thoroughly un-German methods.

June 20.—Boarded and sank 3 sailing *dhows* . . . towed the crew inshore and gave them some biscuit, beef, rum, and water, as they were rather wet.'

June 22.—Let go passenger ship.'

June 23.—Burnt two-master, and started to tow crew in their boat, but had to dive. Stopped two *dhows*: they were both empty and the crews looked so miserable that I only sunk one and let the other go.'

June 24.—Blew up 2 large *dhows*: there was another one about a mile off with no boat . . . and thought I saw two heads in the water. Turned round and found that there were 2 men in the water at least half a mile from their *dhow*. Picked them up: they were quite exhausted: gave them food and drink, and put them on board their ship. They had evidently seen the other two dhows blown up and were frightened out of their wits.

There is nothing here to boast about—to us, nothing surprising. But it brings to mind inevitably the evidence upon which our enemies stand convicted. We remember the long roll of men and women not only set adrift in stormy seas, but shot and drowned in their open boats without pity and without cause. We admit the courage of the Hun, but we cannot admire it. It is too near to animal ferocity, and stained with a cruelty and callousness which are not even beast-like.

On June 21, Commander Boyle had rendezvoused with E. 12, Lieut.-Commander K. M. Bruce. 'I got her alongside, and we remained tied up for 3 hours.' From this time onward the reliefs were arranged to overlap, so that there were nearly always two boats operating at the same time in the Marmora. Lieut.-Commander Bruce came up on June 19, and found, like others, that the chief difficulty of forcing the passage was the heating of the main motors on so long and strenuous a run.

The one great day of his nine days' patrol was June 25, when he brought off a hand-to-hand fight on the surface with three enemy ships. At 10.45 in the morning he sighted, in the Gulf of Mudania, a small two-decked passenger steamer. 'She looked,' he says, 'rather like a tram-car, and was towing two sailing-vessels. In the distance was a sister of hers, towing three more.' He chased, and soon stopped the nearer steamer. He could see, as he steamed round her, that she was carrying a lot of stores. She had no boat, and all the crew appeared to be on deck in lifebelts. He could see no sign of guns, so he ran his bow up alongside and sent his first lieutenant, Tristram Fox, to board her. But guns are not the only risk a submarine has to take on such occasions. As the boarding party stepped on board the steamer, a Turk heaved a bomb over the side. It hit E. 12 forward, but did not explode, and no second one followed.

The Turks, however, meant fighting, and they opened fire with rifles and a small gun, concealed somewhere aft. The situation was a very anxious one, especially for Lieutenant Fox and his boarding party; for they knew their own ship must open fire in return, and it was difficult to take cover on an enemy ship in action. Lieut.-Commander Bruce was in a very tight corner, but he kept his head and played his game without a mistake. He did not hesitate to open fire with his 6-pounder, but he began upon the enemy's stern, where the gun was concealed, and having dealt with that he turned to her other end and put ten shots into her from fore to aft. His men shot steadily, though under gun and rifle fire at a range of only ten yards, and his coxswain, Charles Case, who was with him in the conning-tower, passed up the ammunition.

Spare men, with rifles, kept the Turks' heads down, and all seemed to be going well, when the two sailing-ships in tow began a new and very plucky move of their own. They came in to foul the submarine's propellers, and at the same time opened fire with rifles, taking E. 12 in flank. But by this time the steamer was beaten, and the British rifles soon silenced those in the sailing-ships. Then, as soon as Lieut.-Commander Bruce had cleared the steamer, he sank the three of them. The steamer had probably been carrying ammunition as well as stores, for one of the shots from the 6-pounder touched off something explosive in her forward part. In fifteen minutes she was at the bottom.

Lieut.-Commander Bruce was already thinking of the other steamer with the three sailing-ships in tow. She was diligently making for the shore, and he had to open fire at her at 2000 yards. As he closed, the fire was returned, not only from the ship but from a gun on shore; but by this time he had hit the enemy aft, and set her on fire forward. She beached herself, and as the three sailing-ships had been slipped and were also close under the shore, he had no choice but to leave them. E. 12's injuries were miraculously slight—her commander's account of them is slighter still.

I was very much hampered in my movements and took some minutes to get clear of the first steamer. But only one man was hurt, by a splinter from the steamer.'

This was quite in accordance with the old English rule of the gundecks: to hit and be missed there's nothing like closing. The story of this fine little scrimmage ends with the special recommendation by Lieut.-Commander Bruce of his first lieutenant, Tristram Fox, 'who behaved exceedingly well under very trying circumstances,' and of his coxswain, Charles Case, and three seamen—they all received the Distinguished Service Medal. Of the commander himself we shall hear again presently.

E. 12 was recalled on June 28, leaving E. 14 still at work; and on the 30th her place was taken by E. 7, Lieut.-Commander Cochrane. On the way up, a torpedo from a tube on shore passed over him, and a destroyer made two attempts to ram him, but he got safely through and rendezvoused with E. 14 on the following evening. His misfortunes began next day, when Lieut. Hallifax and an A.B. were badly burned by an explosion in the hold of a captured steamer. Then dysentery attacked the two remaining officers and the telegraphist. Work became very arduous, but work was done notwithstanding. Ship after ship was sunk—five steamers and sixteen sailing-ships in all. One of the steamers was 'a Mahsousie ship, the *Biga*,' of about 3,000 tons. She was lying alongside Mudania Pier, with sailing-vessels moored outside the pier to protect her. But Lieut.-Commander Cochrane saw daylight between this barrage and his prey; he dived under the sailing-ships, and up went the *Biga* with a very heavy explosion.

On July 17, he tried a new method of harassing the Turkish army.

He came up opposite Kara Burnu and opened fire on the railway cutting west of it, blocking the line—then dived, and went on to Derinjie Burnu. The shipyard there was closed, but he observed a heavy troop train steaming west, towards the block he had so carefully established just before. He followed up at full speed, and after twenty minutes of anxious hope saw the train returning baffled. It eventually stopped in a belt of trees at Yarandji Station; this made spotting difficult, but E. 7's gunnery was good enough. After twenty rounds the three ammunition cars of the train were definitely blown up, and E. 7 could move back to Kara Burnu, where she shelled another train and hit it several times.

All this was very disturbing to the Turks, and they tried every means to stop it at the source. They had already a net in the channel, but it was quite ineffectual. Mr. Einstein says on July 15:

> Now it turns out that they have constructed a barrage of network to keep out the submarines from the Dardanelles, and this explains the removal of the buoys all along the Bosphorus. They need these, and especially their chains, to keep it in place.'

A week later, Lieut.-Commander Cochrane saw these buoys on his way down. They were in a long line, painted alternately red and black, and stretching from a position a mile north of Maitos village to a steamer moored in Nagara Liman. He dived under them and went on his way; but later on, below Kilid Bahr, the boat fouled a moorings forward and was completely hung up, swinging round, head to tide. By admirable management she was got clear in half an hour, and then the same thing happened again. 'This time,' says her commander coolly, 'I think the boat carried the obstruction with her for some distance. I was expecting to see something foul when we came to the surface, but everything was clear then.' What he and his men saw, during those two half-hours, might also be described as 'something foul.'

The cruise of E. 7 lasted for over three weeks, from June 30 to July 24. On July 21, Commander Courtney Boyle brought up E. 14 once more. He, too, saw the new net near Nagara, 'a line of what looked like lighters halfway across, and one small steamship in the vicinity.' But he passed through the gate in it without touching anything. This was lucky, as he had already scraped against an obstruction off Kilid Bahr and cut his guard wire nearly through. Once up, he got to work at once, and in a busy and adventurous three weeks he sank one steamer, one supply ship, seven dhows and thirteen sailing-vessels.

In short, he made himself master of the Marmora. The complete interruption of the Turkish sea communications was proved by the statements of prisoners. The captain of one ship stated that Constantinople was full of wounded and short of food, and that the troops now all went to Rodosto by rail and then marched to Gallipoli—six hours in the train and three days and nights marching, instead of a short and simple voyage. All the Turkish warships were above the second bridge in the Golden Horn, and they never ventured out. There were no steamers going to sea—all supplies to Gallipoli went in sailing craft, towed by destroyers under cover of darkness. It is clear that, to the Turkish imagination, E. 14 was like E. 11—very much in the plural number.

On August 5, E. 11 herself came on duty again, and the two boats met at rendezvous at 2 p.m. next day. Half an hour afterwards, Commanders Boyle and Nasmith started on their first hunt in couples. Their quarry was a gunboat of the Berki-Satvet class. The chase was a lively one, and it was E. 11, in the end, who made the kill with a torpedo amidships. Then the two boats came alongside again and their commanders concerted a plan for shelling troops next day.

They took up their positions in the early morning hours, and waited for the game to come past. Commander Nasmith had been given the better stand of the two; at 11.30 a.m. he observed troops going towards Gallipoli, rose to the surface and fired. Several of his shots dropped well among them and they scattered. In less than an hour another column approached along the same road. E. 11 had retired, so to speak, into her butt; she now stepped up again, raised her gun, and made good shooting as before. 'The column took cover in open order.'

In the meantime Commander Boyle had been diving up and down all the morning between Fort Victoria and a point four miles up the coast to the east, about a mile from shore. Three times he came to the surface, but each time the troops turned out to be bullocks. At 1.30 p.m. (when he came up for the fourth time) more dust was coming down the road, and this time it was the right kind of dust. As he opened fire he heard E. 11 banging away. She had left the place where he had stationed her, to the N.E. of Dohan Aslan Bank, and had come down to join him in his billet. The two boats then conducted a joint action for the best part of an hour. Commander Boyle got off forty rounds, of which about six burst on the road among the troops, and one in a large building.

But the distance was almost beyond his 6-pounder's reach. He had to put the full range on the sights, and then aim at the top of the hill, so that his fire was less accurate than that of Commander Nasmith with his 12-pounder. E. 11 had strewed the road with a large number of dead and wounded, when guns on shore came into action and forced her to dive. She came up again an hour and a half later and dispersed the troops afresh, but once more had to dive for her life.

Next day, Commander Boyle ordered E. 11 to change billets with him, and both boats had luck, Commander Boyle destroying a 5,000-ton supply steamer with torpedo and gunfire, and Commander Nasmith bagging a battle-ship. This last was the *Haireddin Barbarossa*. She was passing about five miles N.E. of Gallipoli, escorted by a destroyer. E. 11 was skilfully brought into position on her starboard beam, and the torpedo got home amidships. The *Barbarossa* immediately took a list to starboard, altered course towards the shore, and opened a heavy fire on the submarine's periscope. But she was mortally hit. Within twenty minutes a large flash burst from her forepart, and she rolled over and sank. To lose their last battleship, and so near home, was a severe blow for the Turks, and they made every effort to conceal the depressing details. Mr. Einstein, however, heard them and makes an interesting entry.

The *Barbarossa* was sunk in the Marmora and not in the Dardanelles, as officially announced. She was convoying barges full of munitions and also two transports, when she found herself surrounded by six submarines.

It is creditable to Commander Nasmith that he did so well with only six of his E. 11 flotilla. Einstein continues: 'The transports were supposed to protect her, but the second torpedo proved effective and she sank in seven minutes. One of the transports and a gunboat were also sunk, the other ran aground. Of crews of 700, only one-third were saved.' And on August 15 he records further successes by Commander Nasmith—a large collier, the *Ispahan*, sunk while unloading in the port of Haidar Pasha, the submarine creeping up under the lee of another boat; and two transports with supplies, the *Chios* and the *Samsoun*, sunk in the Marmora.

Commander Boyle returned to his base on August 12, with no further difficulty than a brush against a mine and a rough-and-tumble encounter with an electric wire obstruction, portions of which he carried away tangled round his periscope and propellers. His boat had

'She was mortally hit.'

now done over 12,000 miles since leaving England, and had never been out of running order—a magnificent performance, reported by her commander to be primarily due to the excellence of his chief engine-room artificer, James Hollier Hague, who was accordingly promoted to warrant rank, as from the date of the recommendation.

E. 14 was succeeded on August 13 by E. 2, Commander David Stocks, who met Commander Nasmith at 2 p.m. next day, and handed over a fresh supply of ammunition for E. 11. He also, no doubt, told him the story of his voyage up. Off Nagara his boat had fouled an obstruction, and through the conning-tower scuttles he could see that a 3½-inch wire was wound with a half turn round his gun, a smaller wire round the conning-tower itself, and another round the wireless standard aft. It took him ten minutes' plunging and backing to clear this and regain control; and during those ten minutes, small explosions were heard continuously. These were apparently from bombs thrown by guard boats; but a series of loud explosions, a little later, were probably from shells fired by a destroyer which was following up, and was still overhead an hour afterwards.

The two boats parted again, taking separate beats, and spent a week in sinking steamers, boarding hospital ships, and bombarding railway stations. When they met again on the evening of August 21, Commander Nasmith had a new kind of yarn to tell. His lieutenant, D'Oyly Hughes, had volunteered to make an attack on the Ismid Railway, and a whole day had been spent behind Kalolimno Island in constructing a raft capable of carrying one man and a demolition charge of gun-cotton. Then the raft had been tested by a bathing party, and the details of the plan most carefully laid out.

The object was to destroy the viaduct if possible; but, in any case, to blow up part of the line. The risk involved not only the devoted adventurer himself, but the boat as well, for she could not, so long as he had still a chance of returning, quit the neighbourhood or even conceal herself by submerging. The approach was in itself an operation of the greatest delicacy. Commander Nasmith took his boat slowly towards the shore until her nose just grounded, only three yards from the rocks. The cliffs on each side were high enough to prevent the conning-tower being seen while in this position. At 2.10 a.m. Lieut. D'Oyly-Hughes dropped into the water and swam off, pushing the raft with his bale of gun-cotton, and his clothes and accoutrements, towards a spot some sixty yards on the port bow of the boat. His weapons were an automatic service revolver and a sharpened bayonet.

He also had an electric torch and a whistle.

At the point where he landed he found the cliffs unscalable. So he relaunched his raft and swam along to a better place. He reached the top after a stiff climb, approached the railway line by a careful prowl of half an hour, and went along it for five or six hundred yards, hugging his heavy and cumber-some charge. Voices then brought him up short. He peered about and saw three men sitting by the side of the line. After watching them for some time he decided that they were not likely to move, and that he must make a wide detour in order to inspect the viaduct. He laid down his gun-cotton, and crept inland, making good progress except for falling into a small farmyard, where the fowls, but luckily not the household, awoke and protested. At last he got within three hundred yards of the viaduct. It was easy to see, for there was a fire burning at the near end of it; but there was also a stationary engine working, and a number of workmen moving about. Evidently it would be impossible to bring up and lay his charge there.

He crept back therefore to his gun-cotton and looked about for a convenient spot to blow up the line. The best place seemed to be a low brick-work support over a small hollow. It was only 150 yards from the three men sitting by the line; but there was no other spot where so much damage could be done, and Lieut. D'Oyly Hughes was a volunteer, prepared to take risks. He muffled the pistol for firing the fuse as tightly as possible, with a piece of rag, and pulled off. On so still a night it made a very loud noise. The three Turks heard it and he saw them instantly stand up. The next moment they were running down the line, with Lieutenant D'Oyly Hughes going his best in front of them. But a chase of this kind was not what he wanted. His present object was to find a quiet spot on the shore where he could take to the water undisturbed, and he had no time to lose. He turned on his pursuers and fired a couple of shots; the Turks were not hit, but they remembered their own weapons and began firing too, which was just the relief Lieut. Hughes needed.

He had already decided against trying to climb down by the way he had come up; but after a considerable run eastward, he struck the shore more conveniently about three-quarters of a mile from the small bay in which E. 11 was lying. As he plunged into the water, he had the joy of hearing the sound of a heavy explosion. His charge had hung fire for a long time, but when it went it went well; fragments were hurled between a quarter and half a mile, and fell into the sea near the boat. There could be no doubt that the line was effectively cut; and he could now give his whole attention to saving an officer to the service.

This was the most desperate part of the affair. After swimming some four hundred or five hundred yards out to sea, he blew a long blast on his whistle; but the boat was behind the cliffs in her little bay and failed to hear him. Day was breaking rapidly; the time of waiting for him must, he knew, be limited. With a decision and coolness beyond comment he swam ashore again and rested for a short time on the rocks—then swam off once more, directly towards the boat. Before he reached the bay, he had to discard in turn his pistol, his bayonet, and his electric torch. At last he rounded the point and his whistle was heard; but, at the same moment, shouts came from the cliffs overhead, and rifle fire opened on the boat.

She immediately backed, and came slowly astern out of the bay, intent only upon picking up Lieut. D'Oyly Hughes. But now came the most extraordinary part of the whole adventure. In the early morning mist the bow, the gun, and the conning-tower of the submarine appeared to her distressed officer to be three small rowing-boats advancing towards him, and rowing-boats could only mean enemies. He turned, swam ashore, and tried to hide himself under the cliffs. But he did not lose his head, and after climbing a few feet he looked back and realised his mistake. He shouted and plunged in again. Forty yards from the rocks he was at last picked up, nearly done, for he had run hard for his life and swum a mile in his clothes. But he had done his work and E. 11 was proud of him, as appears from the concluding sentence in her log: '5.5 a.m. Dived out of rifle fire, and proceeded out of the Gulf of Ismid.'

Commander Nasmith ended his cruise with a brilliant week's work. On August 22 he fought an action with three armed tugs, a *dhow*, and a destroyer; succeeded most adroitly in evading the destroyer, sinking the dhow and one of the tugs by gunfire, and capturing a number of prisoners, among whom was a German bank manager with a quantity of money for Chanak Bank. The prisoners willingly helped to discharge the cargo of another captured ship—they were apparently much surprised at being granted their lives. On the 25th, two large transports were sunk with torpedoes; on the 28th, E. 11 and E. 2, in company, bombarded the magazine and railway station at Mudania. On September 1, Commander Nasmith had an hour's deliberate shooting at the railway viaduct, scoring a large number of hits; and on the 3rd he returned without misadventure to his base.

Left to herself, E. 2 now found that she also possessed a heroic lieutenant. Under the date September 7 there stands the brief record: 'Lieutenant Lyon swam to and destroyed two *dhows*.' The story, so well begun, ends next day. At 2.15 a.m. this adventurer, like the other, swam off with a raft and bag of gun-cotton. His object, like the other's, was to destroy a railway bridge. His friends watched him until, at seventy yards' distance, he faded into the dusk. From that moment onwards no sound was ever heard from him. The night was absolutely still, and noises on shore were distinctly audible; but nothing like a signal ever came. It had been agreed that if any trouble arose he should fire his Webley pistol, and the submarine should then show a red light and open fire on the station, which was 300 yards distant. For five hours she remained there waiting.

An explosion was heard, but nothing followed, and broad daylight found Commander Stocks still waiting with desperate loyalty. At 7.15 he dived out to sea. An hour later he came to the surface and cruised about the place, hoping that Lyon had managed somehow to get into a boat or *dhow*. There were several near the village, and he might be lying off in one. But no boat drifted out, then or afterwards. Commander Stocks came again at dawn next day—perhaps, as he said, to bombard the railway station, perhaps for another reason. Six days later he dived for home, breaking right through the Nagara net, by a new and daring method of his own.

It was now Lieut.-Commander Bruce's turn again, and he passed all records by patrolling the Marmora successfully in E. 12 for forty days. He had two other boats in company during part of this time—E. 20 and H. 1—and with the latter's help he carried out a very pretty 'spread attack 'on a gunboat off Kalolimno, on October 17. The intended manoeuvre was for E. 12 to rise suddenly and drive the enemy by gunfire over H. 1, who dived at the first gun. The first drive failed, the second was beautifully managed; but, in the bad light of an approaching squall, H. 1's torpedo missed. In a third attempt the bird was reported hit by several shells, but she escaped in the darkness. Lieut.-Commander Bruce also did good shooting at a powder factory near Constantinople; sank some shipping, and made some remarkable experiments with a new method of signalling. But his greatest experience was his return journey.

He had passed through the net, he thought, but suddenly observed that he was towing a portion of it with him. The boat began to sink quickly, bows down; the foremost hydroplane jammed. He immediately forced her nose up, by blowing ballast tanks and driving her at full speed. But, even in that position, she continued to sink till she reached 245 feet. At that depth the pressure was tremendous. The conning-tower scuttles burst in, and the conning-tower filled with water. The boat leaked badly, and the fore compartment had to be closed off to prevent the water getting into the battery, where it would have produced the fatal fumes of chlorine gas.

For ten mortal minutes the commander wrestled with his boat. At last, by putting three men on to the hydroplane with hand-gear, he forced the planes to work and the boat rose. He just managed to check her at twelve feet and got her down to fifty, but even at that depth six patrol vessels could be heard firing at her—probably she was still towing something which made a wake on the surface.

Blind, and almost unmanageable, E. 12 continued to plunge up and down, making very little way beyond Nagara. The conning-tower and its compass were out of action, but the commander conned his boat from the main gyro compass, and when both diving gauges failed he used the gauge by the periscope. The climax was reached when at eighty feet, just to the south of Kilid Bahr, another obstruction was met and carried away. But this was a stroke of luck, for when the commander, by a real inspiration, put on full speed ahead and worked his helm, the new entanglement slid along the side of the boat and carried away with it the old one from Nagara. The boat rose steeply by the bow and broke surface. Shore batteries and patrols opened fire, and a small shell cracked the conning-tower; others hit the bridge, and two torpedoes narrowly missed her astern. But she came safely through to Helles, and reached her base after a cruise of over 2,000 miles.

H. 1 also put nearly 2,000 miles to her credit, though her cruise lasted only thirty days, as against E. 12's forty. Lieutenant Wilfred Pirie, her commander, took a hand in Lieut.-Commander Brace's signalling experiments and co-operated in several of his military enterprises, as we have already seen. He also worked with E. 20 and was the last to meet her. This was on October 31, the day before he dived for home. After that, nothing more was heard of her till December 5, when Commander Nasmith, who was once more in the Marmora with E. 11, captured a Shirket steamer and obtained much information from the captain, a French-speaking Turk. According to his statement, E. 20 had been ambushed, and her officers and crew taken prisoners. He also gave details of the German submarines based at Constantinople— he thought there were ten of them, including three large ones.

Before accepting this, we shall do well to refer again to Mr. Einstein, who reports four small boats coming from Pola, of which only three arrived; and one larger one, U. 51, of which he tells an amusing story. U. 51 had been at Constantinople, but during August she went out and did not return; it was rumoured that she had gone home, or been sunk. Then the Turks were electrified by news of the arrival of a new German super-submarine, over two hundred feet long. All Constantinople crowded to see her go out on August 30.

> Departure from Golden Horn of a new giant German submarine, the U. 54, over 200 feet long and with complete wireless apparatus.

Next day:

> The U. 54 turns out to be our old friend U. 51, with another number painted.

On September 2 Mr. Einstein adds sarcastically:

> Report that U. 54 was badly damaged by a Turkish battery at Silivri. . . . To mask this, they are spreading the rumour that an English submarine ran aground, and will doubtless bring in the German boat under a false number as though she were a captured prey.

And two days later he was justified:—

> U. 54 lies damaged in the Golden Horn from the fire of a Turkish battery. The reported sinking of an English boat is a downright lie.

Commander Nasmith went down the Straits on December 23, after a record cruise of forty-eight days. In that time he sank no less than forty-six enemy ships, including a destroyer, the *Var Hissar*, and ten steamers. A fortnight before he left, E. 2, Commander Stocks, came up, and did good work in very bad weather, until she was recalled on January 2, 1916. The season was over, and she found, in passing down the Straits, that the Turkish net had apparently been removed, either by the enemy themselves, or perhaps by the wear and tear of British submarines repeatedly charging it and carrying it away piecemeal.

So ended our Eastern submarine campaign a campaign in which our boats successfully achieved their military objects in which, too, the skill of our officers and men was only surpassed by their courage, and by their chivalrous regard for the enemies whom they defeated.

CHAPTER 10

The U-Boat Blockade

Nothing in the history of the past four years has more clearly brought out the difference between the civilised and the savage view of war, than the record of the German U-boat campaign. All civilised men are agreed, and have for centuries been agreed, about war. In their view war may be unavoidable, in so far as all order and security are ultimately dependent on force; but it is a lamentable necessity, and when unnecessary—that is, when undertaken for any object whatever except defence against aggression or tyranny—it is an abominable thing, a violation of human nature. This view is not inconsistent with the plain truth that the act of fighting is often pleasurable in itself, and that, when fighting in a right spirit, men often reach heights of nobility which they would never attain in peaceful occupations.

The savage is in accord with this view on one point only. He has the primitive joy of battle in him; but he cares nothing for right or wrong, and his military power is exerted either wantonly, or with the object of plunder and domination. So long as he gratifies his selfish instincts, he does not care what happens to the rest of the human race, or to human nature. Civilised men have for centuries laid down rules of war, that human industry and human society might suffer only such damage as could not be avoided in the exercise of armed force; and above all, that human nature might not be corrupted by acts done or suffered in brutal violation of it.

These rules of chivalry were not always kept, but by civilised nations they have never been broken without shame and repentance. Savage races sometimes have a rudimentary tradition of the kind—the less savage they. But, in general, they have a brute courage and a brute ferocity, without mercy or law; and the worst of all are those who, living in community with races of merciful and law-abiding ideals, have themselves never been touched by the spirit of chivalry, and have ended by making the repudiation of it into a national religion of their own.

It has long been a recognised characteristic of the British stock, all over the world, to regard a stout opponent with generous admiration, even with a feeling of fellowship; and to deal kindly with him when defeated. But this chivalry of feeling and conduct, now so widespread among us, is a spiritual inheritance and derived, not from our Teutonic ancestors, but from our conquest by French civilisation. It has never been shared by the Germans, or shown in any of their wars. Froissart remarked, five and a half centuries ago, on the difference between the French and English knights, who played their limited game of war with honour and courtesy, and the Germans, who had neither of those qualities. A century later, it is recorded of Bayard—'*Le chevalier sans peur et sans reproche*'—that whenever he was serving in an army with a German contingent, he was careful to stay in billets till they had marched out, because of their habit of burning, when they left, the houses where they had found hospitality.

In the sixteenth and seventeenth centuries their barbarity was unbounded; the Thirty Years' War was the lasting shame of Europe, and the Sack of Magdeburg a final example of the triumph of the wild swine in man. In the eighteenth century, Prussia produced a grotesque anticipation of Zulu ideals, and called its chief Frederick the Great. In the Napoleonic wars, the cruelty of his German allies disgusted the Iron Duke, who had commanded many ruffians and seen some appalling days of horror. In our own time, we have witnessed the brutal attacks on Denmark and Austria, the treachery of the Ems telegram, and the development of Bismarck's blood-and-iron policy into the complete Machiavellism of Wilhelm II and his con-federates. It is not a new character, the German; it is an old one, long inherited. *Nemo repente fit Tirpissimus.*

If anyone doubts this, or wishes to doubt it, let him look through the criminal statistics of the German Government for the ten years preceding the war, and read the book of Professor Aschaffenburg, the chief criminologist of Germany, published in 1913. He will there find it stated and proved, that the most violent and abominable forms of crime were then prevalent in Germany, to a degree beyond all our experience—beyond all imagination of what was possible in a human community—and that the honest and patriotic writer himself regarded this ever-rising tide of savagery, among the younger generation, as 'a serious menace to the moral stability of Europe.'

It is against this younger generation, with these old vices, that we have had to defend ourselves; and now that we have beaten them, now that the time has come when, if they had been clean fighters and fellowmen, every British hand would have been ready for their grip, we can but hold back with grave and temperate anger, and the recollection that we have first to safeguard the new world from those who have desolated and defiled the old.

Anger it must still be, however grave and temperate. Look at the conduct of the war, and especially at the conduct of the submarine war, as coolly and scientifically as you can, you will not find it possible to separate the purely military from the moral aspect. Technically, the Germans were making trial of a new weapon which it was difficult to use effectively under the old rules. They quickly determined, not to improve or adapt the weapon, but to abandon the rules. For this they were rightly condemned by the only powerful neutral opinion remaining in the world. But they not only broke the law, they broke it in German fashion. Their lawlessness, if skilfully carried out with the natural desire to avoid unnecessary suffering, might have been reduced to an almost technical breach, involving little or no loss of life.

But they chose instead to exhibit to the world, present and to come, the spectacle of a whole service practising murder under deliberate orders; and adding strokes of personal cruelty hitherto known only among madmen or merciless barbarians. Finally—and this concerns our future intercourse even more nearly—the German people at home, a nation haughtily claiming pre-eminence in all virtue, moral and intellectual, accepted every order of their ruling caste, and applauded every act of their hordes in the battle, however abhorrent to sane human feeling. In all this, we need make no accusations of our own; we have only to set out the facts, and the words with which the German people and their teachers received them and rejoiced in them.

It was towards the end of 1914 that the German Admiralty conceived the idea of blockading the British Isles by means of a submarine fleet. There were, as we have already seen, great difficulties in the way. For the pursuit and capture of commerce, a submarine is not nearly so well fitted as an ordinary cruiser; is not, in fact, well fitted at all. To hold up and examine a ship on the surface is too dangerous a venture for a frail boat with a very small crew; to put a prize crew on board, and send the captured-vessel into port, is generally impossible.

As an exception, and in case of extreme necessity, it has always been recognised that a prize may be sunk, if the crew and passengers are safely provided for; but this proviso, too, is almost impossible for a submarine to fulfil. Besides these technical difficulties, there was also the danger of offending neutral powers, especially if their ships were to be sunk without evidence that they were carrying contraband.

Under the advice of Grand Admiral von Tirpitz, it was decided to defy all these risks and difficulties. The question was asked by him, just before Christmas 1914, 'What would America say, if Germany should declare a submarine war against all enemy trading vessels?' and on February 4, 1915, a formal proclamation followed from Berlin. This announced that the waters round Great Britain and Ireland were held to be a war-region, and that from February 18 'every enemy merchant-vessel found in this region will be destroyed, without its always being possible to warn the crews or passengers of the dangers threatening.'

No civilised power had ever before threatened to murder non-combatants in this fashion; but there was even worse to come—the seamen of nations not at war at all were to take their chance of death with the rest.

'Neutral ships will also incur danger in the war-region, where, in view of the misuse of neutral flags ordered by the British Government, and incidents inevitable in sea warfare, attacks intended for hostile ships may affect neutral ships also.'

No 'misuse of neutral flags' has ever been ordered by our government, The destruction of a merchant-vessel or liner without warning or search, is not an incident 'inevitable in sea warfare;' it is an incident always avoided in any sea warfare except that waged by barbarians.

A fortnight later the sinkings began; and on March 9 three ships were torpedoed, without warning, in one day. In the case of one of these, the *Tangistan*, 37 men were killed or drowned out of the 38 on board. On March 15 the stewardess and five men of the *Fingal* were drowned. And on the 27th the crew of the *Aguila* were fired upon while launching their boats; three were killed and several more wounded. On the 28th, the Elder-Dempster liner, the *Falaba*, from. Liverpool to South Africa, was stopped and torpedoed in cold blood. As the crew and passengers sank, the Germans looked on from the deck of the U-boat, laughing and jeering at their struggling victims, of whom 111 perished. 'The sinking of the *Falaba*,' said the *New York Times*, 'is perhaps the most shocking crime of the war.'

It did not long remain unsurpassed. In April, the German Embassy at Washington publicly advertised that vessels flying the flag of Great Britain or her allies were liable to destruction, and that travellers sailing in them would do so at their own risk. Intending travellers smiled at this outrageous threat and went on booking their passages to Europe. Even when those about to sail in the huge liner *Lusitania* received anonymous telegrams, warning them that the ship would be sunk, no one believed that the government of a great power could seriously intend such a crime. Not a single berth was countermanded, and, on May 1, the *Lusitania* sailed from New York, carrying, besides her crew of 651, no less than 1,255 passengers.

On the morning of Friday, May 7, she made her landfall on the Irish coast. The sea was dangerously calm; but Captain Turner, wishing 'to reach the bar at Liverpool at a time when he could proceed up the river without stopping to pick up a pilot,' reduced speed to 18 knots, holding on the ordinary course. At 2 p.m. the *Lusitania* passed the Old Head of Kinsale; at 2.15 she was torpedoed without warning, and without a submarine having been sighted by anyone on board. Her main steam-pipe was cut, and her engines could not be stopped; she listed heavily to starboard, and while she was under way it was very difficult to launch the boats. At 2.36 she went down, and of the 1,906 souls on board, 1,134 went down with her, only 772 being saved in the boats which got clear.

This was, for the German Government and the German Navy, an unparalleled disgrace. The German nation had still the chance of repudiating such a crime. But they knew no reason for repudiating it; it was congenial to their long-established character, and differed only in concentrated villainy from the countless murders and brutalities which had troubled the criminologists before the war. The German people adopted the crime as their own act, and celebrated it with universal joy. The well-known *Kölnische Zeitung* said:

> The news will be received by the German people with unanimous satisfaction, since it proves to England and the whole world, that Germany is quite in earnest in regard to her submarine warfare.

The *Kölnische Volkszeitung*, a prominent Roman Catholic and patriotic paper, was even more delighted.

> With joyful pride we contemplate this latest deed of our navy, and it will not be the last.

The two words 'joyful' and 'pride' are here the mark of true savagery. Only savages could be joyful over the horrible death of a thousand women, children, and non-combatants; only savages could feel pride in the act, for it was in no way a difficult or dangerous feat. But this half-witted wickedness is clearly recognised in Germany as the national ideal. In the midst of the general exultation, when medals were being struck, holidays given to school children, and subscriptions got up for the 'heroic' crew of the U-boat, Pastor Baumgarten preached on the 'Sermon on the Mount,' and gave his estimate of the German character in these words:

> Whoever cannot prevail upon himself to approve, from the bottom of his heart, the sinking of the *Lusitania*—whoever cannot conquer his sense of the gigantic cruelty to countless perfectly innocent victims, and give himself up to honest delight at this victorious exploit of German defensive power—him we judge to be no true German.'

'It will not be the last.' The threat was soon made good. On August 9, of the same year, the White Star liner *Arabic*, one day out from Liverpool, was 60 miles from the Irish coast when she sighted the ss. *Dunsley* in a sinking condition. She naturally steered towards her; but as she approached, a submarine suddenly appeared from behind the *Dunsley* and torpedoed the *Arabic* without a moment's warning. Boats were got out, but the ship sank in eight minutes and 30 lives were lost out of 424.

In both these cases the Germans, feeling that their joy and pride were not exciting the sympathy of neutral nations, afterwards tried to justify themselves by asserting that our liners carried munitions of war. This was obviously impossible in the case of the *Arabic*, which was bound from England to America. With regard to the *Lusitania*, an inquiry was held by Judge Julius Meyer of the Federal District Court of New York, who found that the *Lusitania* did not carry explosives, and added:

> The evidence presented has disposed, without question and for all time, of any false claims brought forward to justify this inexpressibly cowardly attack on an unarmed passenger steamer.

The year closed with the torpedoing, again without warning, on December 30, of the P. and O. liner *Persia*, from London to Bombay. She sank in five minutes, and out of a total of 501 on board, 335 were lost with her. Four of her boats were picked up after having been thirty hours at sea.

The year 1916 was a not less proud one for Germany; but it was distinctly less joyful. The American people took a fundamentally different view of war, especially of war at sea, and they began to express the difference forcibly. The German Government, after months of argument, was driven to make a show of withdrawing from the most extreme position. They admitted, on February 9, 1916, that their method was wrong where it involved danger to neutrals, and they offered to pay a money compensation for their American victims. They also repeated the pledge they had already given, and broken, that unarmed merchantmen should not be sunk without warning, and unless the safety of the passengers and crew could be assured; provided that the vessels did not try to escape or resist. This again is a purely savage line of thought; no civilised man could seriously claim that he was justified in killing unarmed non-combatants or neutrals by the mere fact of their running away from him. As for the 'safety of passengers and crew,' we shall see presently how that was 'assured.'

But it matters little how the pledge was worded; it was never intended to be kept. Only six weeks after it was given, it was cruelly broken once more. On March 24, 1916, the French passenger steamer *Sussex*, carrying 270 women and children, and 110 other passengers, from Folkestone to Dieppe, was torpedoed without warning as she was approaching the French coast. Many were killed or severely injured by the explosion, others were drowned in getting out the boats. There were twenty-five Americans on board, and their indignation was intense; for the ship was unarmed, and carried no munitions or war stores of any kind. Nor, as President Wilson pointed out, did she follow the route of the transports or munition ships. She was simply a well-known passenger steamer, and eighty of her company on board were murdered in cold blood by pirates.

The President went on to say that the German Government:

Has failed to appreciate the seriousness of the situation which has arisen, not only out of the attack on the *Sussex* but out of the whole method and character of submarine warfare as they appear in consequence of the practice of indiscriminate destruction of merchantmen, by commanders of German submarines. The United States Government has adopted a very patient attitude, and at every stage of this painful experience of tragedy upon tragedy, has striven to be guided by well-considered regard for the extraordinary circumstances of an unexampled war. . . . To its pain, it has become clear to it that the standpoint which it adopted from the beginning is inevitably right—namely, that the employment of submarines for the destruction of enemy trade is of necessity completely irreconcilable with the principles of humanity, with the long existing, undisputed rights of neutrals, and with the sacred privileges of non-combatants.

This note touches the real point, and settles it; until the submarine is as powerfully armed and armoured, and manned with as large a crew as a cruiser of the ordinary kind, it is not a ship which can be used for the general purposes of blockade by any civilised nation. And it may be added that, even if the Germans had possessed submarines of a suitable kind, they could not have brought their prizes into port, because our fleet and not theirs had the control of the seas. As it was, they pretended once more to submit, and gave nominal orders that merchant-vessels 'shall not be sunk without warning and without saving human lives, unless these vessels attempt to escape or offer resistance.'

It was not intended that this third promise should be kept; there were other ways of evading the issue. The *Rappahannock*, a ship which sailed with a crew of 37, from Halifax, on October 17, 1916, was never heard of again, except in the wireless message by which the German Admiralty reported her destruction. The plan of sinking without a trace was first officially recommended by Count Luxburg, the German diplomatic agent in the Argentine; but the German Professor Flamm, of Charlottenburg, has also the honour of having proposed it in the paper *Die Woche*.

> The best would be if destroyed neutral ships disappeared without leaving a trace, and with everything on board, because terror would very quickly keep seamen and travellers away from the danger zones, and thus save a number of lives.

No doubt the *Rappahannock* was '*spurlos versenkt*;' so was the *North Wales*, and so were many others meant to be. The German method, in 1916, was to torpedo the ship, and then shell the survivors in their open boats. This was done in the cases of the *Kildare* and the *Westminster*, both sunk in the Mediterranean; but on neither occasion were the pirates successful in killing the whole of the crew, and their crime was therefore known and doubly execrated by the whole civilised world. None the less, they continued the hideous practice, and in the following eight months fired upon the helpless survivors of at least twelve ships, enumerated with authentic details in a list published by the *Times* on August 20, 1917.

On the whole, the year 1916 was a difficult one for the German people. The objections of America to the practice of piracy were becoming uncomfortably urgent; promises had to be made under compulsion, and the 'joyful pride' of the nation would have been much diminished if it had not been reinforced by two successes of a new kind. On March 17, 1916, the Russian hospital ship *Portugal* was torpedoed off the Turkish coast in the Black Sea. She carried no wounded, but had on board a large crew and a staff of Red Cross nurses and orderlies. It was a clear morning, the ship was flying the Red Cross flag, and had a Red Cross conspicuously painted on every funnel; but she was deliberately destroyed, with 85 of those on board, including 21 nurses and 24 other members of the Red Cross staff. On November 21, a British hospital ship, the *Britannic*, was sunk in the same way. She was a huge vessel, and had on board 1,125 people, of whom 25 were doctors, 76 nurses, and 399 medical staff. The outrage was said by the Germans to be justified by 'the suspicion of the misuse of the hospital ship for purposes of transport.' This suspicion was wholly unfounded, and the submarine commander had taken no steps to enquire into the truth.

In 1917 and 1918, the 'proudest' and most joyful 'period in the short history of the German Navy, there was no longer any need for the humiliation of excuses. On January 31, 1917, Germany proclaimed her intention of sinking at sight every ship found in the waters around the British Isles and the coast of France, or in the Mediterranean Sea. It was at the same time announced—quite falsely—that the German Government had conclusive proof of the misuse of hospital ships for the transport of munitions and troops, and that therefore the traffic of hospital ships within certain areas 'would no longer be tolerated.' President Wilson dealt promptly with this infamous proclamation. On February 3, he told Congress that he had severed diplomatic relations between America and Germany; on April 6, he formally declared war.

The savages were now entirely free to take their own way, and they took it. On the night of March 20, 1917, the hospital ship *Asturias*, steaming with all navigating lights, and with all the proper Red

Cross signs brilliantly illuminated, was torpedoed and sunk without warning. Of the medical staff on board, 14 were lost, including one nurse, and of the ship's company 29, including one stewardess. On March 30, the *Gloucester Castle* was torpedoed without warning, but her wounded were all got off in safety. On April 17, the *Donegal* and the *Lanfranc* were both sunk while bringing wounded to British ports. In the *Donegal*, 29 wounded were lost, and 12 of the crew. The *Lanfranc* carried, besides 234 British wounded and a medical staff of 52, a batch of wounded German prisoners to the number of 167, including officers. A British officer on board wrote:

> The moment the torpedo struck the *Lanfranc*, the Prussians made a mad rush for the life-boats. One of their officers came up to a boat close to which I was standing. I shouted to him to go back, whereupon he stood and scowled, "You must save us." I told him to wait his turn. Other Prussians showed their cowardice by dropping on their knees and imploring pity. Some cried "*Kamarad*," as they do on the battlefield. I allowed none of them to pass me. . . . In these moments, while wounded Tommies lay in their cots unaided, the Prussian moral dropped to zero. Our cowardly prisoners made another crazy effort to get into a life-boat. They managed to crowd into one—it toppled over. The Prussians were thrown into the water, and they fought with each other in order to reach another boat containing a number of gravely wounded British soldiers. . . . The behaviour of our own lads I shall never forget!

But there is no need to tell that part of the story; it is old, centuries old, and is repeated unfailingly whenever a British ship goes down.

In July 1917, a new type of 'heroic deed' was added to the 'proud and joyful' list. At 8 p.m., on July 31, the *Belgian Prince* was torpedoed without warning; the crew escaped in three boats. The submarine then ordered the boats to come alongside, took the master on board and sent him below. Mr. Thomas Bowman, chief engineer says:

> Then, all the crew and officers were ordered aboard, searched, and the life-belts taken off most of the crew and thrown overboard. I may add, during this time the Germans were very abusive towards the crew. After this the German sailors got into the two life-boats, threw the oars, bailers, and gratings overboard, took out the provisions and compasses, and then damaged the life-boats with an axe. The small boat was left intact, and five

German sailors got into her and went towards the (sinking) ship. When they boarded her, they signalled to the submarine with a flash-lamp, and then the submarine cast the damaged life-boats adrift and steamed away from the ship for about two miles, after which he stopped. About 9 p.m. the submarine dived, and threw everybody in the water without any means of saving themselves.

Mr. Bowman swam till daylight, and was picked up by a chance patrol-boat. The only other survivors were a man named Silessi, and an American named Snell, who had succeeded in hiding a life-belt under his overcoat.

The intention here was, of course, that the *Belgian Prince* should be '*spurlos versenkt;*' and in other cases the same result was aimed at by ramming and sinking the boats with the shipwrecked men in them. The crews of the French steamers *Lyndiane* and *Zumaya* were destroyed in this way in the summer of 1918; and on June 27 the case of the *Llandovery Castle* marked, perhaps, the highest pitch of German 'pride.' This hospital ship was torpedoed and sunk without warning, though she was showing all her distinguishing lights. After she had gone down, the pirate commander took his U-boat on a smashing-up cruise among the survivors; and by hurling it hither and thither, he succeeded in ramming and sinking all the boats and rafts except one, which escaped. The survivors in this boat heard the sound of gunfire behind them for some time; it can only be conjectured that the murderers were finishing their work with shrapnel. The number of those cruelly done to death in this massacre was 244.

The deeds here enumerated form a small but characteristic part of the German submarine record. The total number of women, children, and non-combatants, murdered in the course of the U-boat blockade, is more than seventeen thousand. It has been a failure as a blockade; nine million tons of British, and six million of allied and neutral shipping have been sunk; but the U-boats have never, for a day, held the control of the sea. The policy was a device of savages, and of a nation of savages. There is no escape from this charge; for the policy was approved and deliberately adopted, by the representatives of the whole German people, with the exception only of the few despised and detested Minority Socialists. In October 1918, Herr Haase testified in the Reichstag:

Most of the parties are now trying to get away from the accentuated submarine war . . . in reality all the parties, except the Socialist minority, share the guilt. The first resolution in favour of submarine war was drafted by all the leaders, including Herr Scheidemann and Herr Ebert. The accentuation of submarine warfare was a natural consequence. You Socialists are also guilty because, to the very last, you gave the old *regime* the credits for carrying on the war.

The Germans do not yet realise the crime they confess; they have corrupted one of the oldest and noblest bonds in human life—the brotherhood of '*them that go down to the sea in ships, and have their business in great waters.*' And this they have done because they are, by nature, not seamen but savages.

CHAPTER 11

Trawlers, Smacks, and Drifters

Our Destroyer Service is perhaps as efficient, and as dashing, as anything ever seen in the way of organised human activity. It is long established, and its very perfection seems almost to stand in the way of our wonder at its achievement. The performance of our trawlers and drifters, on the other hand, is the more astonishing because it was an afterthought, the work of a service called into being suddenly created, as it were, out of nothing—to meet the need of a grave moment which no imagination could well have provided against. When the moment came, everyone knew what might be expected from our navy. It had not occurred to anyone that our fishermen might help to keep the sea against an outbreak of piracy, not only with courage but with marked success. Yet this they did; and of all the disappointments which the war has brought our enemies this must have been one of the most unexpected and unpleasant.

In reading the accounts which follow, it will be remarked that the work to which our trawlers and drifters set themselves, with such admirable readiness and courage, was not only new to them, but was continually taking new and unforeseen forms, so that they have been called upon to show quickness and adaptability, as well as the capacity for training and discipline. The armament and methods of the submarine of 1915 were different from those of the later and more dangerous boats of 1917. The trawlers, too, were much less adequately armed and equipped. Our men had at first to play a game in which there were no certain rules, and no standard weapons.

We can hardly over-praise the officers of the R.N.R. who, in those critical days, took command of the special-service trawlers and fought them with the native skill of the Elizabethan sea-dogs. Nor can we admire too heartily the ready pluck and patriotism with which the skippers, mates, deck-hands and boys of our fishing-fleets turned their hands at a moment's notice from nets to depth-charges and twelve-pounders, and undertook the daily sweeping of mines, in seas now doubly treacherous, and a hundred times more deadly. There is a strange and almost pathetic sound, even in the names of the little ships themselves—names bearing none of the splendour of history or the prestige of war, but the humble and intimate memories of wives and children, or the jesting pride of the homely seaport where they lived in the time of peace.

The *Ina Williams* (now His Majesty's Trawler, *Ina Williams*) was steaming towards the Irish coast at seven o'clock, one evening in early summer, when she sighted a large submarine on her port beam, some two-and-a-half miles away. The enemy had just come to the surface; for there was no sign of him in that direction a few moments before, and he had not yet got his masts or ventilators up. The *Ina Williams* was armed, fortunately, with a 12-pounder gun, and commanded by Sub-Lieutenant C. Nettleingham, R.N.R., who had already been commended for good conduct, and after nine months' hard work was not likely to lose a fighting chance.

He headed straight for the U-boat. She might, of course, submerge at any moment, leaving the pursuer helpless. But Mr. Nettleingham calculated that she would disdain so small an enemy, and remain upon the surface, relying upon her trained gunners and keeping her superiority of speed, with her torpedoes in case of extreme necessity. He was right in the main. The U-boat accepted battle by gunfire; but a torpedo which missed the starboard quarter of the *Ina Williams* by only 10 feet must have been fired at least as soon as the trawler sighted her, and showed that the enemy was not disposed to underrate even a British fishing-boat. Mr. Nettleingham had saved his ship by the promptness with which he turned towards the submarine, and he now opened fire, keeping helm to avoid any further torpedoes.

The fight was a triumph for English gunnery. The *Ina Williams* had the good fortune to have fallen in with a wild-shot. All his five shells were misses some short, some on the trawler's starboard side. The gunner of the *Ina Williams* had probably had no experience of firing at a moving target, almost level with the water. The U-boat was going 10-12 knots, too, and that was faster than he expected. The result was that his first three shots failed to get her; they fell astern, but each one distinctly nearer than the last. The pirate commander did not like the look of things; he called in his guns' crews and prepared to submerge.

Too late. The British gunner's fourth shot caught the U-boat on the water-line, half-way between conning-tower and stern. A fifth followed instantly, close abaft the conning-tower itself. The wounded submarine was probably by this time out of hand, for she continued to submerge.

Just before she disappeared, the sixth shell struck the conning-tower full at the water-line, and the fight was over. It had lasted fifteen minutes, and the *Ina Williams* was still 3,400 yards away when the enemy sank. She steamed straight on to the position of the U-boat, and found that even after the ten minutes which it took her to reach the spot, large bubbles of air were still rising, and the sea was being more and more thickly covered with a large lake of oil. The depth was fifty fathoms, and out of that depth, while the *Ina Williams* steamed round and round her buoy, she had the satisfaction of seeing the dead brute's life-blood welling up with bursts of air-bubbles for nearly an hour, until the sea was thick for five hundred yards, and tainted for a much further distance. The smell of the stuff was peculiar, and new to the trawler's crew; they could not find the right word to describe it. But they were eager to scent it again, and as often as possible, for it meant good work, good pay and a good report.

This was a thoroughly professional bit of service, a single fight at long range; but it was no smarter than the sharp double action fought by His Majesty's Armed Smacks *Boy Alfred* and *I'll Try* against two German submarines. The British boats were commanded by Skipper Walter S. Wharton, R.N.R., and Skipper Thomas Crisp, R.N.R., and were out in the North Sea when they sighted a pair of U-boats coming straight towards them on the surface. The first of these came within 300 yards of *Boy Alfred* and stopped. Then followed an extraordinary piece of work, only possible to a German pirate. The U-boat signalled with a flag to *Boy Alfred* to come nearer, and at the same time opened fire upon her with a machine-gun or rifles, hitting her in many places, though by mere chance not a single casualty resulted.

Skipper Wharton's time had not yet come; he was not for a duel at long range. He threw out his small boat, and by this submissive behaviour encouraged the U-boat to come nearer, which she did by submerging and popping up again within a hundred yards. A man then came out of the conning-tower and hailed *Boy Alfred*, giving the order to abandon ship as he intended to torpedo. But 100 yards was a very different affair from 300. It was, in fact, a range Skipper Wharton thought quite suitable. He gave the order 'Open fire' instead of 'Abandon ship,' and his gunner did not fail him. The first round from the 12-pounder was just short, and the second just over; but having straddled his target, the good man put his third shot into the submarine's hull, just before the conning-tower, where it burst on contact. The fourth shot was better still; it pierced the conning-tower and burst inside. The U-boat sank like a stone, and the usual wide-spreading patch of oil marked her grave.

In the meantime the second enemy submarine had gone to the east of *I'll Try*, who was herself east of *Boy Alfred*. He was a still more cautious pirate than his companion, and remained submerged for some time, cruising around *I'll Try* with only a periscope showing. Skipper Crisp, having a motor fitted to his smack, was too handy for the German, and kept altering course so as to bring the periscope ahead of him, whenever it was visible. The enemy disappeared entirely no less than six times, but at last summoned up courage to break surface.

The hesitation was fatal to him—he had given the smack time to make every preparation. He appeared suddenly at last, only 200 yards off, on *I'll Try's* starboard bow; but his upper deck and big conning-tower were no sooner clearly exposed than Skipper Crisp put his helm hard over, brought the enemy on to his broadside and let fly with his 13-pounder gun. At this moment a torpedo passed under the smack's stern, missing only by ten feet, then coming to the surface, and running along on the top past *Boy Alfred*. It was the U-boat's first and last effort. In the same instant, *I'll Try's* shell—the only one fired—struck the base of the conning-tower and exploded, blowing pieces of the submarine into the water on all sides.

The U-boat immediately took a list to starboard and plunged bows first—she disappeared so rapidly that the gunner had not even time for a second shot. *I'll Try* immediately hurried to the spot, and there saw large bubbles of air coming up and a large and increasing patch of oil. She marked the position with a Dan buoy, and stood by for three-quarters of an hour with *Boy Alfred*. Finally, as the enemy gave no sign of life, the two smacks returned together to harbour.

For this excellent piece of work the two skippers were suitably rewarded. Skipper Wharton, who had already killed two U-boats and had received the D.S.C. and the D.S.M. with a bar, was now given a second bar to his D.S.C. Skipper Crisp already had the D.S-JVL, and now received the D.S.C. But with regard to the gratuity given to the whole crew of each boat for the destruction of an enemy submarine, a distinction was made, *Boy Alfred* being rewarded for a 'certainty' and

I'll Try for a 'probable' only. This is interesting as showing the scrupulous caution with which our anti-submarine returns have been made up. The Germans have tried to persuade their public, at home and abroad, that many of the U-boats claimed to have been destroyed by us have, in fact, escaped, with more or less injury, and made their way home to refit.

The exact contrary is the case. No one, with any power of judging the evidence, could examine our official reports without coming to the conclusion that the number of our successes has been greatly underestimated in the published records. The Admiralty have no doubt felt that, where so much is at stake, it is better to run no risk at all of misrepresenting the situation and its possibilities. If certainties only are counted, and the campaign judged and conducted accordingly, there will be no disillusionment for us, and the long list of 'probables' will give us a margin, uncertain in quantity, but absolutely sure to be on the right side of the account. This policy has entirely justified itself. In the long record of the anti-submarine work of these four years, only one complete disappointment has occurred, only one dead U-boat has come to life again.

On the other hand, the first list of certainties published by the Admiralty—the list of 150 pirate commanders put out of action—could not be disputed, even by the authors of the German *communiqués*. It is not an estimate, it is a statement, beyond suspicion or dispute; but to ensure this result restraint was necessary, and the restraint was often regretted by the authorities as much as by the British crews who felt themselves stinted of their full reward. There was probably no member of the board who did not wish that more could be done for the gallant men of *I'll Try*; but her report, as here paraphrased, just fell short of the full evidence required by the rules. She killed her bird; but she could not *prove* that he was not a runner.

The same year, in the second week of August, two other smacks distinguished themselves in action. The first of these was the *G. and E.*, commanded by Lieutenant C. E. Hammond, R.N. She was sailing at mid-day in company with the smack *Leader*, and about a mile to north of her, when she saw a submarine break surface about three cables beyond to the south-east. Lieutenant Hammond must have found it hard to play a waiting game, but to go at once to the help of his consort would have revealed that he was no unarmed fishing-boat. The pirate, therefore, was able to board and blow up *Leader* with a bomb, after ordering her crew into their small boat. He then came on fear-

'*I'LL TRY*'S SHELL STRUCK THE BASE OF THE CONNING-TOWER.'

lessly, closing, as he thought, another helpless victim. When within 200 yards he fired a rifle, and *G. and E.'s* crew encouraged him by getting out a boat; but when he came to forty yards and slewed round, parallel to the smack, Lieutenant Hammond hoisted the White Ensign and opened fire. The U-boat appeared to be paralysed with astonishment. For a whole minute she lay motionless, and that minute was just long enough for *G. and E.'s* gunner. He got off five shots in a tremendous hurry. One was a miss, and two hit the rail of the smack; but one of these went on, and penetrated the enemy very usefully in the lower part of the conning-tower. The other two were clean hits in much the same spot. Down went the enemy—not in the way a submarine would dive by choice, but nose first, and with stern up at a very high angle. The five men who had been on her deck and conning-tower, for the purpose of enjoying a little shooting at British fishermen, got an entirely new view of sport in these sixty seconds. One was killed with a rifle-shot by a petty officer on the *G. and E.*, three disappeared in the shell bursts, and the fifth was seen still clinging to the conning-tower, as the U-boat carried him down to death. The tide made all hope of rescue vain—it was too strong even for a buoy to be put down to mark the spot.

Four days later, on the same ground, the smack *Inverlyon*, commanded by Skipper Phillips, with an R.N. gunner, Ernest M. Jehan, sighted a submarine at 8.20 p.m., steering right towards her in the twilight. When the two boats were within less than thirty yards of each other, the submarine was seen to be a U-boat flying the German ensign, with an officer on deck hailing 'Boat!' Evidently he expected to be obeyed, for he stopped dead and gave no sign of action. He had no gun mounted, and appeared to be out of torpedoes.

Mr. Jehan might well have been taken by surprise by this sudden meeting at close quarters in the dusk; but he was not. In an instant the White Ensign was hoisted, and he himself was firing his revolver at the officer steering the enemy boat. This was his pre-arranged signal for his mates to open fire, and it was obeyed with deadly quickness and precision. The gun was a mere pop-gun, a 3-pounder, but at the range it was good enough. Of the first three rounds fired, the first and third pierced the centre of the enemy's conning-tower and burst inside, while the second struck the after part of the same structure and carried it away, ensign and all. The officer fell overboard on the starboard side.

The submarine was now out of hand. The tide brought her close round *Inverlyorn's* stern, within ten yards, and the pun was instantly slewed on to her again. This time, six rounds of extra-rapid fire were got off. The first hit the conning-tower, the second and fourth went over, the third, fifth and sixth hulled the U-boat dead. She sank, with the same ominous nose-dive, her stern standing up at an angle of 80°. The swirl was violent, and in it three bodies were flung to the surface. A shout was heard from one of them—a pirate, but a man in agony. Skipper Phillips stripped, took a lifebuoy in his arms and leaped overboard. He swam strongly, but vainly, in that rush of wild water and oil, and at last had to be dragged home on his own buoy. The smack meantime was drifting over the dead submarine, and brought up when her trawl got fast upon it.

The trawl was even more useful in another action, where it actually brought on the fight at close quarters and made victory possible. One day in February, H.M. Trawler *Rosetta*, Skipper G. A. Novo, R.N.R., had gone out to fish, but she had on deck a 6-pounder gun concealed in an ingenious manner which need not be described. She joined a small fleet of four smacks and two steam trawlers some forty-five miles out, and fished with them all night. Before dawn next morning a voice was heard shouting out of the twilight. It came from one of the steam trawlers: 'Cut your gear away! there's a submarine three-quarters of a mile away; he's sunk a smack and I have the crew on board.'

'All right, thank you!' said Skipper Novo—to get away from the pirate was precisely what he did not wish to do. For some fifteen minutes he went on towing his trawl, in hope of being attacked; but as nothing happened, he thought he was too far away from the smacks, and began to haul up his trawl. He was bringing his boat round before the wind, and had all but the last twenty fathoms of the trawl in, when the winch suddenly refused to heave any more, and the warp ran out again about ten fathoms—a thing beyond all experience. 'Hullo!' said the skipper, 'there's something funny.' He jumped off the bridge and asked the mate what was the reason of the winch running back.

'I don't know, skipper—the stop-valve is opened out full.' The skipper tried it himself; then went to the engine-man and asked him if full steam was on.

'The steam's all right.'

'Then reverse winch!' said the skipper, and went to give a hand himself, as was his custom in a difficulty. The hauling went on this time, all but to the end.

Suddenly the mate gripped him by the arm—'Skipper, a submarine on board us!'—and there the enemy was, a bare hundred yards off on the starboard quarter.

'Hard a-starboard, and a tick ahead!' shouted the skipper, and rushed for the gun, with the crew following. The gun was properly in charge of the mate, and he got to it first; but the brief dialogue which followed robbed him of his glory.

'Right, skipper!' he said, meaning thereby 'This is my job.'

But in the same breath the skipper said: 'All right, Jack. I got him! You run on bridge and keep him astern.' The *Rosetta's* discipline was good—the mate went like a man, and the skipper laid the gun. He was justified by his success. The enemy was very quickly put out of action, being apparently unable to cope with the whirlwind energy of Skipper Novo. From the moment of breaking surface less than sixty seconds had gone by, when the gun of the *Rosetta* began speaking, and spoke nothing but hard words directly to the point. The target was 250 feet long, and only 300 feet away. Every shot was a hit. The fourth caused an explosion, and flames shot up four or five feet above the submarine. Evidently she could no longer submerge, and she attempted to make off upon the surface. But Skipper Novo was right in his estimate of his own chance—he had 'got him.' His fifth, sixth, seventh and eighth shots were all direct hits on the receding target, and at the eighth the enemy sank outright.

Rosetta then spoke the smack *Noel*, which had been close to her during the action, and now confirmed all her observations. Skipper Novo had no doubt that the U-boat had been the obstruction which was tangled in his net. She had carried it all away, and to get clear had been obliged to come to the surface without knowing where she might find herself. As to her fate, there was no reasonable doubt. But since neither debris nor survivors were seen, the case, with rigid scrupulosity, was refused a place among the certainties. The enemy are no better off for that.

The story of two trawlers, *Lark II* and *Lysander III*, will show how much difference luck may make in giving or withholding the evidence necessary to prove a complete success. These two boats were included in a small division patrolling off the Cornish coast, and hunted two submarines with apparent success, one in March and one in April, but obtained the maximum award on the first occasion only. The third ship of the division was then the drifter *Speculation*, and the division commander was Chief Skipper Donald McMillan, R.N.R. He was in a certain position close inshore on March 10, listening with hydrophones for a U-boat which was known to be on the prowl, when he sighted a steamer about four miles away in the act of being blown up. He made for her with all speed, but she sank in four minutes; twenty-one of her crew of twenty-five were found still floating in one small boat and a raft. The Chief Skipper 'interrogated' the poor men, and found that the ship was a Spanish steamer, the *Christina*. Then he put them on board *Speculation*, and ordered her to take them at once into St. Ives, while *Lark* and *Lysander* carried out their hydrophone work as before.

When *Speculation* had gone about 2½ miles on her way, the Chief Skipper suddenly heard her fire a shot; and the same moment she changed course and blew her siren. *Lark* and *Lysander* raced to join the hunt with their utmost speed. They found *Speculation* cruising round, with depth-charges ready to drop. She had already dropped two, besides firing her 3-pounder into the wake of the enemy's periscope, and had seen not only oil, but some wreckage, and a large object which rolled over and disappeared again. The Chief Skipper ordered her to proceed on her course to St. Ives, and then instructed *Lysander III* to stand by and drop her depth-charges on the chance of stirring up the wounded U-boat. Within five minutes he sighted the wake of a submarine on his own port bow, only 100 yards distant but going fast. He made a bee line for the wake, thinking it possible he might ram her, and when just over the disturbance on the water he dropped his first depth-charge. Then, as the submarine was still making headway, he closed again and dropped his second charge right over the wake. The enemy thereupon showed oil and ceased to make headway; so *Lark* and *Lysander* alternately bombed his supposed resting-place with no less than eight charges.

After nearly an hour of this, they stood by, listening on hydrophones and watching the oil still rising. Then a destroyer arrived, asked questions, heard the whole story and steamed away without comment. Two hours later a motor-launch came by, and was good enough to examine the spot and contribute one more depth-charge. Two hours more, and *Speculation* returned to spend the night with her division— all listening keenly, but without result. Finally, next morning, two sweepers, *John Kidd* and *Castor II*, arrived and swept round about the buoy which had been put down. The three boats of the division stood by and watched anxiously; they felt sure that the sweep fouled some object between 9 and 10 a.m., but at 11.15 they received the order to resume their patrol and went reluctantly away, fore-boding a verdict of 'probably damaged.'

Twelve days later they had a joyful surprise. It had been decided that as the depth of water, the season, and other circumstances were all favourable, it was worthwhile to send a diver to explore the spot. Accordingly, on March 25, an officer diver went down and succeeded in finding and examining the submarine. She was lying on her port beam-ends in twenty-four fathoms. Her conning-tower had been practically blown off—evidently by a depth-charge which had made a direct hit or something very near it. She had also a large fracture in the hull, on the port side amidships. This was, of course, conclusive, and the division received the maximum award. They were the more jubilant, because they had been quite certain of their kill, and had picked up what they considered first-rate evidence—not debris indeed, nor survivors, but a lot of onions, which must have been brought there by somebody. Also they had been told that their 'obstruction' was the wreck of an Italian ship, torpedoed just about there only a few days before. It was a consolation to have so annoying a suggestion conclusively disproved.

The next action of *Lark II* and *Lysander III* fell short of this final felicity. In April the division passed under the command of Chief Skipper G. Birch, R.N.R., and the third place in it was filled by the drifter *Livelihood*. They were patrolling one evening off Tintagel Head, when a periscope was sighted by *Lark II*, about 500 yards away on the starboard quarter, and going N.N.W. at the very slow speed of two knots. It was noted as being very high, quite three feet out of the water. The Chief Skipper came round immediately in order to bring his guns to bear; but the periscope had disappeared before he could accomplish this. He then hoisted the necessary signals for warning the rest of the division, steamed towards the last position of the submarine, lay to, and listened with the hydrophone. But at this moment the periscope reappeared; it was now only one foot above the surface and not more than twenty yards away, on the starboard beam. This was, of course, too near for a torpedo, and *Lark II* accordingly got her chance.

The first shot from her 12-pounder was an extraordinarily happy one—it hit the periscope and scattered it in splinters. The Chief Skipper lost not a moment—he rang the telegraph for full speed, turned towards the enemy, and as soon as he got way on the ship dropped a depth-charge set for fifty feet. His miniature fleet was perfectly in hand, and seconded him brilliantly. Drifter *Livelihood* closed on his port quarter, and dropped her depth-charge almost on the same spot; trawler *Lysander III* followed with another. The three boats continued to play the game in combination; the leader dropping five depth-charges in all and the others three each.

All these exploded satisfactorily, and one of the Chief Skipper's produced a second heavy underwater explosion, after which large quantities of dark oil and air bubbles rose to the surface. The position was then buoyed, and the division patrolled the area all night, using hydrophones at intervals. Next morning a wireless message was sent to Penzance, and another trawler took the watch as relief. Sweeping operations followed, but the bottom was reported rocky and foul, and no satisfactory result was obtained. Diving was not possible in such a place, and in the end the official verdict was one of 'Probably seriously damaged.'

For this the reward was only half of what would have been given for a certainty; and, to the gallant trawlers and drifters, that was probably the smallest part of the disappointment. It is trying to end so exciting a chase with a cry of 'gone away,' and especially so when you are positive that the cry is a mistaken one. The evidence for a kill was very strong—the enemy's speed was slow, his periscope was blinded, he was liberally depth-charged at close quarters—there was a violent double explosion to be accounted for, and a good uprush of oil and bubbles. But the line is strictly drawn, and this time the conclusive evidence was unprocurable.

Among the many cases of fine team-work by these gallant little fishing-boats two more must be given here—one as an example of the deadly thoroughness and precision with which our trawler and drifter divisions can do their hunting, and the other to show how keenly they will fight against an enemy armed with vastly superior guns.

A division of four drifters *Young Fred*, *Pilot Me*, *Light*, and *Look Sharp*—under Lieutenant Thomas Kippins, R.N.R., was patrolling one afternoon in April, when at 5.25 p.m. Skipper Andrew Walker, R.N.R., sighted a periscope about 150 feet away on the starboard quarter of his ship, *Pilot Me*. He immediately altered course to starboard, and the submarine thereupon submerged entirely. Skipper Walker passed over the spot where she was last seen and dropped a depth-charge, altered course rapidly and dropped another, fired a red rocket to warn the division, dropped a third and fourth depth-charge, and hoisted the signal asking his commander to come north at full speed. He then stopped his engines and listened on his hydrophone.

Hearing no sound, he made for *Young Fred*, who had altered course and was now closing him. When the two boats were only 300 yards apart, the submarine came to the surface right between them. She rose at an angle of 45°, bows up, and hung so for about two minutes, during which *Pilot Me*, *Light*, and *Look Sharp* all opened fire, and the two last claim to have hit her. At any rate she went down again, stern first; but Lieutenant Kippins, who was steaming straight for her in hope of ramming, was not disposed to take any chances. He took *Young Fred* exactly over her, dropped two depth-charges and passed on. The explosion which followed was a very heavy one; the fountain of water which rose was mast high and completely hid the drifter flagship from her companions, who thought for a moment that she 'had gone.'

The Chief Skipper was far from gone. The spray was hardly off his deck, and the *Young Fre*d was still rocking, when he turned again and then again, dropping two more depth-charges, and ordered *Pilot M*e to put down a Dan buoy to mark the position. This was done, but it was but marking a grave. H.M.S. *Express*, who had received a wireless signal and hurried to the spot, reports that she found the sea covered with oil, which had extended in a long stream to the northward on the ebb tide. Thick oil was still rising to the surface, and there were streaks of dark brown colour, very noticeable, and distinct from oil. Even when four miles to leeward, whilst approaching, the new comers had been struck by a very strong smell of petrol, which naturally gave them hopeful expectations.

The expectations were fulfilled; in fact the evidence brought on board the *Express* went almost beyond what was acceptable to a British ship's company who had not just been fighting for their lives. The articles of wreckage which it is possible to mention included a quantity of brand-new woodwork, with bright brass fittings, a large portion of a white wooden bunk, bits of furniture and living-spaces, a shot-hole plug, two black-painted gratings, a mattress and bedcover, two seamen's caps, with cap ribbons of the IV and V *Untersee Boot Flotille*, and their owners' names, a vest and two pairs of drawers; also a red flag, a fit ensign for these lawless savages. For their destruction, it is hardly necessary to say, the full reward was given. Lieutenant Thomas Kippins and Skipper Andrew Walker also received the D.S.C. and two of their men the D.S.M.

This was an execution rather than a fight; but our fishermen can show their battles too, battles worthy of the sea-dogs who kept the narrow seas against more worthy enemies. In the Downs, and in the first twilight of a November morning, three of His Majesty's armed drifters—*Present Help, Paramount* and *Majesty*—were beginning their daily sweep, when Skipper Thomas Lane, R.N.R., of the *Present Help*, which was spare ship at the moment, sighted an object one mile distant to the eastward. As day was breaking, she was quickly marked for a pirate submarine a huge one, with two big guns mounted on deck, one a four-inch and one a 22-pounder. Nevertheless *Present Help, Paramount* and *Majesty* opened fire at once with their 6-pounders, not standing off, but closing their enemy, and continuing to close her under heavy fire until they were hitting her with their own light guns. Even our history can hardly show a grander line of battle than those three tiny ships bearing down upon their great antagonist; and if U. 48 did not fall to their fire, it is none the less true that her surrender was due in the first place to their determined onset.

It was *Paramount* who took and gave the first knocks. Her searchlight was shot away, and she in reply succeeded in putting one of the pirate's guns out of action. In the meantime—and none too soon—*Present Help* had sent up the red rocket; it was seen by two other armed drifters, *Acceptable* and *Feasible*, who were less than two miles off, and by H.M.S. *Gipsy*, who was four miles away. Skipper Lee, of the *Acceptable*, immediately sang out 'Action,' and both boats blazed away at 3,000 yards' range, getting in at least one hit on the enemy's conning-tower. At the same moment came the sound of the *Gipsy's* 12-pounder as she rushed in at full speed.

The U-boat started with an enormous, and apparently overwhelming, advantage of gun power. She ought to have been a match, twice over, for all six of our little ships. But she was on dangerous ground, and the astounding resolution of the attack drove her off her course. In ten minutes the drifters had actually pushed her ashore on the Goodwin Sands—*Paramount* had closed to thirty yards! Drake himself was hardly nearer to the galleons. Then came *Gipsy*, equally resolute. Her first two shots fell short; the third was doubtful, but after that she got on, and the pirate's bigger remaining gun was no match for her 12-pounder. After two hits with common pointed shell, she put in eight out of nine lyddite, smashed the enemy's last gun and set him on fire forward. Thereupon the pirate crew surrendered and jumped overboard.

It was now 7.20 and broad daylight. Lieutenant-Commander Frederick Robinson, of the *Gipsy*, gave the signal to cease fire, and the five drifters set to work to save their drowning enemies. *Paramount*, who was nearest, got thirteen, *Feasible* one, and *Acceptable* two, of whom one was badly wounded. The *Gipsy's* whaler was got away, and her crew, under Lieutenant Gilbertson, R.N.R., tried for an hour to make headway against the sea, but could not go further than half-a-mile, the tide and weather being heavily against them. They brought back one dead body, and one prisoner in a very exhausted condition; afterwards they went off again and collected the prisoners from the other ships. Then came the procession back to port—a quiet and unobtrusive return, but as glorious as any that the Goodwins have ever seen. Full rewards followed, and the due decorations for Skippers Thomas Lane, Edward Kemp and Richard William Barker. But their greatest honour was already their own—they had commanded, in victorious action, His Majesty's Armed Drifters, *Present Help*, *Paramount* and *Majesty*.

'THE U-BOAT STARTED WITH AN ENORMOUS ADVANTAGE OF GUN POWDER.'

CHAPTER 12

The Destroyers

The war record of our destroyers is unsurpassed. We know that to the Grand Fleet we owe, as to a vast and solid foundation, the unshaken fabric of our sea power, and that in the day of battle it has always proved itself incomparable. But we hardly, perhaps, realised that in our destroyer force we have a second Grand Fleet, equal to the other in spirit and seamanship, greater in numbers, and counting its days of battle not by twos or by twenties, but by the thousand. The work of the destroyers has been unceasing. Setting apart such service as their whirlwind attacks at Jutland, they have done perhaps nine-tenths of the hard work of the war, cruising and reconnoitring, convoying or rescuing our ships, and hunting the pirate submarine. The strain has been great, for they have been called upon incessantly to do the work of twice their number; they have answered the call, not with a dogged or defensive courage, but with unfailing readiness and dash. They have shown themselves the true successors of the frigates arid ships that were the pride of our proudest days in the old time; their commanders are the right heirs of the Brookes and Blackwoods, Parkers and Pellews.

In considering the anti-submarine work of the destroyers, it must be remembered that hunting is not, generally speaking, their first object. They are out, not for sport, but for 'business as usual.' They have a large number of U-boats to their credit, but in most of these cases the kill was incidental; it resulted from the perfection of skill and smartness with which some professional duty was being performed, at the moment when the opportunity occurred. A few typical examples will make this clear.

In August 1917, an upward sweep of the Norwegian coast was being carried out by a light squadron, consisting of three cruisers and six destroyers, the whole under the orders of H.M.S. *Yarmouth*, Captain Thomas D. Pratt, R.N., with Commander Geoffrey Corbett, R.N., as Senior Officer of Destroyers. The light cruisers were in line abreast, visibility distance apart—anything from five to ten miles—and each was screened by two destroyers. The cruiser on the port wing was *Birkenhead*, and the destroyer on her port bow was the *Oracle*, which was therefore outside ship of the whole squadron.

Just before dark, Lieutenant-Commander A. Grendon Tippet, R.N., commanding *Oracle*, was informed that very strong German wireless from two different sources was being intercepted; and as one of the sources was evidently nearby, he decided to keep all hands closed up to their quarters throughout the night. Nothing, however, happened until broad daylight, when, at about 6 a.m., Lieutenant Claude Butlin, officer of the watch, sighted a vessel on the horizon. No one else on the bridge could see it, but Mr. Butlin reported it, and his captain, who knew his exceptional alertness and powers of vision, ordered him to continue the look-out and report again. Shortly afterwards the vessel was sighted by the midshipman and the signalman of the watch, and was pronounced to be a trawler.

But a few minutes after this Mr. Butlin saw a bow and stern lift out of the water, well to left and right of the vessel's sail, and decided that she was a submarine. He at once informed his commander, who ordered full speed, course to be altered, and the proper signals to be made. The sail then disappeared, and the submarine's conning-tower became clearly visible, at a distance of something under seven miles.

At 6.7 the U-boat dived. The alarm had evidently been given, and it was not likely that she would be seen again on the surface; so at 6.10 Lieutenant-Commander Tippet slowed down. But at 6.13 the submarine unexpectedly broke surface less than three miles away on the port bow; her conning-tower, or part of it, could be seen moving fast through the water in a cloud of spray. She submerged again in 10 seconds, and *Oracle's* course was at once altered to cut her off. At 6.15 the enemy reappeared once more. Her bows shot up out of the water at a steep angle, about half a mile ahead. *Oracle's* course was instantly altered one point to port, telegraphs were put to full speed, and the forecastle gun was ordered to fire common shell at the conning-tower, which was then the only object visible. The U-boat just then lifted her stern out of water, showing a large vertical rudder on top of it, and the gunner's point of aim was shifted accordingly. Four rounds were fired, but the target was a very difficult one and was not hit.

At 6.15 events happened and orders were given in very rapid succession. The U-boat was apparently not inclined to dive and risk paravanes or depth-charges. Lieutenant Commander Tippet no sooner grasped this than he changed his tactics, and determined to ram. It was, of course, desirable to strike the enemy at right angles, and he endeavoured to con his ship so as to secure this position. He gave the orders 'Prepare to ram' and 'Secure the depth-charge,' and steadied the ship on a point midway between the submarine's conning-tower (the top of which was just showing) and the stern, which was about four feet out of water. Then, at 27 knots, he drove *Oracle* straight at her.

The crash came with lightning speed. At 6.17 *Oracle* cut into the submarine's back, exactly in the desired spot. It was, at the moment, inclined down-wards at an angle of 15°, with the top of the conning-tower showing on the port side of the destroyer, and on the starboard side about three feet of the freeboard at the stern. The impact was heavy, and two officers on *Oracle's* deck, who had not 'prepared to ram' by taking a completely prone position, were flung forward several feet. At the same moment an explosion was heard astern. It leaped into the commander's mind that this was either a paravane detonating, or his own depth-charge, which he had ordered to be secured, with the object of avoiding any chance of a disaster from the shock. It was, in fact, the depth-charge that exploded; but in the right way, and not by shock. The order had been misreported to the sub-lieutenant in charge of the after-quarters—as it reached him, it was 'Let go the depth-charge.' This he did personally and with great accuracy, a few seconds before ramming, so that when the explosion came, *Oracle's* stern was well clear and no one was injured, except possibly the enemy.

Oracle, having cut through the U-boat, drifted on for about 150 yards. The bows of the dying submarine appeared momentarily above water, projecting some 3 feet at an angle of 45°. Then she sank, stern first, in 137 fathoms. For half a minute the surface showed a big bubbling brown disturbance, and in the oil patch appeared a quantity of debris, mainly large pieces of unpainted cork, whose curved shape suggested that they formed part of the lining of the hull. *Oracle* herself was not undamaged, as may be imagined; her bows were smashed from the water-line downwards, and a considerable quantity of naval stores were floating around her. She reported accordingly by searchlight to the *Birkenhead*, who could just be discerned at a distance of ten miles, and then returned to her base to refit.

For this fine piece of work Lieutenant-Commander Tippet received the D.S.O., and Acting-Lieutenant Butlin the D.S.C. Nine of the crew were also decorated or mentioned.

Here the destroyers were screening a line of warships, who formed in themselves a fast and powerful force. The convoying of slow and unarmed or lightly armed ships is a very different business, but it is done every day by our destroyers with amazing efficiency and success. A good example is the case of the *Racoon*, who destroyed an enemy submarine in the Mediterranean while on escort duty.

In March 1917, the ss. *Osmanieh*, 4,440 tons gross, owned by the Khedivial Mail Company, but chartered by the Admiralty, was on passage from Malta to Madras when, at about 5.40 p.m., a hostile submarine was sighted. The ship was commanded by Lieutenant Mason, R.N.R., and was flying the White Ensign; she was zigzagging, and was escorted by a single destroyer, the *Racoon*, Lieutenant-Commander Kenneth F. Sworder, R.N. The weather was fine, the sea calm, and visibility good—about eight or nine miles.

The submarine when sighted was about 1,500 yards distant, and two or three points on the *Osmanieh's* starboard bow. Only six feet of her length was visible, and she appeared to be drifting; puffs of blue-grey vapour were coming from her, which seemed to hang in the air and float away without disappearing. When nearer—at 800 to 1,000 yards—she was seen to be moving, for a 'feather' was visible as well as the vapour.

The *Osmanieh's* head was put two points to star-board to steer for the submarine; but as it changed position rapidly, helm was put hard a-port, the whistle was blown to draw the escort's attention, and the alarm gong was sounded. The ship then opened fire with her two guns. The second round from the after gun appeared to score a hit; but the U-boat was at that time almost astern and shining brightly in the sun, so that it was not possible to observe with certainty. *Racoon*, when *Osmanieh* opened fire, was ahead of her, on the port bow and going 16½ knots; but the moment the guns were heard, Lieutenant-Commander Sworder increased speed to 23 knots, put his helm hard a-port, and sighted the U-boat. It had at first 'the appearance of a calcium light giving off intermittent puffs of smoke;' but when the ship's head was turned towards it, a periscope and distinct feather were seen, as the submarine came out of the trough of the swell.

The manoeuvre which followed was a very skilful and effective one. *Racoon* came to meet *Osmanieh*, who had now turned sixteen points to starboard and was on the other side of the submarine and overhauling her. *Osmanieh* continued firing till she saw her escort only 400 yards from the target. She had intended to try a depth-charge herself, and as soon as she passed the U-boat she had stopped her port propeller for this purpose, hoping to get the ship's stern back into or near the enemy's course; but she now gave this up and turned sharply away to port. As she did so, *Racoon* crossed her stern at full speed, and immediately saw the submarine on her own starboard side, the periscope just showing about five yards off and moving almost directly to meet her. Those on the destroyer's deck had a glimpse of about ten feet of a grey hull with green and rust-coloured marks showing; then, as the ship passed over this, she dropped her starboard depth-charge, set to eighty feet, turned swiftly to port and dropped her port depth-charge, four seconds after the first.

Eight or nine seconds passed while *Racoon* swung round on her circle; then came the two explosions in quick succession, throwing up columns of water with bits of black debris in them. The ship continued to turn to port, and completed nearly two circles round the spot, ready to attack again. But nothing more was needed, and she may even be said to have witnessed the dying breath of her enemy. Some twenty or thirty seconds after the explosions, the men stationed in the after part of the destroyer, looking over the stern, saw a fresh upheaval twenty-five yards or more to the right of where the first columns of water had risen. This 'seemed to come from below as if being pumped up,' and it rose to about a foot above the level of the water, making a ripple where the surface had teen very calm. On examination, it proved to be a fountain of dark and very thick brown oil. *Racoon* and *Osmanieh* proceeded accordingly, leaving that dark and evil-smelling blot of oil upon the bright sea to give the 'all clear' to every passing ship.

Lieutenant-Commander Sworder received the D.S.O. on this occasion, Lieutenant Berthon the D.S.C., and three men the D.S.M.

It may be noted that in neither of these two cases did the submarine attempt to escape by submerging entirely. We can only guess at the reasons. Possibly the U-boat which attacked *Osmanieh* thought she could win in a single fight against a lightly armed ship, and was too much preoccupied to see *Racoon's* deadly onset until it was too late to avoid it. But *Oracle's* enemy had certainly sufficient time to make her choice between the ram and the depth-charge; and the fact that she decided to keep near the surface is very suggestive. The combination of the hydrophone and the depth-charge is a terrible one to contend against. The submarine which dives is under the double disability of

147

being both blind and audible. The depths of the sea are no safe hiding-place for the assassin flying from justice; given a sufficient patrol, his undersea refuge is gone.

On the other hand, the surface is hardly better, when it is covered by an adequate number of destroyers, manned by British seamen. The vigilance and decision with which they mark and seize their opportunities are well shown in the following case of the destruction of a submarine in the dead of night.

Early in May 1917, three destroyers—*Miranda*, *Lance* and *Milne*—were patrolling a well-known area, where the enemy has once or twice attempted runaway raids under cover of night. This was a likely enough evening for him; for there was a moon only two days past the full, and from time to time a drift of rainy cloud across it. Tonight, however, it was not with a flurry of destroyers that he came, but-with a creep of mine-layers—U.C.-boats stealing in across the black and silver water to lay their deadly eggs close to our barrage.

One of these was sighted by *Lance*, and killed by her, in the belief of the look-out who were watching from *Miranda*; but with that one we have nothing to do. Another, U.C. 26, is our concern, and about her we know all that there is to know. She was travelling on the surface about an hour after midnight—she had finished laying her mines, and was heading about east—when she suddenly sighted the dark form of an English destroyer within a dangerously short distance of her. At the same moment *Milne*—or rather the perfectly trained team of men who were the eyes, the brain and the heart of her—sighted their enemy.

Lieutenant Leonard Pearson and leading signalman William Smith were the first, and their commanding officer, Commander V. L. A. Campbell, reports that it was only by reason of their exceptional vigilance that the attack could be so timed as to achieve success. The submarine, without losing a moment, dived—or rather attempted to dive. But Commander Campbell was as quick as his look-out, and his helmsman and engine-room watch were as quick as their commander. A trace of hesitation—an order not caught, or misheard, or obeyed with less than absolute precision—and U.C. 26 would have been in hiding. But she was hardly sighted and reported before the fatal orders were sharply and clearly given. Commander Campbell's voice had hardly reached his chief petty officer, Frederick Robinson, before the helm had brought the ship upon her altered course; and even as she turned Ernest Pike and John Reason down below were repeating the

'U.C.-BOATS STEALING IN ACROSS
THE BLACK AND SILVER WATER,'

call for full speed to the chief engineer.

No greater tension can be imagined than that on board the two boats during the few interminable seconds of the onset. This submarine, at any rate, was not unconscious of her danger. She was wide awake, with a possible margin of one second between safety and destruction. Her deck was already awash; only her conning-tower was still clear above the surface when the destroyer struck her just before it, and cut clean through her hull. She took in water in an overwhelming rush, and went straight to the bottom. Scarcely had she reached it when the pressure of air, increasing as the water rose inside her, seemed to give her unhappy crew a last forlorn chance of escape. The captain was in the engine-room, so that the exit by the conning-tower hatch, which would have been his prerogative, was left to the second officer, who succeeded in reaching the surface. Of the remaining 26 members of the crew, 7 got the engine-room hatch open, and 5 at least escaped by it; but only one of the whole number was picked up alive. He was a Dane from Schleswig-Holstein, and had been pressed for submarine service.

For this smart piece of work, in every way characteristic of our Destroyer Service, Commander V. L. A. Campbell received a bar to his D.S.O. Lieutenant L. Pearson was awarded the D.S.C., and the other four men already mentioned received the D.S.M.

The next case is also typical, being a patrol action; but it differs from the last in that the success was due to combined work by three destroyers, and not only by a single crew. There are also one or two exceptional circumstances which distinguish it from other actions of a similar kind—the presence of the rear-admiral commanding the local force, and the additional evidence which eventually settled the classification of the result.

It was on the morning of a day in March 1918 that a light-cruiser squadron was cruising in the North Sea; and at 9.25 a.m. three destroyers—*Thruster*, Commander A. D. Gibbs; *Retriever*, Commander E. W. Taylor; and *Sturgeon*, Lieutenant-Commander Henry Coombs—were ordered to take up a screening position ahead of the force. As they were in the act of moving to their stations an object was sighted, two points on *Sturgeon's* port bow, and about one mile distant. A moment afterwards it was recognised as the conning-tower of a submarine. In order to understand what followed, it is necessary to have the positions clearly before the mind's eye. *Thruster* and *Retriever* were immediately ahead of the squadron, to starboard and port respectively, and *Sturgeon* was ahead of the flotilla, in the act of crossing from starboard to port.

She had just passed *Thruster* and was on her port bow, going towards a point ahead of *Retriever*, when she sighted the submarine on her own port bow and therefore almost enclosed in the triangle formed by the three destroyers. The U-boat dived immediately, and *Sturgeon* fired as she did so, but without effect a late shot at a disappearing target. Lieutenant-Commander Coombs at once increased to full speed, and altered course to pass over the position. He arrived accurately, and in time to sight the track of the submarine as she tried to bolt through the only opening left to her, between her pursuer and the advancing *Retriever*. Her underwater speed was quite unequal to this effort, and in a moment *Sturgeon* was passing along her track and overhauling her. Another moment and the destroyer's depth-charges, set to forty feet only, were dropped—one on either side of the track and a little ahead of it.

Sturgeon put her helm over in the usual way to avoid the explosion area, but turned again on hearing the detonations and had the satisfaction of seeing the U-boat shortly afterwards break surface with her bows up at an ominously high angle. She was by this time near closing *Retriever*, but Lieutenant-Commander Coombs considered her as still his hare. He turned again and raced for her like a greyhound. She tried to submerge, but could not get down quickly enough. Every one of the three destroyers could have rammed her, for as they came up to her in succession they could all see some thirty feet of her bows, with hydrophones and net-cutters, lying almost under them. But there was no need to take the risks of a concussion—this was a plain case for more depth-charges. *Sturgeon*, as she passed over a second time, dropped the remainder of hers.

Then came *Retriever* an instant later, with two more; and she also dropped a Dan buoy, to mark the exact spot for *Thruster*, who was coming across from a greater distance. By the time *Thruster* arrived, she found the U-boat entirely submerged, but she methodically added her two depth-charges and both of them exploded within five yards of *Retriever's* buoy, and probably not more from the submarine, which they followed down to eighty feet.

So far, no one had thought of doubting the success of this very well executed triple attack; and indeed the evidence was both strong and plentiful. The U-boat was clearly seen to have been damaged by the *Sturgeon's* first two charges, for she reappeared almost at once and at an unmistakable angle. The six other charges dropped over her were none of them blind shots—*Sturgeon* and *Retriever* both saw their target plainly, and *Thruster* had the Dan buoy to guide her. The rear-admiral, in reporting the case, added that he was himself a witness of the attack and was of opinion that the submarine was destroyed. As corroborative evidence, he named the following articles, which were picked up near the spot: 1 wooden ladder, 1 red *kisbie* lifebuoy, 1 calcium float, and 1 steel buoy with fractured wire pendant attached. The lifebuoy and calcium float were not of British make, and the former was marked with letters and numbers not used in our service. Finally, the area round the Dan buoy was thick with oil, which came gradually up during the two hours succeeding the chase.

Notwithstanding this evidence, and the opinion of so many competent witnesses, the Admiralty rule held good. There were no survivors or dead bodies, no debris which might not have come from the submarine's deck, no certainty that she could not have righted herself and crawled home to the repairing yard. The report was marked 'Probably sunk,' and a letter of appreciation was directed to be forwarded to each of the three commanders, with an intimation that if any subsequent information should be received which would cause any revision of the classification, the case should be resubmitted. Less than seven weeks afterwards the 'subsequent information' was forthcoming and thereupon Lieutenant-Commander Coombs was awarded the D.S.O., and 'Mentions' were given to Commanders Taylor and Gibbs, as well as to two ratings from *Sturgeon*, and one rating each from *Retriever* and *Thruster*. So ends the plain story of what is, to the Destroyer Service, a day's work in the ordinary routine. But any other service in the world will tell you that there is nothing ordinary about it.

CHAPTER 13

P-Boats and Auxiliary Patrol

The trawler is a fishing-boat by birth, and a mine-sweeper by necessity; the destroyer is first of all a fighting ship, and a protector of the weak. They will both kill a submarine when it comes their way; but we have ships—classes of ships—whose whole profession and occupation it is to hunt the pirate. Their methods differ as the methods of two kinds of hound. The Q-boat hunts slowly and craftily, the P-boat and the Yacht Patrol by speed, the ram, and the dreaded depth-charge. It is unnecessary to give the technical description of either class. A yacht is a yacht, and for a P-boat you may imagine a long slim boat, with fine lines and a rather low freeboard, three officers, a surgeon, and some fifty-five men—depth-charges round the stern and a gun or two, but no torpedoes.

In September 1917, H.M.S. P. 61 received orders to pick up in a certain roadstead the oiler *San Zeferino* and escort her to her destination. It was no easy job; the *San Zeferino's* steering gear was defective, she could not zigzag; and in the misty showers and very dark weather prevailing, her course was embarrassingly original. But she was a valuable ship, and P. 61 meant to get her in if it could be done.

The sea was moderate, but visibility was no more than three-quarters of a mile. P. 61 kept on the convoy's starboard bow and only about two cables ahead, zigzagging at seventeen knots. At three minutes to six in the morning, the oiler was suddenly observed to be settling by the stern. Lieut.-Commander Frank Arthur Worsley, R.N.R., on the bridge of P. 61, had heard no sound of explosion, and no one in the ship had sighted a submarine. The commander knew, however, that in the thick mist and with a head wind and wash against him, this was natural enough. He immediately circled twice round the convoy, signalling to her: 'Have you been torpedoed?' With some difficulty she

153

replied 'Yes,' and also that she had sighted the submarine.

Lieut.-Commander Worsley ascertained that the *San Zeferino* had her boats swung out and was in no immediate danger. He then reduced speed, in order not to betray his presence to the enemy, and started off north-west on the chase. Inevitably he soon lost sight of the oiler in the fog, and was obliged to turn in order to regain touch. He found the convoy still heading on her course, though her engines were wrecked; crossed her bows, and passed down her port side and under her stern. Directly P. 61 was clear, Lieutenant J. R. Stenhouse, R.N.R., on her bridge, sighted the enemy about half a mile away on the starboard beam, heading westward at nine knots.

Action stations had already been sounded, and fire was now opened from the port 12-pounder gun. One round of common shell was sent into the submarine, striking her just before the conning-tower. But a gun action was not the final object of P. 61. Lieut.-Commander Worsley had got his engines up to full speed as he came on, and saw that the enemy could not escape his ram. So sure was he that, after three minutes' run, he deliberately stopped both engines, so as to let the ship's bows drop deeper in the water and make a better hit.

The engines stopped, the bows sank two feet, the order 'Stand by to ram' was heard, and P. 61 struck the enemy stem on, on the port side, just abaft the conning-tower. Her speed at the moment was fully 20 knots, and the impact was severe; the submarine rolled over as the stem cut into her; and when P. 61's stern was just above her, a very violent explosion took place, giving Lieut.-Commander Worsley, for an instant, the nightmare that he had been torpedoed by another U-boat in the moment of victory. He was quickly reassured. P. 61 had suffered no damage. But round the place of collision the sea was boiling with foam; immense air-bubbles were coming to the surface in rushes, and continued for some minutes after the explosion.

There was oil upon the surface, and in it two men struggling. Lifebelts were thrown to them, and boats put out. One of the two was rescued and proved to be Ober-Leutnant Alfred Arnold, the commanding officer of the U-boat—the fifth upon the list of 150 published by the British Admiralty. The submarine was U.C. 49 and lies at the bottom in forty-seven fathoms. The *San Zeferino* was taken in tow by P. 61 and came safely in after an arduous twelve hours—an admirable piece of work. Lieutenant-Commander Worsley received the D.S.O., Lieutenant Stenhouse the D.S.C., and two petty officers the D.S.M. for excellent steering and gun-laying.

On this occasion the P-boat had left her patrol duty for the moment, to act as escort. This was not the case with P. 57, who had a similar success in November of the same year. In the dark of early morning, about 6 o'clock, she had just challenged and examined by searchlight a vessel which turned out to be a friend, when the forward look-out reported 'Buoy on the port bow!' Course was altered to examine this buoy, and on approaching it both Lieut.-Commander H. C. Birnie, R.N.R., in command of P. 57, and Lieutenant Isdale, R.N.R., his officer of the watch, simultaneously perceived it to be a large U-boat heading due west and only 200 yards distant.

There was less than no time to be lost. Orders were given and obeyed instantaneously. The engines leaped to full speed as the ship came round sharply to port and steered straight for the enemy. In less than fifteen seconds the crash came—a heavy impact, at seventeen knots, on a point just before the U-boat's conning-tower, very nearly at right angles. P. 57 cut her way right through, and as she did so the order for the depth-charges reached the officer of the watch. The first charge was released with great promptitude and precision as the damaged submarine passed under the ship's stern. P. 57 turned sixteen points and came back over the spot, when a second charge was immediately dropped and a buoy put down.

An hour and a half afterwards Lieut.-Commander Birnie returned, after verifying his position, and found very large quantities of oil rising about fifty yards from his buoy. He dropped a third depth-charge and another buoy, and patrolled the neighbourhood all night. Sweepers arrived next day, located the U-boat with a bottom sweep in thirty fathoms, lowered a depth-charge on the sweep wire and blew the wreck up. For this 'speedy and faultless attack' Lieut.-Commander Birnie received the D.S.O., Lieutenant Isdale the D.S.C., and two A.B.'s the D.S.M.

This feat was a remarkable one, for it was performed in almost total darkness; but success was achieved in even more difficult circumstances by P. 51 towards the end of March 1918. It was 13.30 in the evening; the sea was calm under the moonlight, but great spaces of it were darkened by cloud shadows. The commander, Lieutenant William Murray, R.N.R., was in the chart-house, and Mr. Whittel, the gunner, on watch, when the signalman on the bridge reported a submarine on the surface, about one point before the port beam and less than 300 yards away. Orders were at once given to increase to full speed, and starboard the helm to ram.

As the ship swung, the commander reached the bridge and took charge. He could see the enemy's wash and bow wave. Then she appeared more distinctly as a large U-boat, 350 feet long, with a huge conning-tower and about two feet of freeboard showing. P. 51 continued to swing into the desired position and the moment for a successful ram seemed to have arrived. Then occurred one of those sudden and unforeseen accidents which try a commander's presence of mind and decision to the utmost. To strike the U-boat fair it was, of course, necessary to put the helm over as soon as P. 51's head had swung far enough to be pointing for her, and so steady the ship on her course. But this order could not be obeyed—the helm had jammed. Lieutenant Murray knew that to struggle with it could only at best result in a bungling collision which would injure his own ship rather than the enemy. He made a lightning act of renunciation, kept his helm a-starboard and swung completely round, passing close along the submarine's side and then turning altogether away from her. The helm was soon afterwards found to be acting again; but in the meantime P. 51 had lost sight of the enemy.

She dashed westwards, and in two minutes sighted the U-boat again, a mile away on the port quarter. A new ramming attack was immediately planned, and the guns were ordered to open fire; but the submarine dived completely before they could pick her up in the uncertain light. In ten seconds Lieutenant Murray had brought P. 51 over a patch of oil which betrayed the spot where the U-boat was submerging. Three depth-charges followed her down. The first two produced the usual upheaval of water, but the third blew a quantity of wreckage into the air, of many shapes and sizes. P. 51 continued to circle around, and ten minutes later three shocks were felt below in rapid succession. Nothing more was seen, nor could any movement be heard on the hydrophone.

The official verdict was one of 'Probably sunk,' the evidence being considered good but inconclusive. It was, however, afterwards supplemented by final proof, and the case was remarked 'Known.' Lieutenant Murray accordingly received the D.S.C. and two of his men the D.S.M.

Very little information has been given to the public about the Yacht Patrol; but it is certain that, when all is known, the history of this service will be eagerly read. There is a fine Elizabethan air about the gift of a ship to the navy by a private owner, and we can imagine how keenly the giver would follow the career of his own boat, longing to command her himself, and glorying to catch her name now and then through the gales and rumours and gun-fire of the seas, where she is at last flying the white ensign. Such a gift was the *Prize*, who with the heroic Sanders, her Commander, lies fathoms deep, and still unknown to many; but in time to come she will be remembered with *Farnborough, Pargust* and *Dunraven*, and her owner's name will stand in a unique and honourable list.

Among the victories of the Yacht Patrol, one of the most timely and decisive was that of May 26, 1918. H.M. Yacht 024, *Lorna*, Lieutenant C. L. Tottenham, R.N.R., was on patrol that day in Lyme Bay, intercepting east-bound traffic, and keeping an eye at the same time on the activities of a U-boat off Portland Bill, whom she intended to deal with when opportunity should offer. Soon after 8.0 in the evening, she spoke two ships in succession, the *Jabiru* and *War Cross*, and ordered them both into Weymouth Bay, warning them at the same time of the enemy submarine. At 8.50 p.m. a lamentable signal came back by wireless—'S.O.S., S.S.S.S., 2 miles S.W. of Portland Bill, ss. *Jabiru*, torpedoed.'

Lorna immediately proceeded at full speed, to look for the sinking ship and give what assistance might be possible. But, at 9.14 p.m., she intercepted the reassuring message—'Proceeding to port, torpedo missed fire.' Lieutenant Tottenham at the same moment saw that *War Cross*, which had parted only twenty-five minutes before, had now turned and was steering westward, having evidently also received the S.O.S. signal from *Jabiru*. He altered course and spoke her accordingly, advising her captain to lay the land, and endeavour to round the Bill inside the U-boat's operating radius. He also offered to go with him as escort, but *War Cross* pluckily declined, thinking he could do better by waiting for darkness and running in by himself.

Lieutenant Tottenham left him and searched the horizon for another smoke streamer. His game was to meet every ship which came that way and by closing them one after another, in the falling dusk, to ensure being within striking distance when the U-boat should make the next attempt at assassination. The only success which could satisfy him would be the destruction of the enemy before he had had time to strike the 'live bait'—an ambition which showed great nerve, and a grasp of the principle of the offensive in war. It would have been easy to make all merchantmen give the Bill a wide berth, and perhaps save the next ten of them thereby; but the pest would be active again tomorrow, in the same place or another—destruction, at all risks, is the only cure for U-boats.

Before long another ship was seen approaching from the south, and *Lorna* at once headed towards her. But after steaming for about three and a half miles on this errand, Lieutenant Tottenham perceived that the new-comer was already in good hands, or would soon be so—the armed drifter *Evening Primrose* was closing her, evidently with the intention of acting as escort. At this moment a fresh ship came in sight, approaching the Bill from the west. Lieutenant Tottenham instantly altered course and made straight for her.

At 9.55 p.m., when he had hardly steadied *Lorna* on her new course, he sighted the periscope of a submarine. It was steering due west, almost directly towards the approaching steamer, and seeing the position of the two ships, and their converging courses, he assumed rightly that the enemy was manoeuvring for an attack of the usual kind, without warning. Of *Lorna's* presence the U-boat was apparently quite unaware, though she was now only 150 feet distant and rapidly coming up on the starboard side of the periscope.

But aware or unaware, the pirates were doomed—caught in the act, and helpless as they had thought to find their victim. *Lorna's* helm flew over to starboard. The ship swung, in one swift curve, through the intervening fifty yards, and in two minutes from sighting her enemy she was right over the periscope. The U-boat dipped, but far too late; as *Lorna* passed over the spot a shuddering jar was felt throughout her—her keel had struck the conning-tower, but so lightly that the pirates below probably thought they had escaped destruction for this time. A moment later they knew their error. Down came *Lorna's* first depth-charge, set to fifty feet. The helm went over still further to starboard, and the second charge dropped about fifty feet from the first, and at the same depth.

Both charges detonated, and it was impossible to believe that they could have failed to destroy or seriously cripple the U-boat. They must have exploded in the most dangerous way possible, just alongside and underneath the target, where the resistance would be the maximum. The proof came a few moments afterwards. While continuing his circle, in order to pass again over the spot and make sure, Lieutenant Tottenham suddenly sighted four objects in the water among the disturbance caused by the two explosions. He turned and steered direct for the place, expecting to find wreckage of some kind; but on arriving, at full speed, he saw an astonishing tumult of water, caused by an upward rush of air, gas, and oil, which showed beyond doubt that the U-boat was immediately below.

The next moment was a terrible one. As *Lorna's* third depth-charge dropped into this seething cauldron, cries of '*Kamerad!*' were heard, and those on the yacht's deck, looking back as she raced over, saw the new explosion hurl into the air the bodies of four men, who for a brief instant had been survivors from the sunken U-boat. Lieutenant Tottenham eased down and returned to pick them up. One was found still crying '*Help!*' and '*Kamerad!*' but the other three were already dead, from the effect of the explosion, or of the thick mass of oil in which they were submerged. About the unhappy prisoner there was no doubt. He was seriously injured internally, and was gone in three hours' time. He lived and died in a cruel and cowardly business, but if care and kindness could have saved him, *Lorna* would have brought him into port and been glad to do it.

This submarine was U.B. 74. She was a week out, and had already sunk three ships when she was caught. Her commander was Ober-Leutnant Schtiendorf, and his name will be found in the list of the 150, for his case was among those marked as 'Known.'

One more patrol story must be added—a story in some ways unique, with mysterious details which haunt the imagination, but can never be finally explained. The vessels of the patrol on this occasion were not yachts, or P-boats in the strict sense of the classification. One was the *Sarba*, an armed trawler like those we have already met, and commanded by Lieutenant George G. Astbury, R.N.R.; the other was a small boat, with no name but T.B. 055, commanded by Gunner T.H. Britton.

On the morning of October 81, 1917, T.B. 055 was accompanying the trawlers who were engaged in sweeping an important channel outride a British harbour. At 3.0 p.m. when the sweep was practically over, Mr. Britton noticed an oil track on the surface of the channel. This was in itself an astonishing sight, and not to be accounted for in a moment. How could a submarine have ventured into a channel only thirteen fathoms deep, and daily swept by a highly efficient force of trawlers? And for what possible reason could she be lying there on the bottom at 3 o'clock in the afternoon, in a position where she could use none of her weapons, and was certain to be found and attacked?

Mr. Britton went into the oil track to investigate; stopped his boat and listened on the hydrophone. His astonishment was redoubled—the submarine was there, and not only there, but busy and audible. The case was so extraordinary that he and his trained hydrophone listener took counsel together and classified the sounds they heard. First there were the usual 'water noises;' these were continuous and perfectly familiar. Secondly, there was an almost continuous high-pitched sound, somewhat similar to that of a turbine engine running. Thirdly, at intervals of a few seconds, came a noise as of knocking or hammering upon metal; the speed of the tapping varied from slow to fairly rapid blows. Lastly—and this was the most unexpected and mysterious of all—on two occasions there was audible, over all the other noises, a sound as of wireless letters on a high musical note.

For three minutes these sounds were heard, noted, and compared. T.B. 055 was then taken forward about 203 yards, to the end of the oil track, and the hydrophone was used again. Precisely the same sounds were heard, except that this time the musical note, as of a wireless message, was not repeated. Mr. Britton had no desire to lose time; but he was not troubled with nerves, and he was determined to make sure of his evidence. He took precautions to stop all ship's noises. The fact only became clearer that the sounds below came from a live submarine. What her crew were doing no one could know; but she was there for an evil purpose, and she must pay the penalty.

The oil was still coming up in a visible thin stream from below the surface. T.B. 055 dropped a Reindeer buoy with moorings, to mark the spot exactly, got under way and came back over the position. As she passed, a depth-charge was dropped. The tide was fairly slack at the time, and there was every reason to believe that it found the target. Mr. Britton returned to the spot once more. The volume of oil rising had now increased, and a strong smell of oil fuel was noticed, which had not been there before. The blobs of oil which now came to the surface had brownish air-bubbles and froth among them; in the hydrophone, nothing was to be heard but the ordinary water noises.

It was now 3.35 p.m., and the armed trawler *Sarba* was seen approaching. Mr. Britton reported what he had been doing to Lieutenant Astbury, who at once stopped his own engines and used his hydrophone. Then, as he too could hear no sign of life, he took a sounding, found sixteen fathoms and a sandy bottom, and decided that the enemy must be still there, alive or dead. Accordingly he steamed clear of the position, turned and came back over it at full speed. He determined to set his depth-charge for eighty feet, in spite of the shallowness of the water, because, with the boat on the bottom at ninety-six feet, he would be absolutely certain of getting a very close explosion. The charge detonated, and he returned at once to the spot. Large

'THE DIVER WHO FIRST WENT DOWN FOUND THE SUBMARINE
LYING ON HER SIDE.'

bubbles of air and quantities of oil were coming up, and within a short time the oil was covering a very wide area. *Sarba* stood by all night, using her hydrophone frequently.

It was now evident that the enemy was dead; but the more the circumstances were reflected upon, the more difficult it was to explain them. Next morning, when T.B. 055 had 'proceeded to sea in accordance with programme,' Lieutenant Astbury, in *Sarba*, was left alone, with nothing but two buoys and an oil patch to give so incredible a story any kind of reality. He got out a sweep wire with a sinker of 1¾ cwt. and took a sweep along the position. The sweep brought up on an immovable obstruction, and the incredible seemed once more possible. At 2.0 p.m. arrived the armed drifter *Sunshine* and T.B. 058. They found *Sarba* lying as near as possible in the position where she had exploded her depth-charge, and where her sweep had brought her up. They took a ground sweep under her, and their sweep wire also fouled the same obstruction. *Sarba*, like a faithful dog, remained on guard during the following night. At last, at 2.30 p.m. on November 2, the divers arrived.

Before the day was out, all uncertainty was removed. The diver who first went down found the submarine lying on her side. When visited a second time, she had been righted by the tide or some shifting of weight; but she and all her crew were dead. The main fact was thus proved; but the mystery remained and still remains inexplicable and haunting. Possibly the answer, to the first of the two questions involved, may be a simple one. The U-boat may have got into the channel in a fog, and finding herself there when the weather cleared, she may have dived for safety and decided to remain on the bottom till it was dark enough to steal away.

But the sounds cannot be explained to the satisfaction of those who know most about submarine war. The U-boat commander must have realised the enormous risk he was incurring, when he allowed those noises to be made at such an hour of day. He must have known that the British Patrol is well equipped with hydrophones, with depth-charges, and with sweeps. Either he had some serious injury to repair, and no time to wait; or else his boat was completely disabled at the bottom, and the hammering and other noises were the desperate attempts of the crew to draw attention in the hope of being rescued. 'There is also,' said the admiral of the station, 'the third possibility, that the boat carries inside her a tragedy that will never be known.'

CHAPTER 14

Q-Boats

Everyone who has ever thought about war must know that secrecy is one of the first conditions of military success, whether on land or sea. Yet the secrecy practised by our government and our Higher Command has often been the subject of complaint. The complaint is not the cry of mere sensationalism or curiosity, deprived of its ration of news. Often it is the most patriotic and intelligent who are the most distressed at being kept in the dark. They understand the dangers of a great war, and they desire, above all things, not to live in a fool's paradise. They know that they can bear to hear the worst, and they feel that they deserve to hear the best. The anti-submarine campaign has especially tried their patience. There has been great anxiety to know the exact figures of our mercantile losses; and on the other hand, when naval honours have been given without the usual account of the actions by which they were earned, there has been a tendency to grumble that we are not being helped to bear the strain of war, even when events are in our favour.

These complaints are not justified. Those who make them have failed to realise the deadly earnestness of the struggle we are carrying on. It is hard on the patriotic student of war that we should go short of facts, and hard on the anxious that they should lack encouraging information; but how much harder would it be for our seamen and submarine crews, if the secret of their tactics were given away to an enemy only too quick to take advantage of what he can succeed in overhearing? When one interesting paragraph in a newspaper may possibly mean the sacrifice of many lives, what statesman or staff of-ficer would take the responsibility of passing it for publication? But the secrets of the Admiralty in this war have not been timidly or unin-telligently kept. In spite of the tradition of 'the Silent Service'—which only means that 'the navy doesn't advertise'—there is no general feeling against telling the truth and the whole truth, when it can be done to the advantage of the country.

Those in power have been for the most part in favour of 'taking the lid off' when the right time has come; and in this very matter of the mysterious honours, it was the First Lord himself who at last told the public what could no longer be valuable information for the enemy. So long as the use of disguised Special Service ships, or Q-boats, was a new method, indispensable to us and unsuspected by the Germans, or at least unfamiliar to them, so long was it highly undesirable that we should speak or write publicly of their successes. But now that after many losses, and some escapes, from Q-boats, the enemy's submarine service has found out all their secrets, our own navy has naturally ceased to rely on this kind of surprise, and has invented new devices, even more deadly and more difficult to evade.

Of these we are, very reasonably, forbidden to write; but of the old and well-known hunting methods—of the work of destroyers, patrol-boats, trawlers, submarines, aircraft and Q-boats—we may now give illustrations; for we shall be telling nothing that the enemy does not know to his cost already. The very name, Q-boat, is as familiar in Germany as in this country. The submarine which escaped from the *Dunraven* carried away a very complete understanding of the work of these Special Service ships, and the *Illustrierte Zeitung* of July 12, 1917, contained a full description of a fight between a U-boat and a 'submarine trap,' which took place on February 22 of that year.

It is evident from this, and other articles of a similar kind, that, in German opinion, it is the U-boats, and not their victims, who have the right to complain of barbarous treatment. This view is amazing; but it is in complete accordance with the principle laid down by Major-General von Disfurth, in the *Hamburger Nachrichten*, at the beginning of the war:

> We owe no explanations to anyone: there is nothing for us to justify, and nothing for us to explain away. Every act, of whatever nature, committed by our troops for the purpose of discouraging, defeating and destroying our enemies, is a brave act, a good deed, and fully justified. Germany stands supreme, the arbiter of her own methods, which must in time of war be dictated to the world.

That is the insolence of unmitigated brutality, and the British

Navy took up the challenge with a spirit that will set the standard of the world so long as war remains a possibility in human life. If our men had retaliated on barbarians by methods of barbarism, neither the German Government, as Sir Edward Grey pointed out, nor the German people, would have had any just ground for complaint.

It is not in consideration for their deserts that the Admiralty reject such a policy. They reject it because it is inconsistent with the traditions of the Service for which they are responsible; nor do they now propose to alter their methods of warfare merely because they find themselves in conflict with opponents whose views of honour and humanity are different from their own.

But within the old rules, the rules of law and chivalry, they are right to use every device that native ingenuity and centuries of experience can suggest. There is no German cunning that cannot be matched by British science and discipline, and no German brutality that cannot be overmatched by British daring and endurance. This has been proved a hundred times in the course of the submarine war, and never more brilliantly than by the captains of the Q-boats, of whom the pattern for all time is Gordon Campbell, till yesterday known only as 'The Mystery Star Captain' of the British Navy.

In 1915, Gordon Campbell was just one of the many Lieutenant-Commanders who had never had an opportunity for distinguished service. His hopes rose when he was appointed to command the *Farnborough*, a Special Service ship, formerly a collier, with crew mainly drawn from the mercantile marine and R.N.R. Into these men he infused his own ideas of discipline and training, as well as his own cool and selfless courage. During the whole winter the *Farnborough* faced the gales without a single fight to cheer her; but never for a moment did her commander waver in his faith that her chance would come, and never did his men cease to give him their whole trust and devotion. In the end, he was able to say of them that they understood every move in the game as well as he himself did, and played it with the same keenness. Even if he had met with no other success, this alone was an achievement, and a proof of invaluable power. But other successes were to be added—the power was to be felt beyond his own ship, as an example and an inspiration.

The *Farnborough's* first chance came in the spring of 1916, when she was tramping quietly along at eight knots. Her look-out sighted the enemy at last—a submarine awash, and about five miles distant on the port bow. It remained in view only for a few minutes and then dived, no doubt for the attack. It was the *Farnborough's* part to be blind, stupid, and generally mercantile. She maintained her course and speed as if she had observed nothing. Twenty minutes later a torpedo was seen coming up on the starboard quarter. The bubbles rose right under the forecastle, the torpedo having evidently passed just ahead of the ship. The *Farnborough* maintained her course, as blind and trampish as before.

A few minutes more, and the U-boat, convinced that she had a fool to deal with, broke surface only a thousand yards astern of the ship, passing across her wake from starboard to port. But she was not exactly in a mood of reckless courage—she fired a shot from her gun across *Farnborough's* bows, and at the same time partially submerged. Now came the moment for which Lieutenant-Commander Campbell had trained his men. He stopped, blew off steam ostentatiously, and ordered a 'panic abandon ship' by his stokers and spare men, under Engineer Sub-Lieutenant John Smith, R.N.R. The U-boat was encouraged by this, closed to 800 yards, and a few seconds later reopened fire with a shell which fell about fifty yards short. Then, in the traditional style of the old navy, the captain gave the order to hoist the white ensign and open fire.

The surprise was complete and overwhelming; the pirate made no fight of it at all. *Farnborough* fired twenty-one rounds from her three 12-pounders, one of the guns getting off 13 rounds to her own share; and the Maxims and rifles also expended some 200 cartridges. The range was long, considering the bad light, but several hits were observed before the submarine disappeared. She went down slowly. Lieutenant-Commander Campbell steamed full speed over the spot and dropped a depth-charge. Immediately the U-boat re-appeared. She was only ten yards off the ship, and rose in a nearly perpendicular position, being out of the water from the bow to abaft the conning-tower. She had had one periscope hit, and there was a large rent in her bow, through which no doubt the water had penetrated and run down into her stern compartment, giving her her unnatural position.

All this was remembered and told afterwards. Her reappearance was instantly greeted with five more rounds from the *Farnborough's* after-gun. They all went into the base of the conning-tower at point-blank range, and she sank at once. Oil, not in driblets but in very large quantities, came rapidly to the surface, mixed with pieces of wood, and covered the sea for some distance round. *Farnborough* collected her boats and stokers, and reported her success—a success insured, as was noted on her report, by 'good nerve and thorough organisation.'

Three weeks afterwards, she heard of a U-boat operating on a definite pitch of her own, and set out to put temptation in her way. In the evening, as she was going warily along at five knots, on a calm and misty sea, she observed a ship on her starboard quarter, about two miles distant. Then suddenly, between the two vessels, a submarine broke surface. The blind old *Farnborough* plodded on, taking no notice till the U-boat hoisted a signal, which Commander Campbell could not read. He stopped, however, and blew off steam, with his answering pendant at the dip. He also hoisted the signal 'Cannot understand your signal,' but kept jogging ahead, so as to edge in, and to avoid falling into the trough of the heavy swell. The U-boat was lying full length on the surface. She was a large boat and had two guns on deck, but no men visible.

Presently she began to close, and manned her foremost gun. In the meantime Commander Campbell had turned out the bridge boat and given his 'papers' to Engineer Sub-Lieutenant John Smith, R.N.R., to take over to the submarine. At this moment the enemy fired a shot, which passed over the ship, and one of the *Farnborough's* gunners, thinking that his own ship had opened the engagement, began to fire himself. This forced Commander Campbell's hand; he ran up the white ensign, gave the general order to open fire, and went full speed ahead to bring his after-gun to bear. The range was a long one for a misty evening—900 to 1,000 yards—but the shooting was good enough. The second shot was seen by the neutral sailors on the other ship to strike the U-boat directly; her bow submerged and her stern came up out of the water so that her propellers were visible, and one of them could be seen to be higher than the other. She lay in this position for a good five minutes, and altogether 20 rounds were fired at her from the *Farnborough's* 12-pounders, the last two of which hit either on the conning-tower or just forward of it.

Then there appeared to be an explosion on board the U-boat, and she sank suddenly. There was a great commotion on the water, and a cloud of dense steam or vapour covered the surface for some minutes. *Farnborough* passed over the spot and dropped two depth-charges; but the submarine had gone to the bottom in 81 fathoms and nothing more was seen of her. The neutral ship afterwards observed a large patch of oil upon the surface. She had behaved with strict neutrality, and was good enough to remain some time on the spot, 'looking for drowneds,' but she looked in vain.

By the destruction of these two U-boats, Commander Campbell and his ship's company had done valuable service, and had given remarkable proof of what can be accomplished by discipline and nerve. But the very efficiency and success of their work gave a deceptive appearance to it. The fighting was so smartly done, and so conclusive, that it looked an easier thing than it really was, to trap and sink a brace of pirates in three weeks. The enemy was not long in perceiving that the trade of murder was being rapidly made more difficult and more dangerous for him. Every time a U-boat came home, the need for caution was more strongly impressed upon the directors of the campaign.

The German Press was instructed to complain that the unscrupulous British Navy was using disguised ships and depth-charges against the power which 'stands supreme, the arbiter pf her own methods,' and has alone the right to dress her *Greifs* and *Moewes* as unarmed neutral trading vessels. At the same time the pirate captains were ordered to be less rash in approaching ships they had torpedoed but had not sunk outright. The result was to make Commander Campbell's next encounter a much more anxious affair, and it was only by his incredible patience and judgment, and the wonderful discipline of his crew, that their third victory was achieved. As to the courage of everyone concerned, it would be waste of time to speak of it. Courage of the finest quality was the very breath which these men breathed—all day, and every day.

One morning, then, early in 1917, the Special Service ship Q. 5 was going due east at 7 knots, when a torpedo was seen approaching her starboard beam. This was what Commander Campbell was out for—in the present timid state of the pirates' nerves, there was no hope of drawing any of them into a fight, except by getting torpedoed outright, to start with . They might approach a sinking ship—they would no longer venture to come near a live one. But, at the same time, one need not make the handicap unnecessarily heavy. Commander Campbell valued his men's lives at least as much as his own, and he did his best to save his heroic engine-room staff, who faced the worst of the danger with perfect understanding and perfect self-sacrifice. He put his helm hard aport, and was so far successful that he received the torpedo in No. 3 hold; but, to his regret, it burst the bulk-head between that hold and the engine-room and slightly wounded Engineer Sub-Lieutenant John Smith, R.N.R. Help, he knew, was not far off; but no signal was sent out, for fear some zealous ship might arrive before Q 5 had done her work. 'Action' was sounded, and all hands went quietly to stations previously arranged for such an emergency. Every man, except those required on board for the fight, then abandoned ship—two lifeboats and one dinghy full were sent away, and a fourth boat was partially lowered with a proper amount of confusion. The chief engineer reported the engine-room filling with water. He was ordered to hang on as long as possible, and then hide.

While all this was going on and a most masterly piece of acting it was, the whole company playing perfectly together—the U-boat was observed on the starboard quarter watching the proceedings through his periscope. His carcass he was loath to expose, but he came past the ship on the starboard side, only five yards from the lifeboats, and ten from the ship; so close, in fact, that though still submerged, the whole hull of the submarine could be seen distinctly through the water. The temptation to fire was almost unbearable. But the effect upon the U-boat at that depth was very doubtful, and there would be no time for a second shot before he slid down out of reach. Commander Campbell made no sign, and his gunners lay as steady as if his hand were upon them.

Their patience was repaid. Twenty minutes after firing his torpedo, the enemy passed across the ship's bow and ventured to the surface to finish her off. He was 300 yards away on the port bow when Q. 5 made the signal 'Torpedoed.' He then came down past the port side on the surface, captain on conning-tower, ready to give sentence of death on his victim. But as he came onto the precise bearing on which all Q. 5's guns could bear, Commander Campbell gave the order to open fire at point-blank range.

The 6-pounder got in first, with a shell which hit the conning-tower and removed the pirate captain's head. The U-boat never recovered from the surprise but lay on the surface while the British gunners shattered his hull. The conning-tower was naturally the chief mark. It was repeatedly hit, some of the shells going apparently clean through it. When the boat sank, the conning-tower was shattered and lay completely open, with the crew trying to escape by it to the deck. Commander Campbell ordered 'Cease fire,' and sent one of his lifeboats to their assistance. But the swirl of the sinking vessel, and the density of the oil which poured out of her, proved immediately fatal to those who had succeeded in reaching the water. One officer was picked up alive, and one man.

'A FOURTH BOAT WAS PARTIALLY LOWERED WITH A PROPER
AMOUNT OF CONFUSION.'

Commander Campbell then recalled his boats and inspected his ship, with what feelings only a seaman can imagine. He found that Q. 5 was sinking by the stern. The engine-and boiler-rooms were rapidly filling, and the water was also pouring into three holds. After making the signal for assistance, he placed all hands in the boats, except a chosen few whom he kept on board with him; and as the case was desperate, he gave orders for the destruction of all confidential books and charts.

An hour and a half later the *Narwhal* arrived, and took all the crew on board. Commander Campbell himself—dead set on saving his ship if it could be done—inspected her once more, and then went over to the *Narwhal* to discuss the possibility of towage. Shortly afterwards the *Buttercup* came up, and as Q. 5 seemed by now to have assumed a more stable position and the water was gaining more slowly, Commander Campbell ordered *Buttercup* to take her in tow, which was done in the most seamanlike manner. It was a long and difficult business, almost desperate at times. First the tow parted, owing to Q. 5's helm being jammed hard over and immovable—the result of explosion. But her commander was not defeated. He was hard at work raising steam in her donkey-boiler, so as to be able to steer and veer cable. After four hours he got her in tow again, and she towed fairly well. But water was still gaining; the swell was breaking over the decks, and the after gun-house was at times under water.

Another ship, *Laburnum*, was now standing by, and at dusk suggested that Commander Campbell and his men should come on board for the night; but they refused to give up their ship as long as they could steer her. About two hours after midnight the end seemed to have come; Q. 5 suddenly started to list, the water gained rapidly, the donkey boiler-room was flooded, and the helm could no longer be used. At 3.30 Commander Campbell put the helm amidships, and ordered his men aboard *Laburnum*. He then followed himself, but returned to his own ship at daybreak and resumed towing; then, finding her in a very critical condition, he was compelled to go back to *Laburnum* for the time.

In the evening, when they were at last nearing port, the trawler *Luneta* came out to help. Q. 5 had by now nearly twenty degrees of list, and her stern was nearly eight feet under water; but she was brought in after all, and we may take her commander's word for it that her safe arrival in harbour was due to the splendid seaman-ship of Lieutenant-Commander W. W. Hallwright of the *Laburnum*. In an achievement like this, there is a romantic touch of the old tradition it was by just such seamanship that our frigate captains saved the Fleet after Trafalgar.

We may hear, too, what the commander of Q. 5 said about his officers and crew.

> They may almost be said to have passed through the supreme test of discipline. The chief-engineer and the engine-room watch remained at their posts and kept the dynamos going until driven out by water. They then had to hide on top of the engine-room. The guns' crews had to remain concealed in their gun-houses for nearly half an hour, while we could feel the ship going down by the stern. At that time it appeared touch-and-go whether the ship would sink before we sank the enemy. The officers and men who remained on board during the towing also did splendidly, the conditions at times being most dangerous ... it is difficult to select individuals where all did so well.

But without selecting, we may name two by their names: Engineer-Lieutenant L. S. Loveless, R.N.R., and Lieutenant Ronald Stuart, R.N.R , First and Gunnery Lieutenant, both now members of the Distinguished Service Order. It is hardly necessary to add that their commander received the Victoria Cross. He was born for it.

It is not often that any man, or any ship's company, can repeat their best performance and better it; yet Commander Campbell's third victory was followed by a fourth, of which, as the admiral on his station said truly, it is difficult to speak in sober terms. Four months after Q. 5 had struggled back to port, her men were out again in the *Pargust*, a merchant vessel on the same Special Service. The ship was going 8 knots in heavy rain and mist, with a fresh southerly breeze and a choppy sea. Like Q. 5, she got what she was looking for—what others run fast and far to avoid.

A torpedo was seen coming towards her on the starboard beam. It was apparently fired at very close range, for it had not yet settled down to its depth, but jumped out of the water when only a hundred yards from the ship. This time there was no choice, and no manoeuvring; *Pargust* received the shot in the engine-room and near the water-line. It made a large rent, filled the boiler-room, the engine-room and No. 5 hold with water, killed a stoker, wounded Engineer Sub-Lieutenant John Smith, R.N.R., and blew the starboard lifeboat into the air, landing pieces of it on the aerial.

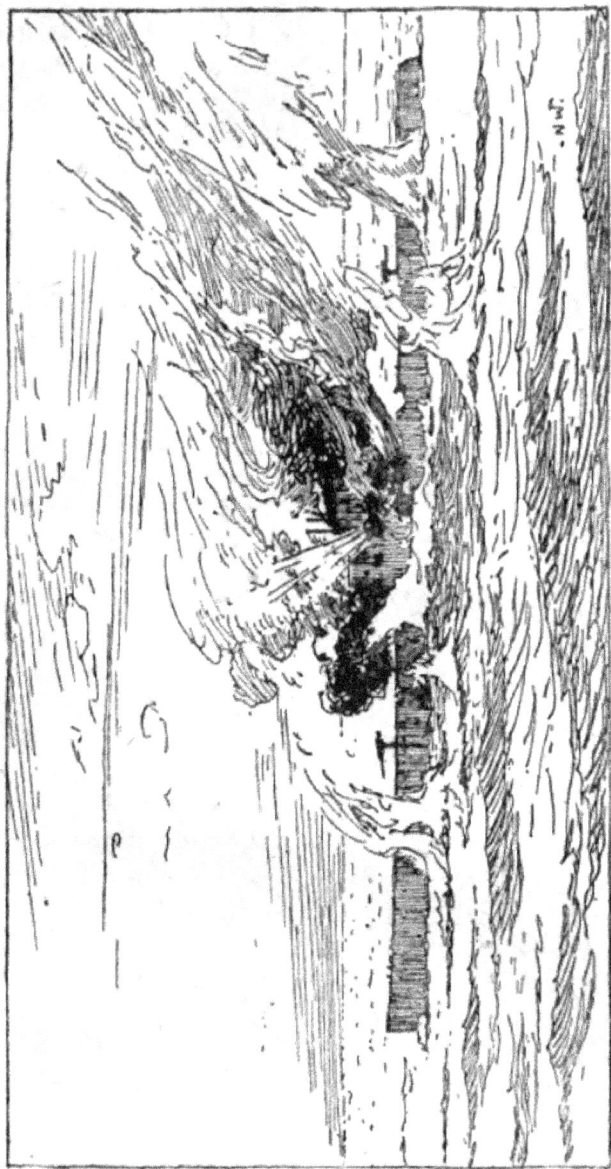

'The U-boat never recovered from the surprise.'

The alarm had already been sounded and 'Abandon ship 'ordered. The three remaining boats—one life-boat and two dinghies—were lowered, full of men, the ship's helm being put hard a-starboard to get a lee for them. Lieutenant F. R. Hereford, R.N.R., as before, went in charge of them and greatly distinguished himself by the coolness and propriety with which he acted the part of master of the supposed merchantman.

As the last boat was pushing off, the enemy's periscope was seen for the first time, just before the port beam, and about 400 yards from the ship. He turned and came straight on; but ten minutes later, when only 50 yards from the ship and close to the stern of the lifeboat, he submerged completely and disappeared. His periscope was sighted again a few minutes later, directly astern; he then steamed to the starboard quarter, turned round and went across to the port beam, turned again towards the ship and lifeboat, and finally, after all this nosing about, broke surface within 50 yards or less. But even now he was extremely cautious, showing only his conning-tower and ends; and when the lifeboat pulled away round the ship's stern, he followed close behind, with only one man visible on top of the conning-tower, shouting directions to those below.

For the next three minutes of this long game of patience, the strain was intense. Commander Campbell was watching the man on the conning-tower carefully, for as long as he saw him perched up there he knew that he could reserve his fire. Lieutenant Hereford was waiting till he was certain that his captain was in a winning position. As soon as that was attained, he pulled deliberately towards the ship. This annoyed the submarine, whose object was evidently, in case of a fight, to keep the boats as much as possible in the line of fire. He came right up to the surface and began to semaphore to the boats, at the same time training a Maxim on them.

But by this time the U-boat was only one point before the ship's beam, with all guns bearing on him at 50 yards' range—Commander Campbell's chance had come. He opened fire with a shot from the 4-inch gun, which struck the base of the conning-tower and also removed the two periscopes. Hit after hit followed, nearly all in the conning-tower, which could no longer be closed. The submarine took a list to port, and several men rushed up, out of the hatch abaft the conning-tower. Then, as the stern began to sink and oil squirted from the boat's sides, the rest of the crew came out, held up their hands and waved in token of surrender. Commander Campbell, of course, ordered 'Cease fire;' but no sooner had the order been obeyed, than the pirate started to move off on the surface, hoping, though listing to port and down by the stern, and in honour bound a prisoner, to get away in the mist. The *Pargust* could not follow, so that she was obliged to open fire again. The U-boat's breach of faith did not save her. In her quick rush, she got to about 300 yards from her captor, whose guns continued to speak straight to her. Then a shot apparently touched off one of her torpedoes there was an explosion forward, and she fell over on her side. For a moment her bow was seen jutting up sharply out of the water, and the next she was gone.

In her reckless rush to escape she had washed overboard her men abaft the conning-tower; one man went down clinging to her bow, and some who came up the fore-hatch were left struggling in the thick oil. The boats of the *Pargust* were sent to the rescue. They had a hard pull to windward in a choppy sea; but they managed to save the only two whom they found alive. The *Pargust* lay tossing helplessly for nearly four hours. Then H.M.S. *Crocus* arrived and towed her into port, escorted by another of H.M.'s ships and the U.S.S. *Cashing*.

Commander Campbell says:

> It is difficult where all did well, to mention individual officers and men, as any one officer or man could easily have spoiled the show. It was a great strain for those on board to have to remain entirely concealed for thirty-five minutes after the ship was torpedoed especially, for instance, the foremost gun's crew, who had to remain flat on the deck without moving a muscle.

And the actual combatants were not the only heroes; for he adds:

> The men in the boats, especially the lifeboat, ran a great risk of being fired on by me if the submarine closed them.

It is difficult for a grateful country, difficult even for the most gen-erously sympathetic of sovereigns, to deal adequately with a ship's company like this. Every man on board had already been mentioned or decorated, most of them more than once, and by the very names of their successive ships they were already marked out for lasting hon-our. Still, for our sake rather than for theirs, we may be glad to know that what tokens could be given them, were given. First, Commander Campbell became a captain, and others were promoted in their vari-ous ranks. Then the memorable thirteenth clause of the Statutes of the Victoria Cross was put into operation. By this it is ordained that in the event of a gallant and daring act having been performed by a ship's company, or other body of men, in which the admiral, general, or other officer commanding such forces may deem that all are equally brave and distinguished, then the officer commanding may direct that one officer shall be selected, by the officers engaged, for the decoration; and in like manner, one man shall be selected by the seamen or private soldiers, for the decoration.

Knowing as we do what Captain Campbell felt about his officers and men, we can imagine something of his satisfaction at being able to recommend that the V.C. should be worn on behalf of the whole ship's company by Lieutenant R. N. Stuart, D.S.O., R.N.R., and by seaman William Williams, D.S.M., R.N.R. The latter, when one of the gun ports was damaged by the shock of the torpedo, saved it from falling down and exposing the whole secret of the ship, by bearing at great personal risk and with great presence of mind the whole weight of the port until assistance could be given him. The former was the captain's first-lieutenant and second self. These two crosses, and his high rank, were the captain's own reward; but to mark the occasion, a bar was also added to his D.S.O.

To these men there was now but one thing wanting—to show their greatness in adversity: and Fortune, that could deny nothing to Gordon Campbell, gave him this too. Less than two months after the *Pargust's* action he was at sea in the Special Service ship *Dunraven*, disguised as an armed British merchant vessel, and zigzagging at eight knots in rough water. A submarine was sighted on the horizon two points before the star-board beam; but the zigzag course was maintained, and the enemy steered towards the ship, submerging about twenty minutes after she was first seen.

Twenty-six minutes later she broke surface on the starboard quarter at 5,000 yards, and opened fire. Captain Campbell at once ran up the white ensign, returned the fire with his after-gun, a 2½-pounder, and ordered the remainder of the crew to take 'shell cover.' He also gave directions for much smoke to be made, but at the same time reduced speed to seven knots, with an occasional zigzag, to give the U-boat a chance of closing. If he had been the merchantman he seemed, he could in all probability have escaped. He was steaming head to sea, and the submarine's firing was very poor, the shots nearly all passing over.

After about half an hour the enemy ceased firing and came on at full speed. A quarter of an hour later he turned broadside on, and reopened fire. The *Dunraven's* gun kept firing short, intentionally, and signals were made *en clair* for the U-boat's benefit, such as 'Submarine chasing and shelling me'—'Submarine overtaking me. Help. Come quickly!'—and finally, 'Am abandoning ship.' The shells soon began to fall closer. Captain Campbell made a cloud of steam to indicate boiler trouble, and ordered 'Abandon ship,' at the same time stopping, blowing off steam, and turning his broadside so that all he did should be visible. To add to the appearance of panic, a boat was let go by the foremost fall on its side. The pirate (thoroughly confident now) closed, and continued his shelling.

One shell went through *Dunraven's* poop, exploding a depth-charge and blowing Lieutenant Charles Bonner, D.S.C., R.N.R., out of his control station. After two more shells into the poop, the U-boat ceased fire again and closed. He was 'coming along very nicely' from port to starboard, so as to pass four or five hundred yards away. But in the meantime, the poop was on fire. Clouds of dense black smoke were issuing from it and partially hiding the submarine. It was obvious to Captain Campbell that since the magazine and depth-charges were in the poop, an explosion must soon take place. He was faced with the choice of opening fire through the smoke, with a poor chance of success, or waiting till the enemy should have got on to the weather side. He decided to wait, trusting his men as faithfully as they were trusting him.

The U-boat came on, but all too slowly. She was only just passing across *Dunraven's* stern when the dreaded explosion took place in the poop. The 4-inch gun and gun's crew complete were blown into the air. The gun landed forward on the well deck, and the crew in various places—one man in the water. This was a misfortune that might well have broken their captain's heart the submarine had only to steam another 200 yards, and he would have had a clear sight and three guns bearing on her at 400 yards range. Moreover the explosion had started the 'Open fire' buzzers at the guns; and the gun on the bridge, which was the only one then bearing, had duly opened fire. The U-boat had already started to submerge, alarmed by the explosion; but it was thought that one hit was obtained on the conning-tower as he disappeared.

Captain Campbell's heart was not broken, nor was his natural force abated. Realising that a torpedo would probably come next, he ordered the doctor, Surgeon-probationer Alexander Fowler, D.S.C., R.N.V.R., to remove all the wounded and lock them up in cabins or elsewhere, so as not to risk detection in 'the next part.' He then turned hoses on to the flaming poop, where, though the deck was red hot, the magazine was apparently still intact and dangerous. At the same time he remembered that a man-of-war had answered his signal for assistance when the explosion took place; and being determined on trying for a second fight, he now signalled to this ship to keep away, as the action was not yet ended. She not only kept away, but kept the ring, by deflecting traffic while these invincibles fought the pirate to a finish.

The torpedo came at last, from a point about 1,000 yards on the starboard side, and it struck abaft the engine-room. Captain Campbell at once ordered a second 'Abandon ship 'or 'Q abandon ship,' as he called it; for by it he was professing to completely abandon a ship whose disguise had been detected. He left his guns visible, and sent a second party of men away on a raft and a damaged boat. The poop continued to burn fiercely, and 4-inch shells exploded every few minutes. The submarine put up her periscope and circled round at various ranges, viewing the position cautiously. After forty minutes she broke surface directly astern, where no gun would bear upon her, and shelled the *Dunraven* at a range of a few hundred yards. Nearly every shot was a hit, but some fell near the boats. Two burst on the bridge and did much damage.

In another twenty minutes the enemy ceased firing and again submerged. Captain Campbell had now no resource left but his torpedoes, of which he carried two—one on each side. He fired the first as the U-boat steamed past the port side at 150 yards—too short a range for certainty of depth. The bubbles passed just ahead of the periscope, and the enemy failed to notice it. He turned very sharply round the ship's bow and came slowly down the starboard side at three knots. The second torpedo was then fired, but the bubbles passed a couple of feet abaft the periscope. This was cruelly hard luck, for the maximum depth was on; but there is no doubt that this torpedo, like the other, must have leaped over, from being fired at so close a range.

This time the enemy saw his danger, and instantly submerged. Captain Campbell had now lost his last chance of a kill, and was bound to signal urgently for assistance. He did so; but in case the U-boat reappeared to torpedo or shell again, he arranged for some of his remaining men to be ready to jump overboard in a final panic, leaving still himself and one gun's crew to fight a forlorn hope. This last extremity was not reached. The U.S.S. *Noma* arrived almost immediately and fired at a periscope a few hundred yards astern until it disappeared. Then came two king's ships, the *Attack* and *Christopher*. Boats were recalled, the fire extinguished, and everything on board having now exploded, arrangements were made for towing.

For twenty-four hours the *Christopher* bore her burden like a saint. Then the weather began to tell upon the half-dead ship, and sixty of her crew and her wounded were transferred to the trawler *Foss*. The next night the sea claimed the *Dunraven* in unmistakable tones. The *Christopher* came alongside and brought off her captain and the rest of her crew; and when she rolled end up, gave her a gunshot and a depth-charge, to take her to her last berth.

In reporting the action, Captain Campbell brought specially to notice the extreme bravery of Lieutenant Bonner and the 4-inch gun's crew.

> Lieutenant Bonner having been blown out of his control by the first explosion, crawled into the gun-hatch with the crew. They there remained at their posts with a fire raging in the poop below, and the deck getting red hot. One man tore up his shirt to give pieces to the gun's crew, to stop the fumes getting into their throats; others lifted the boxes of cordite off the deck to keep it from exploding, and all the time they knew that they must be blown up, as the secondary supply and magazine were immediately below. They told me afterwards that communication with the main control was cut off, and although they knew they would be blown up, they also knew that they would spoil the show if they moved; so they remained until actually blown up with their gun.
>
> Then when, as wounded men, they were ordered to remain quiet in various places during the second action, they had to lie there unattended and bleeding, with explosions continually going on aboard, and splinters from the enemy's shell-fire penetrating their quarters. Lieutenant Bonner, himself wounded, did what he could for two who were with him in the ward-room. When I visited them after the action, they thought little of their wounds, but only expressed their disgust that the enemy had not been sunk. Surely such bravery is hard to equal.'

Hard to equal—harder far to speak about! The king said all that can be said:

> Greater bravery than was shown by all officers and men on this occasion can hardly be conceived.

And again he testified the same by symbols—among them a second bar for Captain Campbell, V.C., D.S.O., R.N.; the Victoria Cross for Lieutenant C. G. Bonner, D.S.C., R.N.R.; and another, under Article 13, for the 4-inch gun's crew, who named Ernest Pitcher, P.O., to wear it to the honour of them all. The whole ship's company is now starred like a constellation; but the memory of their service will long outshine their stars.

CHAPTER 15

Submarine v. Submarine

Since submarines must be hunted, there is something specially attractive in the idea of setting other submarines to hunt them; it seems peculiarly just that while the pirate is lying in wait under water for his victim, he should himself be ambushed by an avenger hiding under the same waters and possessed of the same deadly weapons of offence.

But this method, satisfactory as it is to the imagination, is involved in several practical difficulties. If we put ourselves in the position of a submarine commander with orders to go out and kill U-boats, we shall quickly come up against some of the more obvious of these. The sea is a large place; the submarine moves about it slowly, and therefore takes a long time to patrol a given area. Also the very worst point of view from which to survey that area is the eye-piece of a periscope raised only some two feet above the surface. The strain upon the eye is very severe, when hour after hour is spent in looking for ships of ordinary size, with freeboard, funnels and streamers of smoke. How much more severe, when the object to be looked for is a conning-tower at most, with waves tumbling about it, or possibly only a periscope 4 inches in diameter!

Let us suppose, however, that all the preliminary conditions are as good as they can be; that the commander is in the best of health, with sound nerves and good instruments, and that he is lucky enough to sight a chance near the beginning of his cruise, while his eye is unwearied and his judgment alert. He will still be hampered by two considerations—he must make sure that the boat he is about to attack is an enemy and not a friend, and he must take the not very remote risk of being rammed, bombed, or depth-charged by a British destroyer or a German seaplane, while his attention is fixed entirely on the chase.

Finally, there are the purely technical difficulties of the attack. Manoeuvring for position is not easy, even when the enemy is a large and visible ship of war; it is ten times harder when he is a submerged or nearly submerged vessel, and not steaming straight ahead, but cruising about with sudden and erratic changes of course, as he searches for or sights his intended victims. And here the nature and habits of the torpedo have also to be considered. A periscope, or even a conning-tower, is not a very good object for a distant shot.

On the other hand if the range is too short, say less than 250 yards, the torpedo is very likely to miss. This is due to the fact that a torpedo requires a certain length of run before it can settle to its course evenly at the depth for which it is set. It begins by plunging, then rises, sometimes even breaks surface, and finally takes its proper depth, which may be set for anything from 6 to 22 feet. A torpedo fired at a periscope must be set deep, for the submerged part of the boat will be 15 feet or more below the surface. If it were fired at so short a distance as 100 or 120 yards it would reach the target while still on its upward bound, and might easily leap clean over the U-boat's rounded back.

At a still less range, it would probably dive under the enemy altogether. Moreover, up to a distance of 200 yards—or even more—the explosion of a torpedo is dangerous to the attacker as well as to the attacked. Water, being much less elastic than air, conveys the shock of a blow far more completely; and of course, in such a case, a submarine vessel, being entirely surrounded by water, would suffer much more from the concussion than a ship with only part of its hull below the surface.

If we take account of these obvious difficulties, and remember that there are others of which we know nothing, we shall realise that the destruction of a U-boat by one of our own submarines can only be accomplished by a combination of skill, courage, and good fortune. The examples which follow will make this clear.

Let us take first the case of E. 54, Lieutenant-Commander Robert H. T. Raikes, which shows a record of two successes within less than four months—one obtained with comparative ease, the other with great difficulty. The first of the two needs no detailed account or comment. E. 54, on passage to her patrol ground, had the good fortune to sight three U-boats in succession before she had gone far from her base. At two of these she fired without getting a hit; but the third she blew all to pieces, and picked up out of the oil and debris no less than seven prisoners. Her next adventure was a much more arduous one. She started in mid-August on a seven-day cruise, and in the first four days saw nothing more exciting than a neutral cruiser carrying out target practice. On the morning of the fifth day, a U-boat was sighted at last; and after twenty-five minutes' manoeuvring, two torpedoes were fired at her, at a distance of 600 yards, with deflection for 11 knots. Her actual speed turned out to be more nearly 6 or 7 knots, and both shots must have missed ahead of her. She dived immediately, and a third torpedo failed to catch her as she went down.

An hour and twenty minutes afterwards she reappeared on the surface, and Lieut.-Commander Raikes tried to cut her off, by steering close in to the bank by which she was evidently intending to pass. E. 54 grounded on the bank, and her commander got her off with feelings that can be easily imagined. Less than an hour after, a U-boat the same or another was sighted coming down the same deep. Again Lieut.-Commander Raikes tried to cut her off, and again he grounded in the attempt. He was forced to come to the surface when the enemy was still 2,000 yards away. To complete his ill-fortune, another U-boat was sighted within an hour and a quarter, but got away without a shot being possible.

Twenty-four hours later the luck turned, and all these disappointments were forgotten. At 2.6 p.m., Lieut.-Commander Raikes sighted yet another U-boat in open water, on the old practice ground of the neutral cruiser of three days before. He put E. 54 to her full speed, and succeeded in overtaking the enemy. By 2.35 he had placed her in a winning position on the U-boat's bow, and at right angles to her course. At 400 yards' range he fired two torpedoes, and had the satisfaction to see one of them detonate in a fine cloud of smoke and spray. When the smoke cleared away, the U-boat had entirely disappeared; there were no survivors. Next day, after dark, E. 54's time being up, she returned to her base, having had a full taste of despair and triumph.

Earlier in the year, Lieutenant Bradshaw, in G. 13, had had a somewhat similar experience. He went out to a distant patrol in cold March weather and had not been on the ground five hours when his adventures began. At 11.50 a.m. he was blinded by a snow squall; and when he emerged from it, he immediately sighted a large hostile submarine within shot. Unfortunately the U-boat sighted G. 13 at the same moment, and the two dived simultaneously. This, as may easily be imagined, is one of the most trying of all positions in the submarine game, and so difficult as to be almost insoluble. The first of the two adversaries to move will very probably be the one to fall in the duel; yet a move must be made sooner or later, and the boldest will be the first to move.

Lieutenant Bradshaw seems to have done the right thing both ways. For an hour and a half he lay quiet, listening for any sign of the U-boat's intentions; then, at 1.30 p.m., he came to the surface, prepared for a lightning shot or an instantaneous manoeuvre. No more complete disappointment could be imagined. He could see no trace of the enemy—he had not even the excitement of being shot at. On the following day he was up early, and spent nearly eleven fruitless hours knocking about in a sea which grew heavier and heavier from the S.S.E. Then came another hour which made ample amends. At 3.55 p.m. a large U-boat came in sight, steering due west. Lieutenant Bradshaw carried out a rapid dive and brought his tubes to the ready; courses and speeds as requisite for attack. (These reports often omit superfluous details, while they bristle with intention.) The manoeuvring which followed took over half an hour, and must have seemed interminably long to everyone in G. 13. At 4.30 the enemy made the tension still greater by altering course some 35°.

It was not until 4.49 that Lieutenant Bradshaw found himself exactly where all commanders would wish to be, 8 points on the enemy's bow. He estimated the U-boat's speed at eight knots, allowed 18° deflection accordingly, and fired twice. It was a long shot in rough water, and he had nearly a minute to wait for the result. Then came the longed-for sound of a heavy explosion. A column of water leaped up, directly under the U-boat's conning-tower, and she disappeared instantly. Ten minutes afterwards, G. 13 was on the surface, and making her way through a vast lake of oil, which lay thickly upon the sea over an area of a mile. In such an oil lake a swimmer has no margin of buoyancy, and it was not surprising that there were no survivors to pick up. The only relics of the U-boat were some pieces of board from her interior fittings. G. 13 completed her patrol of twenty-eight days, and returned to her base without sighting another enemy—she had cleared that area for a month.

A successful hunt by Lieutenant North, in command of H. 4, resembles G. 13's exploit in many respects, but has this picturesque difference, that it took place in southern waters and in a bright May midnight. It was more than forty-eight hours since H. 4 had cast off from the pens before she sighted the quarry she was looking for, 3 points on her port bow. The hour was 11.10 p.m. and the moon was nearly full. Lieutenant North at once turned towards the enemy and went to night action stations. The distance between the two boats was about

1,000 yards, and it was desirable to reduce this to a minimum—say to 250 yards—in order to make sure of a hit in the circumstances. The enemy was a large U-boat and was going about 8 knots, in a course which would bring her across H. 4 almost too directly.

But she had not advanced more than 300 yards when she altered course 8 points to starboard. Lieutenant North instantly saw his opportunity, turned first to port to cut her off; and then, when his superior speed had made this a certainty, 8 points to starboard to close her. Within four minutes after sighting her, he had placed himself on her port beam at the desired range of 250 yards. He fired two torpedoes. Both hit and detonated, one under the conning-tower, and one in the engine-room. The enemy sank immediately—in fifteen seconds she had gone completely. Then came the usual search for survivors, and two were eventually rescued; they were the captain of the boat and his quartermaster. H. 4 combed out the surrounding area thoroughly; but no more could be found; and in view of the presence of prisoners, Lieutenant North at once returned to his base.

It is not to our purpose to enumerate successful shots of the simple and easy kind; one or two examples will stand for a number of these. C. 15, for instance, sighted an enemy submarine at 2.43 on a November afternoon, dived and flooded tubes; sighted the U-boat again in the periscope at 3.12; at 3.15 fired at 400 yards. The noise of the explosion was slight, but the enemy—U.C. 65—sank immediately, and C. 15 picked up five survivors. D. 7, Commander C. G. Brodie, sank U. 45 only twenty-two minutes after sighting her, at a range of 1,200 yards. Lieutenant A. W. Forbes, in C. 7, sighted a large U-boat on his port quarter, at 3.32 a.m. of a dark and misty April night. He immediately attacked on the surface, and sank her with a single shot at 400 yards. These prompt and successful shots deserve full credit; but every now and then some exceptional circumstance will add a special reason for satisfaction.

For example, it is always good to catch a pirate red-handed. Lieut.-Commander G. R. S. Watkins, in E. 45, was beginning his day's patrol at 6.15, on a dim October morning, when he observed flashes on his star-board bow. He altered course in that direction, and after five minutes sighted an unhappy merchantman under fire from a U-boat. He dived at once and approached. At 6.37, he was near enough to see through his periscope that the vessel was a steamer with Dutch colours painted on her side. She was a neutral, and of course unarmed, but such considerations meant nothing to the U-boat pirate, who had ceased fire and was coolly waiting for his victim to sink. He was a large submarine, partially submerged, and by way of further caution he was steering about in figures of 8, with his gun still manned. But, for all his caution, just retribution was upon him.

Lieut.-Commander Watkins fired his first shot at 400 yards, and missed—altered course instantly, and in little more than three minutes fired again, from a new angle, two shots in rapid succession. Thirty seconds afterwards, justice was done in full; a loud explosion was heard and there was a tremendous convulsion in the water. For the moment, E. 45 was blinded—her periscope was submerged. With a rebound she came to the surface, saw in one quick glance that her enemy was destroyed, and sank again to 60 feet. When she had reloaded, and re-turned finally Lieut.-Commander Vincent M. Cooper, in E. 43, also had the satisfaction of surprising an enemy at work. This was a U.C. boat, engaged not in actually firing on merchantmen, but in the still more deadly and murderous business of laying mines for them.

When sighted by E. 43, she had evidently just come to the surface, as men were observed on the bridge engaged in spreading the bridge screen. Lieut.-Commander Cooper went straight for her at full speed. But as it was 9.30 a.m., and broad daylight, he was forced to remain submerged, and being in shallow water he soon had to slow down. Again and again he bumped heavily on shoals, but fortunately was never quite forced to the surface. After an hour of this he got into deeper water, and was able to go faster. At 11.0 he rose to 24 feet, and took a sight through the periscope. There was the enemy, about 400 yards away on his port beam. He dived, and five minutes later came up for another sight. This time the U-boat was on his port quarter. He turned towards her, but at the moment of attack, when the sights were just coming on, E. 43 dipped under a big wave and the chance was spoiled.

Her commander was not to be thrown off; he immediately in-creased to full speed, altered course, and planned a fresh attack. By 11.17—nearly two hours after beginning the chase—he was in posi-tion, 2 points abaft the enemy's beam at 550 yards' distance. This time he took every precaution to ensure a kill. On firing he dipped his periscope, so that in case the boat rose suddenly nothing should be visible; and at the same time he yawed to starboard, so as to be ready with another tube if the first shot was a miss. Then came a trying pe-riod of suspense and disappointment; he listened in vain for the sound of an explosion, and after forty-five seconds raised his periscope to see

'WAS STEERING ABOUT IN FIGURES OF 3,
WITH HIS GUN STILL MANNED.'

what had happened.

It was only later, on communicating with his officers and men in the forward and after compartments, that he found, as others have found, how differently sound may affect the different parts of a submarine when submerged. The central compartment may be completely deafened, either by reason of its position, when a detonation occurs directly ahead or astern, or by the much slighter continuous noises of the various electrical machines which are situated there. In this case, the dull report of the under-water explosion, which was not audible to Lieut.-Commander Cooper, was heard in both the other compartments about twenty seconds after he had fired the torpedo.

At the moment when the periscope was raised, the U-boat had disappeared, and there was a great com-motion in the water where she had been. E. 43 hurried to the spot and found the surface covered with a black oily substance which stuck to the glass of the periscope and put it out of action. Lieut.-Commander Cooper rose to 20 feet and put up his second periscope, but the U-boat was gone and had left no survivors.

E. 35 has a chase to her credit, in some respects very similar to this one; but the story is worth adding, because of the masterly precision with which the Commander, Lieutenant D'Oyly Hughes, conducted the manoeuvre and reported it afterwards. At 4 o'clock, on a May afternoon, he sighted in the periscope a low-lying object two to three miles distant on the port beam. His own boat was at 26 feet, and the object was only visible intermittently, when on top of a wave—it was impossible to be certain about it. He turned at once and went straight for it, speeding up as he did so. But this led to immediate difficulties. There was a long breaking swell across his course and a strong wind. Depth keeping was almost impossible, and there was a constant risk of E. 35 breaking surface and throwing away her chance. It was necessary to go down to quieter levels, and for some time she travelled at 40 feet with full speed on.

At 4.18, Lieutenant D'Oyly Hughes reduced speed and brought her up again to 26 feet. His first observation, on looking into the periscope, was that the bearing had changed; and secondly, that the floating object was without doubt a large enemy submarine. He headed at once to cut her off—she was making slowly off northwards—and dived to 40 feet in order to increase to full speed himself.

After a twenty-four minutes' run he slowed down again for periscope observation, ordering the boat to be brought to 23 feet. This was a very anxious moment, for the sea once more all but gave him away. The swell rolled E. 35 up till she was actually for an instant breaking surface, within 1,800 yards of the enemy. She was got down again to 26 feet without having been seen, and her commander then very skilfully placed her in the trough of the sea, where he could pursue the chase on a slightly converging course instead of following right astern.

On this course, which soon became absolutely parallel to that of the enemy, he remained at periscope depth for another half hour; then at 5.20, observing that he was not gaining fast enough, he dived again to 40 feet and speeded up, at the same time bringing a torpedo-tube to the 'ready.' At 5.35 he slowed once more for observation, and found the range had decreased to 1,100 yards. Down he went again for another spurt. At 5.53, he was within 900 yards; but as the parallel courses of the two boats were only a little more than 100 yards apart, he was 'still very fine on enemy's port quarter'—the shot was almost a bow-chaser shot and practically hopeless. He dived again, and for twenty-four more minutes patiently continued to observe and spurt alternately.

At 6.17, a dramatic change occurred in the situation. On rising to observe, he found that the enemy, for some irrelevant reason of her own, had turned 16 points to starboard, and was now actually coming back on a course which would bring her down the starboard side of E. 35 at a distance of scarcely more than 200 yards. This was much too close for a desirable shot—setting aside the dangers of the explosion, it was not certain that the torpedo would have picked up its depth correctly in so short a run, and a miss might put the U-boat on guard. Still, to manoeuvre for a fresh position would take time and the chance was quite a possible one; the torpedo, at the end of 200 yards, would be at any rate near picking up its depth, and might well make a detonating hit on its upward track—it could not miss for deflection at that range; the enemy's length was taking up almost the whole width of the periscope. Even if it were a miss underneath, it would probably escape notice, especially in so heavy a sea.

Lieutenant D'Oyly Hughes took exactly one minute to perceive the change of course and the wholly altered situation, to weigh all the above considerations, and to make his decision. At 6.18 he fired, lowered his periscope, put his helm hard a-starboard, and increased his speed. The hydrophone operator heard the torpedo running on her track, but the sound grew fainter and fainter and died away without a detonation. The shot was a miss beneath the target; after more than two long hours, the chase had failed.

The failure was brilliantly redeemed, and with astonishing swiftness. To realise the swiftness and the brilliancy of the manoeuvre which followed, it is necessary to bring it vividly before the mind's eye. The two boats must be seen at the moment of the first shot, passing one another at 200 yards on opposite courses, E. 35 going N.E., and the U-boat S.W. on her starboard beam. At 6.19 the enemy turned a little more towards E. 35, and began to steer due west under her stern, happily still without sighting her periscope. E. 35 was on her old course, running farther and farther away to the N.E., and there was already some 500 yards between them.

But when the U-boat took up her westerly course, Lieutenant D'Oyly Hughes in an instant sent his boat on a swift curve to port, turning in quick succession N., N.W., W., and S.W., till in less than seven minutes after missing his first shot he was bearing down S.S.W. on the enemy, and therefore only 30 degrees abaft her starboard beam and hardly more than 500 yards distant. By pure luck, the unconscious U-boat had at the first critical moment done precisely the right thing to save herself; by sheer skill, the E-boat had been brought back to a winning position. At 6.25 Lieutenant D'Oyly Hughes—coolly estimating speed, distance, and deflection fired one torpedo at his huge enemy's fore-turret and another at her after-turret.

Both hit where they were aimed to hit. The first made very little noise, but threw up a large column of water and debris. The second did not appear to the eye to produce quite so good a burst; but the noise was louder, and the concussion felt in E. 35 was very powerful indeed, the whole boat shaking and a few lights going out momentarily. When the smoke and water column had cleared away, there was nothing to be seen but a quickly expanding calm area, like a wide lake of oil with wreckage floating in it, and three or four survivors clinging to some woodwork. E. 35, with her sub-lieutenant, her coxswain, and one able seaman on deck, and life-lines ready, went at once to their rescue; but a second U-boat made her appearance at that moment, and Lieutenant D'Oyly Hughes was obliged to dive at once. Three minutes afterwards, a torpedo passed him on the starboard side; but the new enemy was over two miles away, and though he reloaded his tubes and patrolled submerged on various courses, he never succeeded in picking her up in the periscope. She, also, had no doubt dived, and the two boats had scarcely more chance of coming to action than two men miles apart upon the Downs at midnight.

In such a case, only a lucky chance could bring the duellists together; and even then successful shooting would be difficult. But a bold submarine commander, having once closed, would improvise a new form of attack rather than let a pirate go his way. E. 50 was commanded by an officer of this temper when she sighted an enemy submarine, during a patrol off the east coast. Both boats were submerged at the time; but they recognised each other's nationality by the different appearance of their periscopes. The German had two—thin ones of a light-grey colour, and with an arched window at the top, peculiar to their service. The British commander drove straight at the enemy at full speed, and reached her before she had time to get down to a depth of complete invisibility. E. 50 struck fair between the periscopes; her stem cut through the plates of the U-boat's shell and remained embedded in her back. Then came a terrific fight, like the death grapple of two primeval monsters.

The German's only chance, in his wounded condition, was to come to the surface before he was drowned by leakage; he blew his ballast tanks and struggled almost to the surface, bringing E. 50 up with him. The English boat countered by flooding her main ballast-tanks, and weighing her enemy down into the deep. This put the U-boat to the desperate necessity of freeing herself, leak or no leak. For a minute and a half she drew slowly aft, bumping E. 50's sides as she did so; then her effort seemed to cease, and her periscopes and conning-towers showed on E. 50's quarter. She was evidently filling fast; she had a list to starboard and was heavily down by the bows. As she sank, E. 50 took breath and looked to her own condition. She was apparently uninjured, but she had negative buoyancy and her forward hydro-planes were jammed, so that it was a matter of great difficulty to get her to rise. After four strenuous minutes she was brought to the surface, and traversed the position, searching for any further sign of the U-boat or her crew. But nothing was seen beyond the inevitable lake of oil, pouring up like the thick rank life-blood of the dead sea-monster.

CHAPTER 16

The Hunted

The hunter knows little, and cares little, about the feelings of the hunted; and if he is hunting for food, or to exterminate vermin, his indifference is not unreasonable. The submarine may be classed with savage beasts, and is even less deserving of pity; but it is not actually an animal, and the difference is important. It is controlled by beings with human intelligence, speech, nerves and faculties; and since they are our enemies, seeking our destruction while we seek theirs, it must be of interest to us, and may be of advantage, to know what are their feelings during the chase.

Information of this kind is not easy to obtain; but the enemy have thought fit to publish, for their own people, a certain number of accounts by submarine officers, and they have not been able to prevent all of them from finding their way to this country. Here, for instance, is an extract from the *War Diary of U. 202*, by Lieut.-Commander Freiherr Spiegel von und zu Peckelsheim.

At 4 o'clock I again came up to have a look through the periscope. . . . On our starboard bow was a large French torpedo boat with 4 funnels, on the watch. There was no land in sight. 'I should much have liked to sink the smart-looking Frenchman. But the considerable probability, that in such a position I should then have the whole pack hunting me, induced me to refrain. I must admit that I found it very hard not to utilise this opportunity for a shot, and very reluctantly I lowered the periscope and gave orders to dive. This was our salvation. If we had continued a few minutes longer at the level at which here one uses the periscope, I should not be sitting today smoking cigarettes and writing my experiences.

We were still diving, and the depth-gauge showed 17 metres (56 feet). Suddenly we all had the sensation of having been struck on the head with a hammer. For a second we lost consciousness; then we picked ourselves up from the deck, or from the corners into which we had been thrown, feeling pains in our heads, shoulders, and other parts of our bodies. The whole boat throbbed and trembled. Were we still alive? What had happened? Why was it so dark, black as night? Ah! the light was out!

"Examine the fuse!"

"Fuse gone!"

"Put in spare fuse!"

Suddenly we had light again. This was all a matter of seconds, happening in far less time than it takes to describe it.

What had happened? Was it really not the end of us? Was not the water rushing into the boat somewhere, and carrying us down to the bottom? It must have been a mine—a tremendous mine detonation close to the boat. Reports were made automatically; from all compartments. "Bow compartment not making water; stern compartment ,all right; engine-room no water." No water anywhere!

Then the boat inclined itself at a peculiar angle—the bow went down and the stern rose up. The boat was unaccountably trimmed by the bow, although the hydroplanes were hard over in the opposite direction.

"There is something wrong, sir," reported the man at the diving-wheel. "The boat won't answer to her helm. We must be hung up somewhere, by a rope, or perhaps a net!"

The devil! We are in a net, of course, and above us there are mines secured to the net. It is enough to drive one out of one's mind.

"Pay attention!" I shouted from the conning-tower. "We have got to get through! Hydroplanes hard up and hard down, utmost speed ahead with both engines! Don't let her rise! Whatever happens, keep down! There are mines above, us!"

The engines started, revolving at their highest revolutions. The boat shot forward, caught in the net, strained against it, bored itself a way downwards, tugged, tore, and finally left the wire net all ripped apart.

"Hurrah! We are free! The boat answers to her helm!" cried the helmsman from below.

"Go deeper, dive to 50 metres (164 feet)," I ordered. "This is an evil spot hereabouts—it is hell itself."

I sat down on the life-saving apparatus and buried my head in my hands. Everything was going round with me like a mill-wheel. Above my eyes I had a pain as though needles were sticking into my forehead, and I had such a humming in my ears that I stopped them up with my fingers.

"This is certainly an evil spot," I repeated to my-self, "but what luck we had, most extraordinary luck, which has saved us!"

Some time elapsed before the pains in my head allowed me to fit things together and understand what had happened. Yes, it was pure luck that we had dived just in time. We were at a depth of 17 metres when the explosion occurred, our bows touching the net. Things grew clearer and clearer to me as I thought them over.

When we hit against the net we stretched it taut and thus actuated the mine detonators, the mines being attached to the net at the depth at which a submarine usually proceeds. If we had attempted to attack the torpedo-boat, or for any other reasons had remained a little longer at the depth at which the periscope can be used, we should have run into the net in just the way that the enemy would have wished—*viz.*, so that the mines would have exploded alongside or underneath us. What actually happened was that the mine exploded above us, and the main force was expended in the line of least resistance (*viz.*, upwards), and we suffered nothing more than a fearful fright, and perhaps a few disfigurements to the thin plating of the superstructure.

U. 202 was certainly lucky this time. And though she was saved by sheer luck and nothing else, it is not unnatural, considering the ever-growing roll of those which fail to escape, that Lieut.-Commander Freiherr Spiegel von und zu Peckelsheim should enlarge upon his terror at the moment and his self-congratulation afterwards. But he is mistaken if he thinks that he has come through the worst that can happen to a submarine commander. His struggle in the net was short and easy, when compared with the feats of a Bruce or a Cochrane in passing and repassing the barrage off Kilid Bahr; and the jar he got from his mine seems to have affected his head more than his boat. In older navies, and among less excitable nations, these things are reported more quietly—more from a professional than a sensational point of view. Commander Courtney Boyle writes of a very similar accident:

I think I must have caught the moorings of a mine with my tail as I was turning, and exploded it . . . the whole boat was very badly shaken.

Not a word more about it, though his cruise continued for more than ten days afterwards. Without disparaging the German officer (who no doubt shares the national temperament, and knows how to move his audience), we may take pleasure in noting that the steadiness of nerve and the scientific view are in our favour. Given anything like a fair fight, and a reasonable time for play, it will not be the Peckelsheims who will win against our men.

An experience of another kind is described in a number of the *Illustrierte Zeitung* of July 12, 1917. The date of the engagement was February 22, in the same year.

Just at dinner time the watch reports a tank steamer in an E.N.E. direction, steering a course approximately towards the boat. Masts, bridge and funnel are visible above the horizon. Tank steamers are very hard to sink, as they have stray bulkheads fitted to keep their volatile cargo in check. The torpedo must hit the aftermost engine to stop the tank steamer. The periscope must only be shown occasionally for a very short time, so as not to alarm her. The torpedo is fired at 700 metres (765 yards) away, the submarine comes to the surface and fires a shot from her forward gun, as a signal to stop. The steamer understands, lowers two boats, and the crew abandon ship. Steam is blown off in a high white column.

The master appears to be a sensible man, who does not intend to expose himself to shell fire for no purpose. The submarine approaches submerged and takes stock of the vessel—a black tank steamer, grey superstructure, no guns—the naval patent log hanging over the stern. The submarine then makes for the boats. As soon as they see her periscope, they hastily pull away. At length the submarine finds a favourable position to come to the surface, outside the boats, so that the latter are in the line of fire. She rises to the surface, with compressed air in her midship diving-tanks, the conning-tower hatch is opened and the process of blowing out the tanks begins. The boats have pulled away a little further, and just as they are being hailed there is a flash from the steamer.

A submarine trap! Alarm. Flood tanks, dive rapidly! The seconds seem interminable. The super-structure abaft the conning-tower is penetrated, and hardly has the hatch been closed when there is a sharp report in the conning-tower, a yellow flash, and explosive gases fill the air. A shell has penetrated the side of the conning-tower and exploded inside. All the fittings are shattered by splinters; there is a sound of breaking glass. Another shell will fall directly and that will be the end of the war for us, Water is splashing in through the shot hole; the boat is sinking into the shelter of the deep. The conning-tower is cleared, the inner hatch and voice-pipe cock are closed, and the leads laid into the control room.

"Anyone injured in the conning-tower?" Only one, very slightly; but their faces are black and their clothes look as though they had seen service.

At 20 metres (65 feet) there are two sharp explosions, and the boat trembles. The "poor shipwrecked men" have thrown depth-charges after us. A few of the lights go out, and further damage to the main switchboard is averted by timely action. The conning-tower is filling. In theory the boat can still remain afloat, but no one has yet survived to tell us how. The increasing weight causes the boat to sink to 40 metres (131 feet) in spite of her being down by the stern and with the engines at utmost speed. Water spurts through the leaky places, and, owing to short circuits, half the lights and important machinery break down successively—gyro compass, main rudder, forward hydroplane (which, to make matters worse, jams at 'hard down '), trimming pumps, and all control apparatus. The tricolour captured from the full-rigged ship *La Bayonne* is pressed into service to plug the leak. The boat must be lightened by compressed air in the after and amidship diving tanks, and brought on to an even keel. She rises, certainly, but is more down by the stern than ever. The after compressed air service breaks down.

We must avoid coming to the surface, whatever happens, for up above the enemy is lying in wait to fire at us. At 20 metres (65 feet) the diving-tank valves are opened, and all available men sent forward, in order that their weight may cause the bow to sink. The boat sinks by the bow, and the manoeuvre is repeated. In another twenty minutes it becomes impossible to proceed submerged. There is now only one, not very promising, alternative—to come to the surface suddenly and run away, firing as we go.

"Compressed air in all the tanks, open galley ventilator, man the guns, Diesel engines ready, and put to utmost speed as soon as possible."

The boat comes to the surface, the galley hatch is opened. A torrent of water rushes down; never mind, we shall have to swim for it directly, anyhow. Now the way is clear to the surface. The steamer is about 25 hms. (2734 yards) away, and firing as fast as she can. "You haven't got us yet—not by a long way!" The guns quickly reply. Any result? The telescopic sights are still in the flooded conning-tower. The M.A.N. motors are quickly started—much more quickly than is permissible, but when all is staked on one card there is no help for it. All the men who are not occupied below are bringing up supply ammunition.

The sub-lieutenant suddenly feels his feet blown away from under him, and staggers through a cloud of smoke against the gun. Poor fellow, he has probably had both legs shot away. But no, only a few small splinters—nothing more! The shell passed between the legs of the foremost gunlayer, the drum of his ear was perforated by the report, and there are some-lumps and holes in the ready ammunition. The shells pass through, close to the men; they look like black specks in the air just before they fall. One of the railing supports is shattered. A Leipzig man is standing in the stern at the hand-wheel, steering calmly by the verbal directions of the navigating warrant-officer—the compasses can no longer be used.

The telescopic sights can now be recovered from the conning-tower. There is a report, "Destroyer to starboard." Quite right. She is proceeding on a parallel course at 80 hms. (8750 yards) and the fire of her four guns mingles with that of the tank steamer. A destroyer like that has a speed of over 30 knots, and carries 4-inch guns.

"On lifebelts!" Below the horizon, in a S.S.E. direction, there must be a sailing-vessel; we sighted one this morning. Perhaps the boat may be able to reach her, so as to save the crew from a *Baralong* fate.

The guns' crews have become so deaf from the noise of their own guns that it is only possible to direct one gun by verbal orders. The decoy ship is now so far away that there is no further need to fire at her. Open fire on the new foe then! This is not a destroyer, however, but a "submarine-destroyer" of the *Foxglove* class, about twice the size of the submarine, but no faster. At the same moment the second-engineer reports that he can repair the damaged conning-tower, and our hopes soar as far as neutral Spain.

"Open fire at 70 hms. (7655 yards)!" Soon the columns of water from the shells, as high as the funnels, mark the fall of the shots, and the enemy begins to zigzag to avoid the troublesome shells, thereby interfering with the aim of her own guns. Suddenly the superstructure is enveloped in black smoke. A hit! Another! Several shells do not throw up a column of water; they must have buried themselves in her hull. Now she turns away, escapes from the zone of fire, and then follows in our wake.

The damage caused by the short circuit is repaired, ammunition put ready beside the guns, and, like Wellington at Waterloo, we await the coming of night. Our pursuer must have reported the engagement by wireless, with position and course. Soon destroyers will appear and compel the submarine to submerge. The leaking oil supply will leave a track of oil on the surface, and indicate where depth-charges should be dropped.

The wireless aerial, which has been shot away, is repaired in order to keep an eye on the enemy's signals. Nothing to be heard. A lucky shot must have destroyed our pursuer's wireless, and she cannot report. All the men who are not occupied below are on deck smoking, discussing their impressions, experiences, and premonitions; dreams, uncomfortable forebodings, fortune-telling from cards, and all the means—such as green frogs—by which old fortune-tellers and ancient augurs used to foretell the future.

The sun is sinking below the horizon; the chase has already lasted more than three hours. The decoy ship has long passed out of sight, and no new enemies have appeared. Suddenly shells begin falling close by. The *Foxglove* means to have another try as long as the light holds, and we feel that this is an impertinence. "Man the guns!"

Again the after gun carries off the honours of the engagement. The rounds follow close on one another: sometimes three shells are in the air at once. They will soon reach their target; the enemy again tries to zigzag. Range and deflection are quickly adjusted, and the shells leave her no peace. Once again that beautiful cloud of black smoke envelopes her super-structure and several others fail to raise the expected column of water. The enemy has ceased firing; she turns sharply away at 92 hms. (10,000 yards), and follows us only at a respectful distance. An hour later she disappears in the darkness.

The deliberately false German *communiqués*, and even the more craftily composed stories in their press, are, as a rule, distinguished only for their clumsiness and bad psychology. But this is a vivid and quite possible account, and, if the details are accurate, the commander of the submarine had a most trying experience and brought his boat home by great luck. It is hard to imagine a moment more desperate than that in which, after struggling to the surface and escaping from the Q-boat's guns, he heard the report of 'Destroyer to starboard,' and knew that he could neither dive nor run from such an enemy. A good deal might have been made of this by a more inventive writer; the simple comment 'Quite right!' is much more convincing than any highly coloured phrase, and is almost enough by itself to prove the narrative genuine.

Another intense moment lightly touched is that in which the deadly 'destroyer' turns out to be only the little 10-knot patrol boat *Alyssum*, with her small guns, and a flight for bare life becomes suddenly a successful repulse of the enemy. It is noticeable, too, that the commander is not once mentioned, and all his orders are given as uttered rather than as heard; the-narrator, moreover, is familiar with the story of Wellington at Waterloo, and makes a country gentleman's joke about missing a hare. On the whole, I think it is plain that we have here a true account.

Stories such as this are hard to come by, for the hunted seldom escape so narrowly and with so good a tale to tell. But our own records show at least one case of the kind, and it is one in which the crew of the submarine passed through an even severer trial, for they were hunted by their own side and had not the joy of a good fighting chance to sustain them.

In August, 1917, Lieut.-Commander V. M. Cooper, in command of one of H.M. submarines, was ordered to patrol a neighbouring coast, close in, between certain parallels. He was warned not to arrive on his billet before 10 a.m., for the very good reason that some of our own light forces were conducting operations in that direction during the night, and might be met returning at any time in the early morning. It must be remembered that when such a meeting does occur, no system of signalling is to be relied on for safety. A submarine will always be attacked on sight by any ship, friend or enemy, for she is a danger too deadly to be given a moment's chance. Her colours, if she show any, may be false, and only a seaplane can afford her the time necessary for answering a private signal. Commander Cooper knew all about this. He decided to arrive on his billet about noon, when the risk would presumably be over.

At 8 o'clock, then, on the finest summer morning of the year, Commander Cooper was making his passage at normal surface speed, when the horizon on his starboard bow began to be delicately shaded by faint pencilled lines. Ten minutes more and a number of ships were visible, two points on the bow, and five to six miles away. They were immediately in the sun, and blurred by the haze, so that it was impossible to detect their nationality. They might be our own squadron, coming back unexpectedly early, or more likely a hostile force running from them. The only thing certain was that they had sighted the submarine and were bent on her destruction, for they were all bows on, bearing down upon her at high speed—destroyers and cruisers—throwing up clouds of dense black smoke.

Commander Cooper was in no indecent hurry, but he knew what he had to do. He must get down, or be put down. Moreover, he must get well down; for the water was very clear, and the sea flat calm, without a ripple. After a last look at the charging squadron he dived to ninety feet, changing his course to 185°.

His troubles began at once: the helm was reported jammed—it was amidships. He sent the first-lieutenant to inspect, the report was that the gear was all correct—the jamming seemed to be due to the tightening of the rudder-post gland, either from external pressure, or from some distortion of the after compartment of the ship. In any case, nothing could be done for the moment, and there were plenty of distractions coming. At 8.37 the sound of propellers was recorded on the hydrophone—the destroyers were passing from port to starboard overhead, like hounds abreast trying to pick up a scent.

One of them must have thought she had hit it off, for a tremendous explosion shook the submarine—a depth-charge had been dropped not far behind her, shaking her stern violently. In her steering flat, the first-lieutenant and his men were lifted bodily off their feet. The commander continued his dive, and to his great comfort took bottom at 125 feet on the gauge.

Within three minutes of the first explosion, a second one followed. It was equally violent, and to Commander Cooper appeared even louder; but he told himself that this effect was probably due to the relative position of the bomb, which had apparently detonated in a line with the conning-tower. As he was himself in the control-room, in the centre of the ship, the explosion The boat was well built, and the commander had perfect confidence in her. This was not his first experience of the kind. Exactly a year before, he had been out in the Cattegat in an E-boat and had met 'a wrong un'—a *Greif* or *Möwe*, which had opened fire on him with four 6-inch guns at 2000 yards and straddled him at once. The boat had to dive as she was, in complete surface trim. Shot after shot fell close to her; she was shaken by explosives and struck by splinters.

Finally a 6-inch shell came alongside and threw up a huge column of water which fell plump on the commander as he descended through the hatch. Part of it accompanied him down the ladder, but he had the presence of mind to draw the lid down behind him, and he and his boat lived to tell the tale. So he knew that a British submarine can stand a shock or two. But what made him really anxious was the question—which he hoped would occur to no one else on board—why did those two depth-charges fall so near one another: why did the enemy drop the second so close to the first? The horrible suspicion came into his mind that his position was being given away by something that he could only guess at—some noise or some escape of air bubbles or oil which was reaching the surface.

What was to be done? Nothing, but to lie closer than ever, and enjoy the calm of the man who has done all that is possible. The order was given to stop all motors, even the Sperry motor for running the gyro compass. All vent valves, and other possible leaking places, were inspected and reported tight.

Then came the third explosion, the most violent of all. Lights went out suddenly, and the crew—groping in darkness—thought that the end had come.

For a moment the ship seemed to be stunned; then the lights reappeared. They had not been injured, but the shock had thrown all the chopper-switches on the auxiliary switchboard to the 'Off' position. Not a trace of a leak could be discovered—the ship was alive still, and without a mortal wound. In her commander's judgment it would take a direct hit, or something very, near it, to kill her.

Perhaps the most trying time of all was that which now followed. What happened? Nothing happened. It was that which was so trying. From 9.5 a.m., when the third depth-charge exploded, till 4.7 p.m., the submarine lay motionless on the sea-bed; no one on board knew when it would be safe to move, or even whether it would be possible at all—for both helm and hydroplanes were jammed and other defects might be discovered. This was a test of moral stability as severe as any yet recorded, even in the submarine service, and it is not surprising that Commander Cooper was eventually ordered to add to his report a special statement on the moral effects of the strain upon his ship's company.

He reported accordingly, not in the picturesque style of the German officer, exhilarated by his successful fight, but with the brevity of a man of science and the simplicity of a narrator who has nothing to prove. The behaviour of the officers he assumes without a word; that of the men, he says, was admirable. Naturally it varied with the individual; the older and more experienced men observed the demeanour of their officers, and were content to abide by it; the younger ones showed more difference, each in accordance with his temperament; but they, too, did excellently, and having been assured that all was well, the whole company settled down to read or to occupy themselves in other ways. In the majority of cases the events of the day had no permanent effect, though for a short time afterwards some of the men would start on being wakened or touched suddenly by others. As to himself, the commander declares that he thought the chances of being destroyed by depth-charges small.

To retain this opinion in the circumstances was a proof of remarkable constancy; the constancy of the 'man convinced against his will' in the proverb. And he felt at the time, as he frankly says, that he would much rather remain on the surface and engage an enemy, however large, and at all costs, than endure the strain of a further experience of the kind. It would be likely, he thought, to affect the judgment for some days, causing a tendency to act over-cautiously or over-rashly.

None the less he carried on. At 4.7 the submarine left the bottom and rose to a depth of 28 feet; at 8.35 in the evening she came to the surface and proceeded to her billet. There she carried out the duties of her patrol, and six days later, 'at 1 p.m., British Summer Time,' she returned to her base.

Of the hunted who do not return to their base we cannot hope

'A HUGE COLUMN OF WATER WHICH FELL PLUMP
ON THE COMMANDER.'

to hear much. But there was a smart engagement towards the end of 1917 between an American convoy-escort and a German submarine, of which accounts have been given by both sides, those above water and those below. The convoy was approaching our shores towards dusk of a November afternoon when the attack was made. The U-boat's periscope—a 'finger' one, of only two inches diameter—was sighted by the U.S.S. (destroyer) *Fanning*, which was at the moment turning to port at a speed of about fifteen knots. The submarine was 8 points on the *Fanning's* port bow, distant about 400 yards, and going some two knots.

The other destroyers had just passed the spot, where she was seen; the second of these, U.S.S. *Nicholson*, was now on the *Fanning's* starboard bow, and very handy for what was to follow. The commander of the *Fanning*, in order to continue his swing to port, put his helm hard over and at the same time increased speed to full. The periscope, of course, disappeared instantly. But every eye on the *Fanning* had marked her position. The commander, when he had turned about 30°, ported his helm so as to bring his ship right over the desired place, slightly ahead of the periscope's last position, and there he dropped a depth-charge, within three minutes of the first alarm. It was a fine piece of work, and, as it turned out, a decisive stroke.

Nothing was seen for the moment, beyond the upheaval of water caused by the detonation. The *Fanning* continued to turn under starboard helm; the *Nicholson* altered course to starboard, turned, and headed for the spot where the charge had been dropped, intending, no doubt, to drop a shot of her own in the same place. She could not have made a luckier move. The conning-tower of the submarine suddenly broke surface between her and the convoy, about 500 yards from where it had disappeared. The boat was one of the new large-type U-boats, and was evidently hit, for she could neither submerge properly nor keep an even keel, but went rolling up and down like a gigantic porpoise in the direction of the convoy.

The two destroyers headed for her at full speed; *Nicholson*, who was, of course, leading, passed over her, dropped her depth-charge, and turned to port, firing three rounds from her stern gun into the wash. Once more the enemy's bow came up with a bound. This time he made a desperate effort to keep on the surface, and struggled along at two knots, being about 30° down by the stern. Finally he righted himself, no doubt by-filling tanks and crowding men forward, and his speed seemed to increase. But by this time *Fanning's* guns were speaking to him in unmistakable language; after the third shot the hatch opened, a white shirt was waved, and the whole crew came on deck holding up their hands.

It was now 4.28; the fight had taken no more than eighteen minutes from first to last, and ten minutes later the U-boat sank. Her crew had opened the sea valves and nearly paid the penalty, for they were all in the water before they could be got off to the destroyer, and one who could not swim was rescued by two chivalrous Americans. They jumped into the dark, cold sea for him, forgetting all about the German rules of war, and were disappointed when he died on deck.

The account given by the survivors was full of interest. They were forty-one in number, including a captain-lieutenant, a first-lieutenant, a lieutenant and a chief-engineer. The boat had come straight from her base for the express purpose of attacking this particular convoy, and had been lying in wait for two days, paying no attention to any other ships. She carried twelve torpedoes, and she carries them still, for not one had been fired when she went down. The first depth-charge from *Fanning* had been practically a direct hit; it had wrecked her motors, diving gear, and oil leads, and sent her diving entirely out of control to a depth of 200 feet. The commanding officer thought at first that he would never be able to stop her, and that she would go on until the deep-sea pressure burst her sides in.

He had only one possible course—he blew out all his four water-ballast tanks at once. This stopped the dive but brought the boat back to the surface with a rush and made her unmanageable. One witness in the destroyers says that she 'leaped clear of the water like a breaching whale.' It was then that *Nicholson* overtook her and dropped the second depth-charge; but even without this the end was inevitable, for in her porpoise-like gambols she could have been shot or rammed with certainty. Given a sufficient supply of patrol boats and depth-charges in the submarine chase there will be but few and evil days for the hunted. The American naval authorities have grasped this truth at once and founded a building policy upon it. The boats will be provided in any number, and if they are handled as the *Fanning* and *Nicholson* were handled, the U-boat will spend her short life in dodging a perpetual bombardment.

That the end of the pirate, when it does come, is terrible, may easily be conjectured, but probably no imagination could give any idea of the actual experience. There is, however, in existence a narrative, compiled by a neutral from the evidence of two Germans who sur-

'THE SUBMARINE SUDDENLY BROKE SURFACE.'

vived, by an extraordinary chance, the destruction of their ship. These men were among the crew of a U-boat of the largest and newest type, one of the last to come out of Zeebrugge before the harbour was bottled up by the *Intrepid* and *Iphigenia*. She had not gone far from port when she hit a mine and exploded it. The shock was severe, but did not at once appear to be fatal. The electric switches were thrown out of position, the lights in some compartments went out, and the vessel began to sink rapidly by the stern; but the lighting did not take long to restore, and the crew were immediately ordered to trim the boat by making a combined rush forward. This manoeuvre was successful in bringing her to an even keel, but by no effort could she be induced to rise to the surface.

Now began the terror; the plating of the ship had been shaken and forced apart by the explosion; water was pouring in; the leaks were rapidly enlarging, and all attempts to stop them failed. In very few minutes the boat would be filled either with water or with chlorine gas from the batteries. It was hardly possible to escape from the death-trap; but there was one desperate chance, if the conning-tower and forward hatches could be forced open against the pressure of the sea.

The commanding officer and the chief engineer entered the conning-tower and ordered their men to open one of the forward hatches. If this could be done, though the crew would have little hope of pushing their way up through the incoming torrent, the air-pressure inside the boat would be so greatly increased that the officers would be probably enabled to open the conning-tower and escape. But the outside pressure was too great for the hatch to be moved. The most violent efforts were made, the men working in relays and using their strength desperately, while their companions urged them on with terrible cries. Meantime it was becoming more and more difficult to breathe; the salt water was penetrating the batteries and giving off chlorine gas. The stern of the vessel was now fully flooded and the internal air pressure was rapidly increasing as the free space grew less. The moment of suffocation was near. But the hatch could not be raised.

At this point, some of the crew lost control and behaved like madmen. They crammed cotton waste into their ears and nostrils, and plunged beneath the water, which was now knee-deep. One man turned his revolver upon himself; it missed fire; he hurled it from him and plunged after his comrades. One, who still kept his head, with a final effort forced open one of the torpedo tubes and let in the water to end the struggle one way or another. Hope returned for a moment. The internal air pressure increased to such a pitch that the conning-tower and forward hatch could both be opened. Officers and men sprang and fought their way upwards through the inrush.

Perhaps twenty in all made their way out of the ship; but it was only passing from one death to another. Human lungs are not adapted for the sudden change from a deep-sea pressure to surface conditions. The shrieks of these unfortunate men were heard by a trawler which happened to be passing near; but before she could reach them all were dead but two, and those two were broken men, bleeding from the lungs and crushed in spirit. They had digged a cruel pit and fallen into the midst of it themselves.

Chapter 17

Zeebrugge and Ostend

We have long been regretting that the work and the fame of our Submarine Service are for the most part hushed to a kind of undertone. We cannot speak of them as we wish, lest the enemy should overhear and profit by information which he is unable to get for himself. But there are victories that cannot be concealed—blows which must and will reverberate, now and for ages to come. The work of the navy at Ostend and Zeebrugge may openly be spoken of as it deserves. And this is fortunate; for nations, like men, 'live by admiration, hope and love,' and admiration is not the least powerful of the three elements. The double attack of St. George's Day achieved not only a diminution of the enemy's strength, but an increase of our own. All over the world we heard it hailed as a great feat of arms, and a proof of mastery; even our own hearts were stronger for being so vividly reminded that our seamen are what they have always been—the greatest fighting men alive.

The very conception of this attack was in itself conclusive evidence of a high heroic spirit. The enterprise was not a wild-cat scheme, it was both possible and useful, but it was one from which no man or officer could expect to return. It was planned in November 1917, a month in which the long and splendid work of our anti-submarine division was rapidly advancing to success. The imagination of the service rose with the rising tide, and it was determined that the pirates should be not only hunted down at sea, but harried and blocked in their principal submarine sally-ports.

These ports had, during the past two years, become more and more important to the U-boat campaign, and had therefore been more and more strongly guarded and fortified against attack. The section of coast upon which they lie had a system of defensive batteries, which included no less than 120 heavy guns, some of them of 15-inch calibre. A battery of these was upon the Mole at Zeebrugge—a solid stone breakwater more than a mile long, which contained also a railway terminus, a seaplane station, huge sheds for personnel and material, and, at the extreme seaward end, a lighthouse with searchlight and range-finder. An attacking force must reckon with a large number of defenders upon the Mole alone, besides the batteries and reinforcements on shore, and the destroyers and other ships in the harbour. But the attack on the Mole was an indispensable part of the enterprise; for the enemy's attention must be diverted from the block-ships, which were to arrive during the fight and sink themselves in the mouth of the canal. And in order to deal satisfactorily with the Mole, it must be cut off from the reinforcements on shore by the destruction of the railway viaduct which formed the landward end of it.

That was not all. The main difficulty of the plan was the management of the approach and return of the expedition. The conditions were extremely severe. First, the attacking force must effect a complete surprise and reach the Mole before the guns of the defence could be brought to bear upon them. The enemy search-lights must therefore be put out of action, as far as possible, by an artificial fog or smoke-screen; but again, this must not be dense enough to obscure the approach entirely. Secondly, the work must be done in very short time, and to the minute; for though the attack might be a surprise, the return voyage must be made under fire. The shore batteries were known to have a destructive range of sixteen miles; to clear out of the danger zone would take the flotilla two hours, and daylight would begin by 3.30 a.m.

It was, therefore, necessary to leave the Mole by 1.30; and as, for similar reasons, it was impossible to arrive before midnight, an hour and a half was all that the time-table could allow for fighting, blocking, and getting away again. To do things as exactly as this, a night must be chosen when wind, weather and tide would all be favourable. We need not be surprised at hearing that the expedition had twice before started and been compelled to return with-out reaching its objective—once it was actually within fifteen miles of the Mole—but fortunately the Germans, having no efficient patrol at sea, got no hint of what was being planned; and in the end were so completely taken by surprise, that some of their guns when captured had not even had the covers removed from them!

The attack was to be conducted by Vice-Admiral Roger Keyes,

commanding at Dover. The force employed was a large and composite one which required masterly handling. The Ostend expedition was a comparatively simple affair; but for Zeebrugge there were needed, besides the principal ships, a fleet of smoke-boats for making fog, motor launches for showing flares and bringing off men in difficulties, monitors for bombarding the batteries, and destroyers for looking after the enemy ships lying in harbour, besides a submarine of which we shall hear more presently. The landing on the Mole was to be made from *Vindictive*, an old light cruiser of 5720 tons, and she was to be accompanied by two old Mersey ferry-boats, *Daffodil* and *Iris*, with storming and demolition parties. The three destroyers were *North Star* (Lieut.-Commander K. C. Helyar), *Phoebe* (Lieut.-Commander H. E. Gore-Langton), and *Warwick*, in which the admiral himself was flying his flag for the occasion.

It need not be said, except for the pleasure of saying it, that the name of every officer present is worth remembering. Those who died, gave their lives to secure a victory as effective and gallant as any recorded, even in our naval history. Those who returned are marked men, to whom their country will never look in vain for sound and brilliant service. It is an inspiring thought that while their action was unique, they themselves were not. The British Navy is full of such men, and we may jostle them in the corridors of the Admiralty every day in the year. Anyone who happened to be near Room 24 on the morning of Monday, April 22, might have seen two officers come out who bore no sign of a destiny more heroic than the rest. Yet they were, in fact, Captain Alfred Carpenter, who had been selected to command *Vindictive*, and Wing-Commander Brock, who was to create the magic fog, and whose mysterious fate is one of the most heroic and moving episodes of the fight.

To Captain Carpenter we owe the best account yet given of the expedition. If we read the main portion of it, and supplement it with a few notes, we shall get as near to realising the achievement as anyone without experience or expert knowledge can do.

At last, the opportunity we had waited for so long arose, and everybody started off in the highest spirits, and with no other thought than to make the very greatest success of the operation. Fate was very kind to us on the whole, and everything went well—almost as per schedule. The various phases depended on accurate timing of the work of the various units. The smoke-screen craft and the fast motor-boats, at given intervals, rushed on ahead at full speed, laid their smoke-screens, attacked enemy vessels with torpedoes, and generally cleared the way for the main force, in addition to hiding the approach of the latter from the shore batteries. Meanwhile a heavy bombardment was being carried out by our monitors, and the sound of their firing, as we approached, was one of the most heartening things that I can remember.

On arriving at a certain point some considerable distance from shore, the forces parted, some going to Zeebrugge and some to Ostend, the idea being that the forces should arrive at the two places simultaneously, so that communication from one place to the other could not be used as a warning in either case. Precisely at midnight (the scheduled time) the main force arrived at Zeebrugge and two of the block-ships arrived at Ostend. The admiral's signal before going into action was "St George for England!" and the reply from *Vindictive* was "May we give the Dragon's tail a damned good twist!"

At midnight we steamed through a very thick smoke-screen. German star shells w r ere lighting up the whole place almost like daylight, and one had an extraordinary naked feeling when one saw how exposed we were, although it was in the middle of the night. On emerging from the smoke-screen the end of the Mole, where the lighthouse is, was seen close ahead, distant about 400 yards. The ship was turned immediately to go alongside, and increased to full speed so as to get there as fast as possible. We had decided not to open fire from the ship until they opened fire on us, so that we might remain unobserved till the last possible moment. A battery of five or six guns on the Mole began firing at us almost immediately, from a range of about 300 yards, and every gun on the *Vindictive* that would bear fired at them as hard as it could. (Ours were 6-inch guns and 12-pounders.)

In less than five minutes the ship was alongside the Mole, and efforts were made to grapple the Mole, so as to keep the ship in place. The *Iris* was ahead. The *Daffodil*, which was following close astern, came up and in the most gallant manner placed her bow against the *Vindictive* and pushed the *Vindictive* sideways, until she was close alongside the Mole. There was a very heavy swell against the Mole; the ships were rolling about, and this made the work of securing to the Mole exceedingly difficult.

Vindictive was specially fitted along the port side with a high false deck, from which ran eighteen brows or gangways, by which the storming parties were to land. The men were standing ready, but before the word was given a shell killed Colonel Bertram Elliot of the Marines, and Captain Henry Halahan (who was commanding the blue-jackets) fell to machine-gun fire. But no losses could stop the stormers.

When the brows were run out from the *Vindictive*, the men at once climbed out along them. It was an extremely perilous task, in view of the fact that the ends of the brows at one moment were from eight to ten feet above the wall, and the next moment were crashing on the wall as the ship rolled. The way in which the men got over those brows was almost super-human. I expected every moment to see them falling off between the Mole and the ship—at least a 30-feet drop—and being crushed by the ship against the wall. But not a man fell—their agility was wonderful.

It was not a case of seamen running barefoot along the deck of a rolling ship; the men were carrying heavy accoutrements, bombs, Lewis guns and other articles, and their path lay along a narrow and extremely unsteady plank. (Of these plank brows only two were uninjured by the enemy's fire; the rest were riddled.) They never hesitated; they went along the brows, and onto the Mole with the utmost possible speed. Within a few minutes three to four hundred had been landed, and under cover of a barrage put down on the Mole by Stokes guns and howitzer fire from the ships, they fought their way along.

Comparatively few of the German guns were able to hit the hull of the ship, as it was behind the protection of the wall. Safety, in fact, depended on how near you could get to the enemy guns, instead of how far away. While the hull was guarded, the upper works of the ship—the funnels, masts, ventilators and bridge—were showing above the wall, and upon these a large number of German guns appeared to be concentrated. Many of our casualties were caused by splinters coming down from the upper works. (One shell burst in the Stokes battery, another destroyed the flame-throwing house, and a third killed every man in the fighting top except one—Sergeant Finch, who was badly wounded, but kept his machine-gun going and won the V.C. for it.) If it had not been for the *Daffodil* continuing to push the ship in towards the wall throughout the operation, none of the men who went on the Mole would ever have got back again.

But *Daffodil's* men jumped across to *Vindictive*, and so joined the storming party. *Iris*, in the meantime, was trying to grapple the Mole ahead of *Vindictive*; but her grapnels were not large enough to span the parapet, and two most gallant officers—Lieut.-Commander Bradford and Lieut. Hawkins—who climbed up and sat astride the parapet try-ing to make them fast, were both shot and fell between the ship and the wall. Commander Valentine Gibbs had both legs shot away. He came out of action with his ship, but died next morning. His place on the bridge was taken by Lieutenant Spencer, R.N.R., who was already wounded, but refused to be relieved. Finally a single big shell came down through the upper deck and burst among some marines who were waiting their turn for the gangways. Out of 56 only 7 sur-vived, and they were all wounded. Altogether *Iris* lost 8 officers and 69 men killed, and 3 officers and 102 men wounded. But the parapet was stormed all right, and the Germans under it put up no resistance except intense and unremitting gun-fire. Some of them took refuge in a destroyer, and were sent to the bottom with her by a successful bombing attack from the parapet.

After some fifteen minutes of this work the batteries on the Mole were silenced, the dugouts cleaned out, and the whole range of hang-ars and store sheds set blazing, or blown to ruins with dynamite. Then came the first great moment of triumph.

A quarter of an hour after the *Vindictive* took her position, a tre-mendous explosion was seen at the shore end of the Mole. We then knew that our submarine (the old C. 3, who had certainly reached the age for retiring) had managed to get herself in be-tween the piles of the (railway) viaduct connecting the Mole with the shore, and had blown herself up. She carried several tons of high explosive (the equivalent of over 40 good mines) and the effect of her action was effectually to cut off the Mole from the land. Before the explosion the crew of the submarine, which comprised some half-dozen officers and men (under command of Lieutenant R. D. Sandford, R.N.), got away in a very small motor skiff, which lost its propeller and had to be pulled with (a single pair of) paddles against a heavy tide and under machine-gun fire from a range which could be reckoned only in feet.

Most of the crew were wounded, but the tiny boat was picked up by a steam pinnace (commanded by Lieut.-Commander Sandford, who rescued his brother and the other five salamanders when they had struggled only 200 yards away from the point of explosion). It is possible that the Germans who saw the submarine coming in under the play of their searchlights, thought that her object was to attack the vessels within the Mole, and that she thought it feasible to get through the viaduct to do this. Their neglect to stop the submarine as she approached could only be put down to the fact that they knew she could not get through owing to the large amount of interlacing between the piles, and that they really believed they were catching her!

A large number of Germans were actually on the viaduct, a few feet above the submarine, and were firing at her with machine-guns. I think it can safely be said that everyone of those Germans went up with the viaduct. The cheer raised by my men in the *Vindictive* when they saw the terrific explosion, was one of the finest things I ever heard. Many of the men were severely wounded—some had three and even four wounds—but they had no thought except for the success of the operation. (They cheered their captain as he went round the decks and kept asking, "Have we won?"—just as if it had been a football match.) About twenty-five minutes after the *Vindictive* got alongside (and ten minutes after the explosion of C. 8), the block-ships were seen rounding the light-house and heading for the canal entrance. It was then realised on board the *Iris*, *Daffodil* and *Vindictive* that their work had been accomplished. The block-ships came under very heavy fire immediately they rounded the end of the Mole. Most of the fire, it appears, was concentrated on the leading ship, the *Thetis* (Commander R. S. Sneyd). She ran aground off the entrance to the canal, on the edge of the channel, and was sunk, as approximately as possible, across the channel itself, thus forming an obstruction to the passage of the German vessels.

She was coming in in grand style, but had the bad luck to catch her propeller in the defence nets and became a target; but she did fine

'A TREMENDOUS EXPLOSION WAS SEEN AT THE SHORE END OF
THE MOLE,'

work even then, signalling to her sister ships and enabling them to avoid the nets. And she may give quite as much trouble to the enemy yet as the other two, for she lies right in the channel, which must always be kept free from silt if even the outer harbour is to be used.

This co-operation between the three block-ships, carried out under extremely heavy fire, was one of the finest things in the operation.

The second and third ships, the Intrepid (Lieutenant Stuart Bonham-Carter) and *Iphigenia* (Lieutenant E.W. Billyard-Leake), both went straight through the canal entrance until they actually reached a point some two or three hundred yards inside the shore lines, and behind some of the German batteries. It really seems very wonderful. How the crews of the two ships ever got away is almost beyond imagination.

Lieutenant Bonham-Carter, after running *Intrepid* into the canal bank, ordered his crew away in the boats, and blew her up himself. He then escaped on a Carley float, a kind of patent buoy which lights a flare when it takes the water. Very fortunately, Intrepid was still smoking and the smoke partially hid both him and his flare. He was picked up by a motor launch (Lieutenant Deane, R.N.V.R.) which had actually gone inshore to take off another officer who had swum to the bank, and brought away both together. *Iphigenia*, too, after ramming a dredger and carrying away a barge with her up the canal, was even more successfully placed across the channel and blown up with her engines still going, to ensure her sticking her nose fast in the mud. Her crew escaped, some in the motor launches and some in their own boats, rowing for miles out to sea before they were picked up by the destroyers,

The situation, rather more than an hour after the Vindictive got alongside, was this: The block-ships had passed in, had come to the end of their run, and had done their work. The viaduct was blown up and the Mole had been stormed.

Even the lighthouse had been sacked, for Wing-Commander Brock had announced before starting that after seeing to the smoke-screen work, his first objective would be the range-finding apparatus which he knew was up in the lighthouse top. He carried out his intentions. He was seen going into the lighthouse, and coming out again laden with an armful of stuff; then charging a gun single-handed; and, last of all, lying desperately wounded under the parapet wall of the Mole. This was only reported afterwards, and his fate is unknown to this day. If he died, he died as he would have wished, for he was a big man with a big heart, and did his fighting gladly.

Nothing but a useless sacrifice of life could have followed if the three boarding vessels had remained by the Mole any longer. The signal to withdraw was therefore given, and the ships got away under cover of the smoke-screens as quickly as they could. The signal was given by siren, but the noise of the guns was so loud that it had to be repeated many times. Twenty minutes passed before it was definitely reported that there was nobody left on the Mole who could possibly get on board the with-drawing ships.

All three ships got away from the wall; they went at full speed and were followed all the way along their course by salvos from the German guns. Shells seemed to fall all round the ships without actually hitting them. The gunners apparently had our speed but not our range, and with remarkable regularity the salvos plopped into the sea behind us. In a short time the ships were clear of imminent danger, owing to the large amount of smoke which they had left behind them.

Two of the three destroyers also got away safely; the third, *North Star*, was sunk by gunfire near the block-ships but her crew were brought off by *Phoebe*. Her loss was balanced by that of the German destroyer, sunk by bombs under the inner wall of the Mole. Of our motor-launches (under command of Captain R. Collins), many of which performed feats of incredible audacity at point-blank range, all returned but two.

There is no doubt about the complete success of the enter-prise. Photographs taken by our flying-men show that two of the block-ships are in the mouth of the Bruges Canal, well inside the shore line, and lying diagonally across the channel. The third is outside the canal mouth, blocking the greater part of the channel across the harbour. An officer assured me that the bottoms having been blown out of the ships, they are now simply great solid masses of concrete. Blasting, even if it could be attempted without risk to the surroundings (*e.g.*, the walls of the canal and docks) would only divide one solid mass into several masses, just as obstructive as the whole. Moreover, owing to the shallowness of most of the harbour area, every tide will cause sand to silt up about the obstacles and make their removal more difficult. The photographs reveal a clean break in the viaduct at the landward end of the Mole. They also show that the Germans have tried to bridge the gap by planking.

But planking will hardly carry the railway; and as for the block-ships, they were still in position three months later, with dredging parties at work who only offered an excellent target to the bombs of our seaplanes.

During the attack at Zeebrugge the wind changed and blew the smoke off shore. This helped us in the end by enabling the ships to cover their retirement with a thick screen of miscellaneous smoke; but at Ostend it caused a partial failure of the blocking operations. Commodore Hubert Lynes, who commanded this little expedition, successfully laid his smoke-screen, and sent in his motor-boats behind it to light up the ends of the two wooden piers with flares, visible to our ships but not to the enemy. He then sent in two old cruisers, *Sirius* and *Brilliant*, which were to be sunk between the piers. But the moment the wind changed, the enemy, seeing the flares, at once extinguished them, sinking the motor-boats by gunfire, and the block-ships were no longer able to find the entrance. They ran aground about 2000 yards to the east of the piers and were there blown up. Their crews were taken off under heavy fire in motor-launches commanded by Lieutenant K. R. Hoare, R.N.V.R., and Lieutenant R. Bourke, R.N.V.R.

One object had been accomplished—the Ostend garrison had been thoroughly distracted from giving any warning or assistance to Zeebrugge; but the block-ships had only made the harbour-entrance dangerous—they had not closed it. There was no doubt on either side that the attempt would be renewed. Our men were all ready and eager for a fight to a finish; the Germans were quick to take every precaution possible. They removed the Stroom Bank buoy, which marked the entrance to the harbour, cut the wooden piers through, to prevent landing parties from advancing along them, and tried to keep up a patrol of the coast with some nine destroyers. But, in spite of all, they were once more taken by surprise, and this time they lost the game at Ostend as they had lost it at Zeebrugge.

The new expedition sailed on May 9 under command, as before, of Commodore Hubert Lynes. Vice-Admiral Sir Roger Keyes was also present himself, in the destroyer *Warwick*. The flotilla was this time on a larger scale, and the block-ship (which was entrusted to Commander Godsal, late of the *Brilliant*) was none other than the *Vindictive* herself, and was to double her glory by a triumphant death.

The night was a perfect one, calm with light airs from the north, a few faint stars and no moon. The ships came on in silence; for though the monitors were already anchored in their firing positions, and the heavy land batteries towards Nieuport were trained ready for the bombardment, not a shot was to be fired until the signal was given for every arm to attack at the same moment. The whole German front was shrouded in a delicate haze, like a genuine sea fog, but even more impenetrable to sight or searchlight. Under cover of this, Commodore Lynes first took his destroyer in and laid a burning light-buoy as a mark for the block-ship. *Vindictive* followed, and from this point bore up for another flare, lighted by Lieutenant William Slayter on the former position of the Stroom Bank buoy.

Four minutes before she arrived there, and fifteen minutes before she was timed to reach the harbour mouth, the signal was given for a general engagement. Instantly the whole force got to work. Two motor-boats, under Lieutenant Albert Poland and Lieutenant Barrel Reid, R.N.R., dashed in and fired their torpedoes at the two wooden pier ends. The western pier had a machine-gun mounted, and that too went up in the explosion. Then the sea-planes began to bomb the town and the monitors were heard thundering from far out to sea. The German star shells were useless in the mist, but every gun in the batteries and land-turrets opened at once, and the Royal Marine guns on our front replied to them with flanking fire.

At this moment a real sea fog drifted in and mixed with the smoke-screen; our destroyers had to keep touch by siren signals, and *Vindictive* found herself in danger of missing her mark, like *Sirius* and *Brilliant*. She had a motor-boat escorting her on each side with huge Dover flares, but the darkness was too dense even for them. Twice she passed the entrance, and came back at last to her first position. Then, by a happy chance, a breeze cleared the fog for a moment and she saw the piers close to her with the opening dead ahead. Acting-Lieutenant Guy Cockburn, in his motor-boat, saw them too; he dashed in under heavy fire and laid his flare right in the channel; *Vindictive* went straight over it and into goal.

The enemy were now blazing at her with everything they had. A shell hit the after-control and killed Sub-Lieutenant Angus MacLachlan with all his men. Machine-gun bullets made the chart-room and bridges untenable, and Commander Godsal took his officers into the conning-tower. There, after steaming about 200 yards along between the piers, he left them, and went outside, calling back to them to order the ship to be laid bow on to the eastern pier and so swing across the channel.

The order was no sooner given than a shell struck the conning-tower full. It killed the commander outside and stunned Lieutenant Sir John Alleyne, who was inside with Lieutenant V. A. C. Crutchley. Lieutenant Crutchley shouted through the observation slit to the commander, but, getting no reply, he coolly went on with the swinging of the ship by ringing full speed astern with the port engine. But he soon found that she had ceased to move, so he gave the order to abandon ship and sink her. The main charges were accordingly blown by Engineer-Lieut.-Commander William Bury and the auxiliary charges by Lieutenant Crutchley himself. *Vindictive* heaved, sank about six feet, and settled on the bottom at an angle of forty-five degrees across the channel. 'Her work was done,' says the official narrative.

The losses were two officers and six men killed, two officers and ten men missing, believed killed, and four officers and eight men wounded. The greater number of these were hit while leaving the Vindictive. They were taken off under very heavy machine-gun fire by motor-launches under Lieutenant Bourke, R.N.V.R., and Lieutenant Geoffry Drummond, R.N.V.R. When the latter reached the *Warwick* his launch was shot to pieces and unseaworthy, he himself was severely wounded, his second in command, Lieutenant Gordon Ross, R.N.V.R., and one seaman, were killed, and a number of others wounded. Day was breaking and they were still within easy range of the forts, so the good ship motor-launch 254 was sunk by a charge in her engine-room. The triumphant return was made without even the most distant attempt at interference by the nine German destroyers. It was a fine chance for a counterstroke with superior force, but the nine did not see it. Ostend remained, like Zeebrugge, a complete British victory.

ALSO FROM LEONAUR

AVAILABLE IN SOFTCOVER OR HARDCOVER WITH DUST JACKET

THE RELUCTANT REBEL *by William G. Stevenson*—A young Kentuckian's experiences in the Confederate Infantry & Cavalry during the American Civil War..

BOOTS AND SADDLES *by Elizabeth B. Custer*—The experiences of General Custer's Wife on the Western Plains.

FANNIE BEERS' CIVIL WAR *by Fannie A. Beers*—A Confederate Lady's Experiences of Nursing During the Campaigns & Battles of the American Civil War.

LADY SALE'S AFGHANISTAN *by Florentia Sale*—An Indomitable Victorian Lady's Account of the Retreat from Kabul During the First Afghan War.

THE TWO WARS OF MRS DUBERLY *by Frances Isabella Duberly*—An Intrepid Victorian Lady's Experience of the Crimea and Indian Mutiny.

THE REBELLIOUS DUCHESS *by Paul F. S. Dermoncourt*—The Adventures of the Duchess of Berri and Her Attempt to Overthrow French Monarchy.

LADIES OF WATERLOO *by Charlotte A. Eaton, Magdalene de Lancey & Juana Smith*—The Experiences of Three Women During the Campaign of 1815: Waterloo Days by Charlotte A. Eaton, A Week at Waterloo by Magdalene de Lancey & Juana's Story by Juana Smith.

TWO YEARS BEFORE THE MAST *by Richard Henry Dana. Jr.*—The account of one young man's experiences serving on board a sailing brig—the Penelope—bound for California, between the years1834-36.

A SAILOR OF KING GEORGE *by Frederick Hoffman*—From Midshipman to Captain—Recollections of War at Sea in the Napoleonic Age 1793-1815.

LORDS OF THE SEA *by A. T. Mahan*—Great Captains of the Royal Navy During the Age of Sail.

COGGESHALL'S VOYAGES: VOLUME 1 *by George Coggeshall*—The Recollections of an American Schooner Captain.

COGGESHALL'S VOYAGES: VOLUME 2 *by George Coggeshall*—The Recollections of an American Schooner Captain.

TWILIGHT OF EMPIRE *by Sir Thomas Ussher & Sir George Cockburn*—Two accounts of Napoleon's Journeys in Exile to Elba and St. Helena: Narrative of Events by Sir Thomas Ussher & Napoleon's Last Voyage: Extract of a diary by Sir George Cockburn.

www.ingramcontent.com/pod-product-compliance
Lightning Source LLC
Chambersburg PA
CBHW032053080426
42733CB00006B/257